T0358457

SAVING A PLACE: ENDANGERED
SPECIES IN THE 21st CENTURY

Saving a Place: Endangered Species in the 21st Century

Edited by
JOHN A. BADEN
PETE GEDDES

Routledge
Taylor & Francis Group

LONDON AND NEW YORK

First published 2000 by Ashgate Publishing

Reissued 2018 by Routledge
2 Park Square, Milton Park, Abingdon, Oxon OX14 4RN
711 Third Avenue, New York, NY 10017, USA

Routledge is an imprint of the Taylor & Francis Group, an informa business

Copyright © John A. Baden and Pete Geddes 2000

All rights reserved. No part of this book may be reprinted or reproduced or utilised in any form or by any electronic, mechanical, or other means, now known or hereafter invented, including photocopying and recording, or in any information storage or retrieval system, without permission in writing from the publishers.

Notice:
Product or corporate names may be trademarks or registered trademarks, and are used only for identification and explanation without intent to infringe.

Publisher's Note
The publisher has gone to great lengths to ensure the quality of this reprint but points out that some imperfections in the original copies may be apparent.

Disclaimer
The publisher has made every effort to trace copyright holders and welcomes correspondence from those they have been unable to contact.

A Library of Congress record exists under LC control number: 00130116

ISBN 13: 978-1-138-71704-6 (hbk)
ISBN 13: 978-1-315-19672-5 (ebk)

Contents

Part III: Reform

About the Contributors

John A. Baden is Founder and Chairman of the Foundation for Research on Economics and the Environment (FREE) and Gallatin Writers, Inc. FREE conducts environmental economics and public policy seminars for federal judges, law professors, columnists and editors, and environmental writers. Gallatin Writers links essayists and novelists with economists and policy analysts interested in rural areas and communities.

Dr. Baden received his Ph.D. from Indiana University in 1969 and then was awarded a National Science Foundation Postdoctoral Fellowship in environmental policy. Dr. Baden is a leader in developing the New Resource Economics, an incentive-based approach to environmental and natural resource management. He has held endowed professorships, received teaching awards, and is the author or editor of twelve books, numerous articles on the environment and natural resources, and writes a syndicated column originating with Bridge News.

Max H. Bazerman is the J. Jay Gerber Distinguished Professor of Dispute Resolution and Organizations, J.L. Kellogg Graduate School of Management, Northwestern University.

Pete Geddes is the Program Director at the Foundation for Research on Economics and the Environment (FREE) and Gallatin Writers, Inc. Mr. Geddes received his B.S. from St. Lawrence University and his M.S. from the University of Montana School of Forestry.

Michael Gilpin, after early training in theoretical physics and operations research, switched to theoretical population biology in 1970. His first decade of research was on traditional academic topics such as island biogeography, population genetics and community ecology. In the early 1980s with Michael Soule, Gilpin was one of the founders of conservation biology, writing pioneering papers on population viability analysis and reserve design. Since 1985, Gilpin had done extensive consulting on the viability and recovery of endangered species. Among other species, he has carried out analysis on the Stephens kangaroo rat, the desert tortoise, the Colorado River squawfish, the grizzly bear, bull trout, cutthroat trout and blacktailed prairie dogs.

Gilpin has authored over 100 papers and five books, and has received a Guggenheim Fellowship for his work on captive species management.

Daniel Goodman is a Professor in the biology department at Montana State University, where he has taught since 1980. Previous to that, he taught at Cornell University and at Scripps Institution of Oceanography. His PhD was earned in 1972 from Ohio State University. His research is on environmental statistics for decision-making in connection with endangered species management and hazardous waste remediation. He has served on advisory committees for many environmental agencies.

Robert G. Hand, in the past two decades, has acquired international and business credentials, including serving as operational consultant for a major air freight carrier and head of a management consulting firm based in Maine. As a young adult in the U.S. Marine Corps, Mr. Hand served with distinction on the battlefields of Vietnam. That experience, combined with his graduate degree in psychology plays a pivotal role in his understanding of human folly and potential. In addition to three screenplays: Parallel Play, The Baton and The Ghost in the Atom, Mr. Hand has a large body of stories and articles to his credit.

Karl Hess, Jr., is an environmental writer and policy analyst. He holds B.A., M.A., and Ph.D. degrees, respectively, in economics, history and ecology. He has spoken extensively on western land and national environmental issues and has written on those topics in publications that include High Country News, Reason, Human Ecology, Environmental History, The New York Times, The Washington Post, and The Wall Street Journal. His published books include Visions Upon the Land: Man and Nature on the Western Range (Island Press, 1992), Rocky Times in Rocky Mountain National Park: An Unnatural History (University Press of Colorado, 1993), and Writers on the Range (University Press of Colorado, 1998). He is currently a senior associate of the Thoreau Institute, a board member of High Country Foundation and founding member of the High Country News western writers group, Writers on the Range. In addition, he is working on allied wildlife and community-based conservation projects in the Sangre de Cristo Mountains of Colorado, the South Luangwa Valley of Zambia, and the Bubiana and Save conservancies of southern Zimbabwe. His current book, Bridging the Divide: An American Environmental Odyssey, will be completed in late 1999.

Andrew J. Hoffman is Assistant Professor of organizational behavior, School of Management, Boston University.

James L. Huffman is Dean and Professor of Law of the Lewis and Clark Law School in Portland, Oregon. A Montana native, Huffman received his B.S. from Montana State University, M.A from the Fletcher School of Law and Diplomacy at Tufts University, and his J.D. from the University of Chicago Law School. He is author of one book and over 90 articles, chapters and reports on various topics including constitutional law, water law, property rights, public lands law, torts, environmental law, and legal philosophy.

Frederic A. Morris is a Research Leader in the Environmental Policy and Management Group at Battelle Seattle Research Center. Trained as a lawyer and policy analyst, he focuses primarily on addressing regulatory issues in the environmental, nonproliferation, and technology management arenas. Mr. Morris is currently the U.S. team leader of two international projects that are assisting in the establishment of regulatory systems to secure nuclear materials in the Russian Federation.

Mark L. Plummer was born and raised in Seattle, Washington. Dr. Plummer earned a B.A. in Environmental Studies (1976) and Ph.D. in Economics (1982) at the University of Washington. He has worked as a consultant in environmental economics, focusing on the economic value of environmental resources, and as a writer, producing a book on the history of aspirin (The Aspirin Wars, with Charles Mann, Alfred A. Knopf, Inc., 1991), and endangered species (Noah's Choice: The Future of Endangered Species, with Charles C. Mann, Alfred A. Knopf, Inc., 1995). Noah's Choice won the 1995 Washington Governor's Writers Award and was named one of the best science books of 1995 by the Library Journal (March 1, 1996). He has published articles on biodiversity for Audubon, The Atlantic Monthly, and Science.

Randal O'Toole is Senior Economist with the Thoreau Institute, a nonprofit research organization whose goal is to find ways to protect the environment using incentives instead of government regulation. O'Toole is the principle author of The Endangered Species Act, a 60-page report published by the Thoreau Institute in 1996. He was the 1998 McCluskey Conservation Fellow at the Yale University School of Forestry and Environmental Studies and the 1999 Koch Conservation Scholar at the University of California, Berkeley, College of Natural Resources.

Mark Sagoff is Senior Research Scholar at the Institute for Philosophy and Public Policy in the School of Public Affairs, University of Maryland. He is the author of The Economy of the Earth (Cambridge University Press, 1988), was named a Pew Scholar in Conservation and the Environment in 1991, and from 1994-1997 served as President of the International Society for Environmental Ethics. He was a Fellow of Woodrow Wilson International Center for Scholars, part of the Smithsonian Institution, for the year 1998-9. Sagoff has an A.B. from Harvard and a Ph.D. (Philosophy) from the University of Rochester, and he has taught at Princeton, the University of Pennsylvania, the University of Wisconsin (Madison), and Cornell.

Ione Hunt von Herbing, Ph.D., is currently Assistant Professor of Marine Sciences at School of Marine Sciences at the University of Maine, Orono, Maine. Her experience in scientific research was gained in locations around the world including the Caribbean, Europe and Canada, as well as in the United States at the Woods Hole Oceanographic Institution. She is the author of numerous scientific papers on subjects ranging from ecology, physiology and conservation of aquatic organisms.

Todd Wilkinson lives in Bozeman, Montana and writes for a number of national magazines and newspapers. He is a western correspondent to the Christian Science Monitor and a contributor to such magazines as Audubon, Sierra, the Utne Reader, and Orion. He also is author of the recent, critically acclaimed book, Science Under Siege: The Politicians' War on Nature and Truth (Johnson Books) which tells stories from "the trenches of combat biology" and examines the federal government's attempts to silence natural resource scientists whose research challenges the politically driven positions of their superiors.

Steven L. Yaffee is Professor of natural resource and environmental policy, School of Natural Resources and the Environment, University of Michigan.

Foreword

MICHAEL J. BEAN

Last August, the staff at the 10,500-foot high Land's End Visitor Center on Colorado's Grand Mesa was startled by three visitors. Odd-looking, taciturn types were not all that unusual, but nothing like these particular visitors had ever been seen before. They did not ask questions, they merely looked around to satisfy their curiosity and then left without saying a word. Of course, no one really expected them to say anything; they were California condors.[1]

Months earlier, the three wanderers had been released near the Grand Canyon, 250 miles to the south, as part of an experiment to avert the extinction of North America's largest and one of its most endangered birds. Their release followed an uneasy truce between the federal government, charged with promoting the bird's conservation, and local rural landowners, who feared the restrictions they expected to accompany the birds as a result of the Endangered Species Act.[2] That law turned 25 in December and, like the condor, it faces an uncertain future.

Saving endangered species was not always controversial. When Congress passed the first federal endangered species legislation in 1966, few noticed and fewer still objected.[3] A year later, the government compiled the first official list of endangered species. On it were many of the familiar species that have since become synonymous in the public's mind with endangerment: the black-footed ferret, the Florida panther, the whooping crane, the bald eagle, and of course, the California condor.

The 1966 Endangered Species Preservation Act generated little notice or controversy because it did little more than authorize the creation of an official list of endangered species and the development of a largely discretionary program to conserve them. Broader federal legislation three years later prohibited importation of endangered species but did little else.[4] It was soon evident, however, that the causes of endangerment were more varied, the consequences of extinction more serious, and the challenge of preventing it far more difficult than had been previously understood. In 1972, in an environmental message to the nation, President Richard M. Nixon acknowledged that "even the most recent act to protect endangered species, which dates only from 1969, simply does not provide the kind of management tools needed to act early enough to save a vanishing species" and called for "a stronger law to protect endangered species of wildlife."[5]

On 28 December 1973, Nixon signed the stronger law he sought. On the opening day of the 93rd Congress, Michigan Democratic Congressman John Dingell introduced the bill that the House would pass only eight months later by a margin of 390 to 12. Senator John Tunney (D-Calif.) shepherded a similar bill through the Senate on a vote of 92 to 0. Just how much stronger this law would turn out to be neither Nixon nor its congressional champions likely understood. What they must have known, however, was that it contained major changes from the two prior laws. First, every plant and animal was now potentially eligible for protection; previously, only vertebrates, mollusks and crustaceans could be endangered species. Second, the species eligible for protection included not just true species but also subspecies and even discrete populations (later, this last authority was narrowed to apply only to vertebrates). Third, the law would now protect both endangered species and those likely to become endangered, a category known as threatened species. Together, these changes guaranteed two major consequences. First, the list of federally protected species in the United States would become much larger than the 114 that existed as of 1973. Second, it would become much more diverse and include many plants, insects and other organisms far less familiar than the panthers, eagles, wolves and condors found on the original list.

Expanding the size and diversity of the protected species list were not the only important changes. The protection afforded them was also significantly changed. Most obvious was that the 1973 Endangered Species Act (ESA) made it illegal to "take" endangered animals (no comparable prohibition applied to plants) and backed up that prohibition with stiff penalties. The 1973 law also imposed new duties on federal agencies. Earlier legislation required the Interior, Agriculture, and Defense Departments to preserve endangered species habitats on lands under their jurisdiction but only "insofar as is practicable and consistent with the primary purposes" of those agencies. ESA imposed a new duty on all federal agencies to insure that their actions not jeopardize the continued existence of any listed species. Another new concept, that federal agencies had to avoid modifying or destroying critical habitat, was also introduced.

What has happened since these changes were made? First, the list of protected species in the United States has undergone a tenfold increase, from 114 in 1973 to 1,143 today.[6] Its composition has also changed dramatically.

More than two-thirds of the U.S. species on the list in 1973 were birds and mammals; today, nearly two-thirds are plants, and there are almost as many protected invertebrates as there are birds and mammals combined. The familiar and imposing Florida panther and California condor now take their place alongside the Florida ziziphus and California freshwater shrimp.

More importantly, what has happened to the species themselves? Some, like the dusky seaside sparrow and the Maryland darter, have vanished. A few others, like the American alligator and the eastern population of brown pelicans, have recovered and been removed from the protected list. For the overwhelming majority, however, it is too early to tell whether their stories will have happy or tragic endings.

While the final chapter is yet to be written for most endangered species, the outlook for many is sobering. The U.S. Fish and Wildlife Service's (FWS) most recent assessment of the status of species under its care (issued in 1995) concluded that fewer than one in ten could be considered to be improving. Nearly four times that number were declining and for about one third, FWS simply had no idea.[7] Better results are clearly needed, but what would be the best method to achieve those results? To answer that question, this article examines what has worked well and what has not in implementing the Endangered Species Act.

Institutionalizing Conservation in Federal Agencies

As noted, one of the major innovations in 1973 was to impose on all federal agencies a duty to ensure that their actions did not jeopardize the continued existence of any listed species. If Congress did not fully appreciate the ramifications of this innovation at that time, it soon would. In 1978, the Supreme Court decided that this new duty, which was embodied in Section 7 of ESA, required the Tennessee Valley Authority to halt work on the nearly completed Tellico Dam because of its impact on an endangered fish, the snail darter.[8] In the history of ESA, the conflict between the darter and the dam was the law's first wrenching ordeal. The prospect that a $100 million public works project might be halted to prevent the extinction of a tiny, recently discovered fish was unthinkable to many. To the Supreme Court, however, that was exactly what Section 7 required.

Congressional response to the court's decision was swift but in retrospect, restrained. Congress did not change the stringent duty that Section 7 imposed; rather, it created an elaborate mechanism for granting exemptions from that duty in extraordinary situations. Ultimately, the Tennessee Valley Authority failed to win an exemption because of the dam's meager economic benefits, but Congress directed its completion anyway.

If not finishing a nearly completed dam because of an endangered fish was unthinkable to many two decades ago, what would people have thought about drawing down a major reservoir just to benefit an endangered fish? What would they have thought about dismantling an existing dam? In the Pacific Northwest, the former has been done and the latter is under consideration, prompted by Section 7. In that same region, federal timber management has been dramatically changed, driven in significant part by the demands of Section 7 and the presence of the northern spotted owl and other species. Elsewhere, highway construction, federal range management, and a host of other activities—even military training—have been altered in response to Section 7.

Section 7 has not brought the federal government to a screeching halt, however. Although its substantive duty is stringent, the procedures for complying with it have generally enabled federal agencies to accomplish their objectives while avoiding serious adverse impacts to endangered species. By adjusting the alignment of a highway, altering the timing of a beach renourishment project, reconfiguring a timber sale, or building a protective berm behind a firing range, agencies have generally been able to comply with Section 7's demands and proceed with planned activities.

Indeed, the overwhelming majority of federal actions that go through the Section 7 screening process ultimately proceed with little or no change. That fact is often cited as proof of Section 7's great success and minimal adverse impact. The statistics, while consistent with that conclusion, do not necessarily prove it, however. First, a number of federal projects have been given an undeserved green light under Section 7, causing the statistics to overstate the harmony between conservation and other federal goals.

Conversely, Section 7 may cause federal agencies not to pursue projects that they would otherwise regard as desirable. While this benefits conservation, it also means that the oft-cited statistics understate the negative impact to other interests.

Notwithstanding the inability to gauge precisely either the benefits or costs of Section 7, it is almost certainly the one provision of ESA that has led to the most profound and generally beneficial changes. It has forced federal agencies not merely to scrutinize their planned actions but to modify them to reduce their negative impacts. The fact that, in general, species whose habitats occur almost exclusively on federal land are faring better than those found elsewhere is a strong indication that Section 7 has been one of the more successful innovations of the Endangered Species Act.[9]

Critical Habitat

Birdwatchers who would like to spot an endangered snail kite might be tempted to look for them in Florida's Loxahatchee National Wildlife Refuge. After all, the refuge was made part of the kite's critical habitat 20 years ago. Back then, this was the spot to find kites. Today, snail kites are much more numerous outside the critical habitat than in it, due to ecological changes in both places. As the environment changed, the birds shifted their locale. Critical habitat designation has yet to catch up with the birds and likely never will.

When Congress enacted ESA, it recognized that the major threat to the survival of most imperiled species was not hunting or commercial exploitation but habitat loss. Nevertheless, the law itself scarcely used the word habitat. The only significant use of the word is in the provision creating duties for federal agencies, Section 7. There, Congress required agencies to ensure that their actions not modify or destroy habitat determined to be critical. Though commentators hailed critical habitat as one of the important innovations of the law, Congress neither defined nor explained it.

Of all the innovations of the 1973 law, critical habitat has been one of the least successful and most controversial. Its minimal success stems from several sources. Because critical habitat duties are lodged in Section 7, they apply (directly at least) only to federal agencies. But federal agencies are already required by Section 7 to ensure that their actions do not jeopardize the continued existence of listed species. It is not readily evident whether the critical habitat duty adds anything to that, and in fact, the government has concluded that the duty toward species essentially subsumes the duty toward their critical habitats. Critics have attacked this interpretation as negating any independent significance for the critical habitat duty.[10] What they have not done, however, is offer a compelling alternative interpretation. The definition that Congress added to the law five years after ESA was passed only compounded the confusion.

Convinced that critical habitat adds little to the protection of imperiled species, the government has generally declined to designate it. Critical habitat has been designated for only about one in ten listed species. In allocating its scarce resources for adjusting the list of protected species and critical habitats, FWS has made critical habitat designation its lowest priority.

Conceptually, critical habitat is hobbled by the fact that it assumes stasis where dynamism often prevails. For example, many endangered species are associated with ecosystems subject to periodic natural disturbances, such as fire or flooding.[11] These species are imperiled because the natural disturbance regimes have been altered by human action. For these species especially, critical habitat is a difficult concept. Today's strongholds will cease to be of much value if the disturbance regime is not restored (or if management to replicate it is not implemented). Conversely, areas unoccupied by the species today could become strongholds for it through purposeful disturbance. The choice between defending the current strongholds against both humans and nature— or creating new ones elsewhere ought to be addressed in plans for the recovery of the species. Unfortunately, endangered species recovery planning has proven less useful than many had hoped.

Recovery Planning

In 1983, shortly before his tenure as Secretary of the Interior ended, James Watt appeared before a congressional committee to discuss his accomplishments with respect to ESA. Characterizing the recovery planning process as a major thrust of his leadership, Watt sought to distinguish his record from that of the Democratic administration that preceded him. In his first two years as secretary, he asserted, FWS had "approved or reviewed 160 plans," which he hailed as a "160 percent increase over the previous four years." [12] Whether those plans provided a reliable roadmap to recovery and whether the government would assiduously implement them were questions no one thought to ask. Yet ultimately, those are perhaps the questions that matter most.

When ESA was passed, nothing in it mentioned recovery plans. It simply directed the government to save imperiled species. FWS, the agency charged with this task, needed some way of systematically organizing its efforts. Recovery plans grew out of this need, a practical and flexible response to the challenge FWS faced.

The first mention of recovery plans was added to the law in 1978. It did little more than direct the government to develop recovery plans when doing so would be beneficial. Subsequent amendments have been increasingly prescriptive. Today, ESA spells out the types of species to which priority is to be given in preparing plans, specifies the necessary elements of each plan, requires cost and time estimates, and mandates planning procedures. The trend toward legislating even more prescriptive recovery planning requirements seems likely to continue. In the just-ended 105th Congress, the major bills supported by rival interests had little in common except a desire to reform the recovery planning process by adding new deadlines, new procedural requirements, and new substantive elements, as well. The question of whether that is a useful direction in which to proceed is seldom asked.

A host of problems afflict recovery plans. Nearly 500 listed species still lack them, and even for species with recovery plans, the plans are often outdated. Recovery plans also rarely give sufficiently clear direction to serve as a guide for the day-to-day decisions the government must make. For example, few recovery plans provide clear guidance as to when a federal action would have the prohibited effect of jeopardizing the continued existence of the species. Fewer still articulate principles for mitigating the adverse impacts of actions that cause some amount of harm to species but not enough to jeopardize its existence.

When a recovery plan addresses an important issue, it often does so with dazzling vapidity. Take the black-capped vireo, a rare bird that occurs largely on privately owned land in Texas and Oklahoma. Influencing what private landowners do is likely to be vital to the success of conservation efforts for this species. The recovery plan offers the following trenchant recommendation: "Use various methods to protect vireos and their habitat on private lands. This should be a major part of recovery because little public land occurs in the vireo's range."[13] What those various methods might be and how to persuade private landowners to cooperate in their use are left undefined.

Sometimes, the weakness of recovery plans stems from lack of information about basic biology. For example, some songbirds fare best in interior habitats, while others thrive in edge habitats. The recovery plan for the golden-cheeked warbler notes that this fundamental aspect of its biology is unknown:

At present, there is no quantitative evidence suggesting that warblers lining along woodland "edges" are more abundant, more frequently paired with a female, or more productive along edges than in woodland interiors. Conversely, there is also no evidence that the species does best in woodland interior locations. [14]

Constructing a rigorous plan in the absence of such basic biological information is nearly impossible. Recovery plans have also been criticized for setting the bar of recovery too low. One much-noted study concluded that "recovery goals have often been set that risk extinction rather than ensure survival."[15] That study's conclusions, however, may have been overstated. Those conclusions rested on the fact that in some plans, the goal of recovery can be achieved with fewer individuals (or fewer populations) than existed at the time the species was listed. According to the study, this meant imperiled species were being managed for extinction. However, recovery plans typically set population (or number of populations) goals on securely protected habitat, whereas no such habitats may exist at the time of listing. Thus, it is in fact possible that a species could be less abundant when it meets its recovery goals than it was at the time of its listing. The adequacy of recovery plan goals therefore remains an open question.

President Dwight D. Eisenhower is reported to have said that "in preparing for battle, I have always found that plans are useless, but planning is indispensable." In the battle to save species from extinction, the same is almost certainly true. Unfortunately, however, Congress seems increasingly inclined to see the solution to many of ESA's problems in the faster preparation of more detailed recovery plans into which a broader array of interests have had input. The experience to date suggests that a much different approach is needed. A planning process that guides the practical decisions that the relevant agencies will be faced with making over the near and intermediate terms seems more likely to be productive than the increasingly sclerotic long-range plan envisioned by many in the latest congressional debate.

Experimental Populations

The California condors that paid an unexpected visit to Colorado's Land's End Visitor Center were part of a small population released two years earlier in the Grand Canyon. Their release was done under authority of a provision added to ESA in 1982. That provision, codified in Section 100, authorized the establishment of experimental populations of endangered species under rules less restrictive than those normally applicable to endangered species. For the condor, the gray wolf in Yellowstone, the red wolf in coastal North Carolina, and others species, these experiments appear to be headed for stunning success.

Section 10(j) was a response to a practical problem. Many endangered species have been so diminished that the only hope for their recovery is to reestablish them where populations formerly occurred. Yet because the restrictions imposed by ESA are so significant, both for federal agencies under Section 7 and for private landowners and others under other provisions, endangered species reintroduction proposals have often generated intense controversy. Controversy itself is not an insurmountable barrier, but as a practical matter, many reintroduction efforts are unlikely to succeed without at least a measure of cooperation from local landowners, public officials and others.

To win that cooperation, Section 10(j) authorized the government to relax the rules for certain reintroduced populations, allowing, for example, reintroduced wolves to be shot when they attack livestock or assuring that certain land uses will not be restricted as a result of nearby condors. This flexibility has never eliminated opposition to experimental reintroductions, but it has usually dampened it. The condor again provides an illustration. The first release of condors near the Grand Canyon in 1996 was opposed by many local ranching interests, notwithstanding efforts made to accommodate their concerns. Two years later, however, as plans to carry out another release proceed, there is no visible opposition to it, due apparently to the success of the earlier releases and the lack of problems they generated. [16]

To date, the authority to establish experimental populations has not been extensively used. It remains a cumbersome bureaucratic process, although that may be inherent in the fact that it is used only when reintroduction is highly contentious and controversial. The results, however, have been among ESA's more conspicuous successes because the species that have been reintroduced have been some of the best known and most "charismatic" of endangered species. The unexpected sight of condors in Colorado and the opportunity that thousands of visitors have had to see wolves in Yellowstone National Park for the first time in 60 years are testimony to the provision's success. But they also carry a larger lesson: The path to recovery will not necessarily require the same restrictions, applied in the same way, for every species. Experimentation is essential.

Private Lands: The Act's Achilles Heel

The lesson that experimentation is essential is only beginning to be learned for endangered species that depend heavily on privately owned lands. As it turns out, most of them do.[17] To date, on privately owned lands, ESA has had only modest beneficial impact and some unintended negative consequences, including antagonizing many of the landowners whose actions will ultimately determine the fate of many species. Improving the effectiveness of conservation efforts on private lands is ESA's most pressing need.

As stated above, one of the major changes wrought by Congress in 1973 was the prohibition against taking endangered wildlife. Congress defined "take" to include not only hunting, shooting and trapping, but also actions that harm an endangered animal. What Congress intended was never clearly articulated. As early as 1975, however, FWS promulgated regulations defining harm to include some forms of habitat modification. Thus, a forest landowner harvesting timber, a farmer plowing new ground, or a developer clearing land for a shopping center potentially stood in the same position as a poacher taking aim at a whooping crane. It was not until 1995, however, that the Supreme Court resolved whether FWS's broad definition was within its legal authority. The definition, the court said, was lawful.[18] As to what the definition actually meant, however, the court was silent.

At the very least, major land clearing activities that destroy habitat and kill endangered animals in the process constitute a prohibited taking. Nonetheless, prior to 1982 this extraordinarily broad prohibition had no discernible impact on private landowners, who developed, farmed, logged and otherwise behaved pretty much as they always had. The government was reluctant to enforce such a rigid prohibition and landowners had no reason to seek approval that the government could not give. Ironically, it was a 1982 amendment relaxing this absolute prohibition that gave the government its first practical tool for influencing private land use. The amendment authorized permits allowing the taking of endangered species incidental to otherwise lawful activities. To get a permit, a landowner had to develop a habitat conservation plan that mitigated the impacts of the authorized taking.

For major development projects and nonfederal timber management, habitat conservation plans have become the primary tool for addressing conflicts between private land use and endangered species conservation. Their use has been spurred in part by Interior Secretary Bruce Babbitt's willingness to offer landowners who prepare satisfactory plans an assurance that the government will not unilaterally impose new requirements for the conservation of species covered by the plan because of unforeseen future circumstances.[19] Though this "no surprises" policy has been sharply criticized, it is hard to dispute Babbitt's belief that offering some form of certainty is essential to securing major conservation commitments from landowners. Many habitat conservation plans have, in fact, secured major conservation commitments, including actions that the taking prohibition could never have compelled, such as the restoration of degraded habitats, the control of exotic species on protected habitats, and the conservation of sites currently unoccupied by an endangered species but suitable for future occupation. Other plans, however, have yielded more questionable results.

Though habitat conservation plans have often done significant good, unintended, negative consequences have sometimes been produced on other lands where such plans have not been prepared. Fearing that no good deed will go unpunished, some landowners have actively eliminated habitats that could eventually support rare species or refrained from beneficial management practices that could increase the number of those already present. To overcome those fears, safe harbor agreements have met with noteworthy success. Under these, a landowner creates, restores or enhances habitat or otherwise cooperates in a species conservation effort but does not incur added liabilities as a result of his or her beneficial practices.[20] These agreements represent a small but significant breakthrough in designing an endangered species program that makes landowners allies, not adversaries. A telling example is the safe harbor program for the Attwater's prairie chicken in coastal Texas. In a state where landowner hostility to the federal endangered species program has often been intense, several ranchers and an oil company are restoring tens of thousands of acres of coastal prairie habitat upon which this critically imperiled species depends.

If landowners are going to become full partners in the endangered species conservation effort, genuine incentives will need to be offered to cover some of the costs of habitat restoration and management. Even if all of the best habitat for endangered species is eventually brought into public ownership, other lands will still have to be managed to contribute to conservation. At present, most landowners have no financial incentive to practice beneficial management, and most have a strong regulatory disincentive for doing so. Safe harbor agreements address the disincentive, but unless Congress seriously tackles the job of providing positive incentives for conservation by private landowners, many rare species will surely be lost.

Conclusion: What Lies Ahead?

Since 1992, Congress has been deadlocked over what to do with the Endangered Species Act. One camp, consisting of regulated interests, insists that the law is too onerous, particularly for landowners. Many in that camp advance a constitutional claim that every diminution in property value from governmental regulation must be fully compensated. No court has ever agreed with that argument, so partisans endeavor to sell it to Congress instead. Others in that camp appear satisfied to tie the administrators of ESA in a morass of new procedural requirements regarding the listing of species, the development of recovery plans, and other actions. Like Gulliver tied down by Lilliputian ropes, a government that is believed to be untrustworthy can be restrained through these new procedural manacles.

Another camp, mainly composed of environmentalists, insists that ESA has been too ineffective and must be strengthened. They would also like to forge a set of procedural chains for a government that they too distrust, but for quite different reasons. This camp would strengthen ESA by tightening the screws on landowners and others. In their view, more aggressive enforcement, less agency discretion, more independent oversight and far more money will fix the current problems with ESA.

Neither camp sees much legitimacy in the other's position, and in the sharply polarized Congress that exists today, the result is total impasse, particularly given the lack of any major change in congressional makeup in the most recent election. There is little prospect for that impasse ending, at least not until more members of the two camps acknowledge that both sides have legitimate concerns. The Endangered Species Act has often been too much of a burden for landowners and others, but it has also been much too ineffective for many of the species it seeks to conserve. Crafting new ideas, even experiments, that aim to reduce the burdens of ESA while increasing its effectiveness is the key to breaking the impasse.

For the immediate future, the likely venue for most of these new ideas will continue to be the executive rather than the legislative branch. The key need for a more effective and less onerous Endangered Species Act is the creation of positive incentives for conservation. For that, congressional action is nearly essential. But the job of experimenting with new approaches to conservation has not been stymied by the legislative impasse. Safe harbor agreements and similar agreements for private landowners willing to make significant commitments to benefit species even before they become listed are two conspicuous examples. Another with considerable potential is the use of novel mitigation banking concepts that offer more than just the preservation of the current, unsatisfactory status quo but the opportunity to improve the status of rare species. Under these arrangements, landowners who successfully restore or enhance habitat for rare species may be able to earn credits for doing so that they can sell to others who need to mitigate for adverse impacts to those species from other projects. Still a third is a novel "landowner incentives program" funded by FWS and implemented by the Texas Parks and Wildlife Department. It pays landowners for part of the cost of implementing practices beneficial to imperiled species.

For these and other ideas, resources commensurate with the challenge are indispensable. The administrators of the Endangered Species Act have been easy targets for ridicule because they have been given a Brobdingnagian task and Lilliputian resources with which to accomplish it. Perhaps, however, the real progress that can be made from new approaches that benefit both species and landowners can turn the trickle of resources for one of the nation's most important environmental problems into a respectable torrent.

Michael J. Bean is a senior attorney at the Environmental Defense Fund. He is the author, with Melanie J. Rowland, of The Evolution of Wildlife Law (Praeger Publishers, 1997). He may be reached at the Environmental Defense Fund, 1875 Connecticut Avenue, Washington, DC 20009 (telephone: (202) 387-3500; email: mb@edf.org)

Acknowledgment

Environment 41(2):13-38, 1999. Reprinted with permission of the Helen Dwight Reid Educational Foundation. Published by Heldref Publications, 1319 Eighteenth St., N.W., Washington, DC 20036-1802. Copyright 1999.

Notes

1   The story of the condors' unexpected visit is told in "Endangered Birds Have a Look Around Colorado:" San Jose Mercury News, 28 August 1998.
2   Endangered Species Act of 1973. U.S. Code, vol. 16, sec. 1,531-47 (1973).
3   Endangered Species Preservation Act of 1966, Public Law Number 89-669 (repealed 1973).
4   Endangered Species Conservation Act of 1969, Public Law Number 91-135 (repealed 1973).
5   R. Nixon, Public Papers of the Presidents of the United States: Richard Nixon. 1972 (Washington, D.C.: Government Printing Office, 1974), 183.

6   The official list of endangered and threatened species (as of 1 October 1997) is found in Code of Federal Regulations, vol. 50, sec. 17.11 (animals) and 17.12 (plants) (Washington, D.C.: Government Printing Office, 1997). Subsequent changes in the list are published in the Federal Register (http://www.access.gpo.gov/su_docs/aces/aces140.html).

7   U.S. Fish and Wildlife Service, Report to Congress: Recovery Program. Endangered and Threatened Species, 1994 (Washington, D.C.: Government Printing Office, 1995). The U.S. Fish and Wildlife Service is responsible for administering the law with respect to terrestrial and freshwater species; the National Marine Fisheries Service has parallel responsibilities for marine and anadromous species. Unless otherwise noted, the term FWS refers to both.

8   Tennessee Valley Authority v. Hill, 437 U.S. 153 (1978).

9   D. S. Wilcove et al., Rebuilding the Ark: Toward a More Effective Endangered Species Act for Private Land (Washington, D.C.: Environmental Defense Fund, 1996).

10   See for example, O. Houck, "The Endangered Species Act and Its Implementation by the U.S. Departments of Interior and Commerce:" University of Colorado Law Review 66, no. 2 (1993): 296-315.

11   For a reference to some of the literature, see A. Hessl and S. Spackman, "Effects of Fire on Threatened and Endangered Plants: An Annotated Bibliography," National Biological Service Information and Technology Report 2 (Washington, D.C.: U.S. Department of the Interior. 1995).

12   Hearings on "Violations of the Bald Eagle Act Oversight" before the Subcommittee on Fisheries and Wildlife Conservation and the Environment of the House Committee on Merchant Marine Fisheries, 98th Congress, 1st sess., serial no. 98-13, 23 June 1983, 75.

13   U.S. Fish and Wildlife Service, Black-Capped Vireo Recovery Plan (Washington, D.C.: Government Printing Office. 1991), 45.

14   U.S. Fish and Wildlife Service. Golden-Cheeked Warbler Recovery Plan (Washington, D.C.: Government Printing Office. 1992), 11.

15   T. H. Tear, J. M. Scott, P. H. Hayward, and B. Griffith, "Status and Prospects for Success of the Endangered Species Act: A Look at Recovery Plans:" Science, 12 November 1993. 976-77.

16   S. Yozwiak, "Nine New Condors to Fly over State: Latest Release in Northern Arizona Draws No Protests," The Arizona Republic, 21 September 1998, found at http:Hwww.azcentral.com/news/092 Icondors.slitnil.

17   U.S. General Accounting Office. Endangered Species Act: Information on Species Protection on Nonfederal Lands. GAOIRCED-95-16 (Washington, D.C., 1994).

18   Sweet Home Chapter of Communities for a Great Oregon v. Babbitt, 115 S. Ct. 2407 (1995).

19   U.S. Fish and Wildlife Service. "Habitat Conservation Plan Assurances Policy:" Federal Register 63. no. 35 (1998): 8,859.

20   U.S. Fish and Wildlife Service, "Draft Safe Harbor Policy:" Federal Register 62, no. 113 (1997): 32.178.

Acknowledgements

The Foundation for Research on Economics and the Environment (FREE) is a non-profit educational and research foundation based in Bozeman, Montana. Working with important decision makers and opinion leaders, and focused upon federal judges and law professors, FREE links sound science, economic progress, and environmental quality.

While our programs are explicitly pro-environment, they explain why ecological values are not the only important ones. We stress that trade-offs among competing values are inescapable. We show why it is ethically and materially irresponsible to pretend such choices can be avoided.

For nearly a decade FREE has hosted a series of week-long seminars on environmental economics and policy analysis for members of the federal judiciary. This book had its genesis at such a seminar on the topic of endangered species protection. We are grateful to Dean Jim Huffman of Northwestern School of Law, Lewis and Clark College for co-sponsoring that event and to the M.J. Murdock Charitable Trust for financial support of the same.

This book project was made possible through the generous support of the J.C. Downing Foundation. We thank Stuart Winkleman for his patience and understanding as we herded this project along.

We would also like to thank others who have long encouraged and supported our work. They include Bill Dennis of Liberty Fund, Inc., Barrett Walker of the Alex C. Walker Foundation, Jim Warjone of Port Blakely Tree Farms, and Dick Larry a long-time friend and visitor to Montana.

Introduction
The Endangered Reservoir of Goodwill Towards Endangered Species

JOHN A. BADEN AND PETE GEDDES

The Political Economy of Endangered Species

Congress passed the Endangered Species Act (ESA) in 1973. The Act directed the federal government to devote whatever efforts and resources were necessary to avoid the further loss of the nation's biological legacy. Further, the Act mandated that all federal agencies "shall seek to conserve endangered species" and further defined "conserve" to mean, "to use...all of the methods and procedures which are necessary to bring any endangered species...to the point which the measures pursuant to this chapter are no longer necessary."

However noble the motivations, that act exemplifies the perverse political economy of political decisions. The law as stated is absolute; there is no recognition of the future costs implied by the statement, "whatever efforts and resources" necessary to avoid loss. The implicit but strong implication is that the creatures to be saved, each species of beetle, rat, or toad, has infinite value. There is no recognition of the necessity of trade-offs.

When evaluating environmental policies, we have become far more responsible, reasonable, and rational in the generation since the first Earth Day. Environmental professionals understand that citizens weigh many values and that green values don't necessarily trump all others. At the intuitive level, and sometimes explicitly, environmental advocates understand the pervasive, inescapable reality of the real costs, the opportunities foregone, implied by their preferred policies. They understand that as the cost of environmental policies escalate, support for these policies evaporates.

But back in 1973, politicians and conservationists were naive. They envisioned a deep reservoir of good will for attractive or fascinating beasts and birds. And they assumed saving lives and habitat would be, if not free, nearly costless. After all, who could possibly be against saving the bald eagle, wolverine, and ruby-throated bug catcher?

Just three years later the Act's mettle (and that of its political supporters) was tested by a three-inch long fish in Tennessee. The completion of the Tennessee Valley Authority's Tellico Dam threatened to destroy the habitat of the tiny snail darter. Supporters of the dam argued Congress never intended the ESA to affect projects of such scale. The issue over the snail darter was a mistake, the result of an oversight. The ESA was meant to save "charismatic mega-fauna"–Yellowstone's grizzly bears and bald eagles.

In Tennessee Valley Authority v. Hill, the U.S. Supreme Court affirmed the primacy of species protection. Writing for the majority, Chief Justice Burger noted, "The plain intent of Congress...was to halt and reverse the trend towards species extinction, whatever the cost...the plain language of the Act, buttressed by its legislative history, shows clearly that Congress viewed the value of endangered species as 'incalculable.'"

Americans remain deeply supportive of environmental protection. Ironically, however, the ESA itself may be endangered. While there is widespread verbal support for saving species "at any cost", when trade-offs become obvious, and values compete, support erodes. How have we gone astray with our efforts to save endangered species? This book provides some insights from several disciplines, then offers modest, constructive reforms that may increase the effectiveness and viability of endangered species protection.

Political Economy

Basic economic principles can help us explain the ESA's loss of support

People first consider the personal impact of decisions: How will a decision affect me and those people, beliefs, and things I care about? For example, subjecting hundreds of homes to recurrent fire danger to protect a subspecies of rat may protect that rat, but it erodes support for the ESA.

Second, the only costs people count are those they actually face. When a person is insulated from the consequences of his actions, costs are ignored or discounted. For example, people who do not graze livestock or harvest timber can easily advocate expanding the land protected for the endangered grizzly bear. To these people, increased protection is free.

Others, however, face the direct costs of this protection. For example, the construction of a hospital in California's San Bernadino County was postponed and relocated for the sake of protecting eight Delhi Sands flower-loving flies inhabiting the property. The cost? $4.5 million, or about half a million dollars a fly.

Economists understand that regardless of claims, environmental quality is only one of several competing values people actually seek. Scarcity—the fact that virtually no resources are abundant enough to satisfy all human demands at zero cost—dictates that choices must be made among competing values or goods. It is intellectually and ethically impossible to pretend away the necessity of such choices.

Complexity and Emotion

Environmental issues are almost always scientifically complex and highly emotional. Unfortunately, these are ingredients for error, acrimony, and poor public policy. The debate over the recovery of endangered species may be archetypal.

The controversy over how best to recover endangered species is especially difficult, for several reasons. Paramount among them are perceived threats to the well-being of private landowners. Since only 10 percent of endangered species reside on federal lands, private lands are critical to achieving recovery goals. In a nation whose founding principles sanctify private property, perceived threats to landowners excising normal rights sparks controversy.

Horror stories (some real, some hyperbole) grab media attention. Some in the business and development community believe the ESA is an 800-pound gorilla, manipulated by eco-ring masters with the support of radical elements in the environmental movement. In their view, the real green goal is to halt economic progress.

While stories of economic devastation wrought by ESA may be exaggerated (and when compared to the United States GNP, they are surely trivial), it's irresponsible to ignore the real costs of protecting species. Here, as everywhere else, we'll confront genuine, unavoidable trade-offs. As citizens face the costs of current policies (e.g., of saving gnatcatchers in Southern California and grizzly bears in Idaho and Montana) the noble goals embodied in the ESA collide with financial and social realities. In general, resistance is greatest when policies fail to recognize and respect the importance people place on their own economic progress and property.

Problems Inherent to Governments

We have problems dealing with endangered species, especially those without commercial value. Corporations have weak incentives to preserve their habitat. Non-profits find it difficult to mobilize support for species lacking romantic appeal. All institutions have imperfections. As America's founders understood so clearly, this includes the policies and laws governing federal agencies. They explicitly recognized in the Federalist Papers that each law is an experiment which should be evaluated and perhaps modified in the light of experience.

Historically Americans have relied on the federal government for endangered species protection. While the ESA may provide some protection, many threats remain and the overall efficacy of the Act is questioned by all serious observers. When tasks are given to political organizations, decisions are made by a political calculus. In this inexact but subtle analytic scheme, ecology, economics, and equity are normally trumped by political considerations. The resolution of the snail darter controversy is instructive.

It was decided by a cabinet-level committee (a.k.a. the "God Squad") created by a 1978 amendment to the Act. The committee's charge was to resolve conflict between the Act's strict requirements and political demand for specific federal projects. In 1979 the committee concluded that preservation of the snail darter outweighed the benefits of completing the Tellico Dam.

However, with some adroit maneuvering, Tennessee Senator Howard Baker persuaded his colleagues to exempt Tellico from the ESA, and the dam's gates were closed. The discovery of additional snail darter populations eventually resulted in the delisting of the species. That the political maneuvering of Senator Baker triumphed may surprise some people, but as analysts familiar with the Public Choice school of economics have explained, these are the predictable consequences of bureaucratic management subject to political oversight.

Governments are generally much better at stopping harm than at doing good. But ensuring the persistence of species with large home ranges (e.g., grizzly bears and wolves) requires protection of greater habitat area than previously imagined. Conservationists' efforts are now directed to biologically valuable lands outside our wilderness areas and parks. Habitat corridors between protected areas are especially important in the Western United States. Many of the most ecologically valuable lands are in private ownership. This status creates new challenges for conservationists who traditionally focused on federal lands protection.

Environmentalists are learning that conventional approaches to environmental protection (establishing federally designated protected areas and carefully limiting human use) won't work for the protection of large areas of habitat. Efforts at these scales require the cooperation of private landowners, people with huge emotional and economic investments in their land. Naturally, they will try to protect these investments.

The Role of the Environmental Entrepreneur

Saving species is a management problem, but the ESA precludes efficient management of scarce resources for both human and nonhuman use. A new approach is required to achieve the goals which motivated the ESA. Simply scolding people for wanting the "wrong things," and demanding that they change their values, is naive. We must acknowledge our practical inability to save all species. People are simply unwilling to sacrifice things they cherish to save things they don't. Protecting land to the detriment of those who depend upon it is rarely productive. A more constructive approach would:

- reward those who provide habitat for endangered species,

- foster innovation and entrepreneurship directed toward saving species; and

- respect peoples' rights and compensate them accordingly when these rights conflict with habitat requirements of endangered species.

There is wide recognition that entrepreneurial activity is vital to economic and community development. Successful entrepreneurs identify, create, and act on profitable opportunities, typically by innovative arrangements of people, information, and material.

In stark contrast with America, the Soviet Union had no entrepreneurs; those with the talents and the tolerance for risk became criminals within their bureaucracies. Among the results were some of the world's worst episodes of pollution and resource waste. In this system there could be no entrepreneurs to discover profitable opportunities to address environmental and resource problems. These persistent negative outcomes in the USSR and throughout the communist world demonstrate the importance of entrepreneurial actions.

We Recognize Three Kinds of Entrepreneurs

First, for-profit entrepreneurs range in size from Fred Smith's Fortune 500 Federal Express to Becky Weed's Predator Friendly, Inc. The latter is a tiny firm near Bozeman, Montana, that produces sweaters and other woolen goods from sheep whose herders promise not to use lethal means of predator control. These people perceive and develop unoccupied market niches and provide services that meet people's demands.

Second, non-profit organizations or NGOs create innovative, attractive incentives for individuals, landowners, and communities to practice better conservation. One example is Defenders of Wildlife's "wolf insurance program," an effort to reduce the resistance to wolf recovery by compensating ranchers for wolf predation on livestock.

Third are creative individuals within government agencies who develop and then execute new programs. One local example is a U.S. Forest Service manager in the Gallatin National Forest, in southwestern Montana, who worked with the Bozeman Lions Club to develop a handicapped hiking and interpretive trail in the Hyalite drainage.

Only the first type, economically motivated entrepreneurship, has received wide media attention. But other, newer forms of entrepreneurship are crucial in a rapidly changing West. NGO entrepreneurs, in particular, offer some of the best thinking and best practices to a region torn apart by political polarization, rampant mistrust and enmity between urban and rural residents, and widespread disgust with agencies of government. And environmental entrepreneurs often bridge the gap between public and private land protection.

For example, since the early 1980s, efforts have been made to stem the decline of the red-cockaded woodpecker in the southeastern United States. This non-migratory bird requires mature, fire-maintained pine forests for foraging and nesting. These are forests with high economic value. In addition to protecting habitat on the region's federal lands, successful recovery requires that private timber lands play an important role in recovery.

In 1995 the Environmental Defense Fund, in cooperation with other organizations, began the "safe harbor" program to protect habitat through voluntary agreements with area landowners. Under the program, landowners agree to enhance woodpecker habitat on their lands, maintaining the current or baseline populations of birds present at the time of the agreement. In return, the owners are assured of protection from liability under the ESA if the population of woodpeckers on the land increases.

A "permit" trading scheme is included in the "safe harbors" program. Landowners who increase the population of red-cockaded woodpeckers on their property can sell safe harbor "rights" to landowners seeking permission to modify habitat. In the Sandhill region of North Carolina, these efforts are expected to double the population of woodpeckers over the next 15 years.

"Safe harbors" is successful because it responds to landowner concerns. Previously, the arrival of these woodpeckers meant owners could lose control of their property. Now landowners enrolled in the program have their rights protected. Even if they attract woodpeckers, they may continue active forestry and agriculture. Similar programs can link large tracts of habitat without removing land from all productive uses.

Creativity, flexibility and adaptability are essential in coordinating habitat protection at the scales needed for the future. But these traits are rare in governmental bureaucracies. Environmental entrepreneurs, however, specialize in identifying conservation opportunities and building constituencies for wildlands. For example:

- The Malpais Borderlands Group, an alliance of about 15 ranchers in Arizona and New Mexico, has raised and spent nearly $1 million to protect threatened and endangered species in the region. John Cook of the Nature Conservancy praises their efforts: "Private efforts like these represent the future of conservation. Government can't do it all."

- The Rocky Mountain Elk Foundation, founded in 1984, now has more than 115,000 members who have helped conserve and enhance 2.3 million acres of wildlife habitat in North America.

- Ducks Unlimited's Habitat 2000 campaign has the goals of protecting and restoring 1.7 million acres of wetland and upland habitat in addition to the 2 million acres currently under protection. DU already saves through purchase and contract an area of habitat equal to that administerd by the U.S. Fish and Wildlife Service.

- The Audubon Society operates the 26,000-plus-acre Rainey Sanctuary Preserve in southern Louisiana. Natural gas wells have operated within the preserve for more than 45 years without measurable damage to the surrounding ecosystem. The preserve is home to ducks, geese, and a variety of mammals, including mink, otter and deer. Royalties from oil and gas production have allowed Audubon to purchase additional wildlife habitat while improving the management and ecological integrity of the Rainey Preserve.

Attempts to save species exclusively through federal action is ecologically incomplete and hence doomed to failure. There is an important federal role in monitoring against abuse and adjudicating conflict. But to achieve acceptable results, we should recognize the value of environmental entrepreneurs and create institutions that foster their good works. The key is to create institutional arrangements which involve rather than alienate local communities. The locksmiths will be environmental entrepreneurs.

The Conservatism of Old-Line Greens

It is not unusual to find people who have thrived in one system fearing and resisting change to another. Like cattle barons of the open range, Communist Party apparatchiks in Eastern Europe after the revolutions of 1989, and America's robber barons of the early 1900s, traditional green leaders will find the changes we have outlined and the perspective we have offered difficult to accept.

The early successes of the environmental movement came through political organizing and subsequent agency regulation. The value of entrepreneurship was unknown, discounted or ignored by mainstream environmentalists. The term "entrepreneurship," if used at all, was employed with derision, not respect.

There have been times and places when politics and regulations were appropriate means for achieving ecological ends. Establishing the Endangered Species Act was surely one, if only as a way to constrain political/bureau-cratic/industrial exploiters of the federal lands.

These strategies, however, are doomed to frustration as we move toward efforts to preserve environmental values on the privately owned lands of the West. The creativity and flexibility required for these varied lands and cir-cumstances are antithetical to bureaucratic means. Our experience with the environmental movement suggests that some of today's environmental lead-ers fail to recognize these changes. Their organizations are failing to achieve their claimed objectives. These failures will continue until their boards find leaders who appreciate the environmental value of entrepreneurs.

Conservation, like other long-term movements, requires innovations. It's an evolutionary process. Institutions appropriate for one period often become obsolete. Environmental entrepreneurs are creating new arrangements to de-liver a sustainable future. The future of endangered species substantially de-pends on their success.

Part I

Thinking About
Endangered Species

1 Saving Space for Species: The Conservation Challenge for the 21st Century

KARL HESS, JR.

Predicting the course of nature is fraught with peril. It's a gamble, at best, to project from today to tomorrow when the connection between the two may be more tangled than linear. Yet some things are not so inscrutable. The fate of species is one. Debate as we will over the number and rate of plant and animal extinctions, the fact is that increasing numbers of species are being pushed to the biological and ecological edge. We hear most frequently about the plight of the charismatic megafauna—the bigger-than-life creatures we have seen in zoos, museums, picture books, and sometimes in real life, but whose impending loss seems to us incomprehensible if not unimaginable. Yet for every grizzly, wolf, rhino, whale, panther or tiger facing oblivion, there are dozens of lesser known and less notable critters, plants and insects that face far less celebrated losses.

Saving the species we know, and the species we don't yet know about, starts with understanding why we are losing them in the first place. There are many causes. Bad public policies stand among the most notorious. We know, for example, that leopards and cheetahs teetered on the brink of extinction due, in part, to bounties placed on their hides by farmer-friendly southern African governments. We know that salmonoid species such as the bull trout are under siege from the combined effects of introduction of exotic trout species, sedimentation from badly logged and heavily grazed uplands, and the erection of dams that play havoc with spawning runs. We know that wolves succumbed in the Southwest to an aggressive federal and state campaign to erase them from the landscape. And we know that black-footed ferrets fell victim to a well-orchestrated federal program to purge prairie dogs, the ferret's food source, so that ranchers could stock their lands at levels commensurate with the federal subsidies granted them.

There are other causes, too, often more indirect but no less devastating.

We have just ended a half-century plus of federal agricultural policies that encouraged, and sometimes paid, wheat farmers to drain and fill the once extensive wetlands of the northern prairies. We used public funds to build the irrigation works that transformed California's Central Valley from America's equivalent of the Serengeti to the most intensively farmed landscape in the world. And we are just now putting an end to agricultural policies that have made it profitable for farmers to plow fragile, erosion-prone arid soils and divert the life-sustaining waters of western streams to the production of crops and forage, all on a landscape more suited to cactus and sagebrush than fields of alfalfa.

Public lands fare no better. On western forestlands and rangelands, we know the environmental record of 100 years of wise use policies that have made it the business of government to consume, not conserve, the biological wealth of one-third of the nation. We have seen the legacies of below-cost timber sales and stood amazed at the engineering marvels that symbolize the nation's most ambitious water projects. Yet greening the desert by building dams is nothing compared to the depletion of the same by the power and persuasion of public policies that have made it the compelling interest of ranchers to skim the land of its plants. It's no wonder that a species like the Gila trout is on the edge of extinction when the sole incentive ranchers face on public lands is to use wetlands as watering holes and feeding troughs for thousands of cattle.

More recently, and with the best intentions in mind, policy makers struggled to undo the environmental misdeeds of the past and take an heroic stand for endangered plant and animal species. The 1973 Endangered Species Act signaled a major shift in governmental policy from business as usual to the business of trying to rescue the growing number of species at risk. Today, debate rages as to whether the Act has attained its ends, or not. Critics claim millions of dollars have been spent on species recovery with few results to show. Proponents counter that the Act is the safety net that now protects hundreds of imperiled creatures. Whichever side is right, however, this much is certain: the Endangered Species Act has done little to assuage the fears of property owners or to enlist them in the fight for species protection. Quite the opposite is true. Under the regulatory juggernaut of the Act, endangered species are liabilities, not assets. Property owners may lose part or all of the economic value of their land if and when a listed species is found on their premises. Landowners have incentives—perverse incentives to make certain their properties are not home to either listed species or the habitats of those species. This may explain why the red-cockaded woodpecker is closer to extinction today than it was before the Endangered Species Act, and why habitat for the black-capped vireo and golden-cheeked warbler is rapidly disappearing in much of the historic Texas range of the two species. Small as these species are in real life, they are in the eyes of some landowners two-ton gorillas with chips on their shoulders.

The failures of the Endangered Species Act speak volumes to the causes of animal and plant extinction. We can erase from the law books the ecologically senseless statutes that have laid profligate waste to our native biota. And we are doing this; subsidy programs are falling by the wayside. We can also change the laws and policies that encourage and sustain land uses that are incompatible with protection. And we are doing this, too; we are reconstructing federal land policy and overhauling national agricultural programs. But none of these actions are likely to halt the most alarming—and threatening—development of all: the massive loss of species habitat. No matter how ecologically sound our laws are, the human population of the United States will likely mount for years to come while demand for living, working and recreational space—space that otherwise could be used by wild species—will mount in proportion. Indeed, the evidence is compelling that loss of habitat is the single greatest threat to species viability and richness in the United States. More and more lands are succumbing to some form of development, and as they do, species with highly specialized niches and localized habitats move closer to extinction.

Globally, people are filling in wild spaces with homes, livestock and crops with even greater alacrity, and they are doing so despite the best intentions of statutes such as the Endangered Species Act. And it's no wonder, too. In a world of relative scarcity, laws that convert species and habitats into liabilities give housing developments, cattle pastures and corn fields the clear competitive edge over the world's 1.7 million identified species. Not surprisingly, many of those species are faring poorly as the world's 5 billion human inhabitants, year after year, monopolize more and more of the earth's productivity to feed, cloth and house themselves. And when the domesticated animals and plants of those 5 billion people—the cattle, sheep, goats, horses, chickens, dogs, cats, corn, wheat and other crops—are added to the equation, it is clear that an ever-growing share of the earth's photosynthesis is shifting from the bulk of creation to the thin slice of creation controlled and utilized by humankind. Species are disappearing because their physical, biological, and ecological spaces are disappearing at alarming rates. Moreover, it is, as suggested above, highly unlikely that simply striking bad laws and even worse public policies from the books will change the fate of species. Something more substantial is needed if species are to find the space they need to survive the coming millennium.

Solutions abound, of course, but in a world bound by the inexorable facts of diminishing living spaces, two stand out. First, we can no longer assume that public lands are capable of providing the living species sufficient for the survival of most species. They are not. We must, for that reason, rethink the role of public lands and reconsider the assumptions that underlie state-protected areas. They may well be necessary, but they are not spatially or ecologically sufficient. Second, we must revisit and rediscover the forgotten yet vital role of non-governmental lands in both the history and future of species conservation. The 1.7 million species that occupy earth did evolve on what now constitutes public lands; they evolved across the entirety of the world's landscape. Saving space for them means saving more than the tiny fraction of the world's landmass set aside as government parks and protected areas. It means shifting the focus of conservation to private and communal lands and entrusting the fate of species protection to the men and women who effectively control the bulk of terrestrial earth.

The Limits of Public Spaces

Conservation policy over the past century has focused disproportionately on protecting public spaces. This is not surprising. Well before scientists grasped the vital elements of biological diversity or understood the dynamics of landscape-level ecology, conservationists took it for granted that all the parts of nature would be best served and safeguarded when set aside as publicly owned fortress islands and duly policed by public servants in the public's name. Indeed, it was John Muir, one of America's first and foremost conservationists, who called for a soldier behind every tree as the surest way to protect American forests. "Only what belongs to all alike is [protected]," he declared, "An acre that is left should be held together under the federal government as a basis for a general policy of administration for the public good."[1]

Muir's dictum has, in one fashion or another, helped shape conservation thinking and action at home and abroad. Nearly a third of the United States is now set aside as national forests, public domain lands, wildlife refuges and national parks. Moreover, over five percent of the earth's total surface—a landmass roughly equal to the size of India—enjoys some form of protected status. In fact, protected areas worldwide have increased in total acreage by more than 50 percent since the 1960s. This trend, though, is not translating into more secure spaces for species. As the number of parks and preserves increase, the rate at which species come to risk or simply succumb to extinction mounts. Nations are more aware than ever of the elements of biological diversity and the processes that sustain large landscapes. And they are more willing than ever to wield the regulatory hammer of statutes like the Endangered Species Act. Despite this—or just possibly because of it—species continue to disappear and habitats continue to fall victim to plows, hoofs and bulldozers.

There are good reasons why public spaces are falling short of species needs. The most obvious is that state-protected areas do not always contain the full range of habitat required by species or, for that matter, embrace the most productive lands. Historic settlement patterns in most areas of the world are the root cause. Bottom lands that contain the richest soils and that lie adjacent to and intermingle with wetlands were the first to fall to the plow, the ax and the cattle hoof. Only as settlement advanced did newcomers move up the watershed and away from the deepest soils and the most predictable and perennial waterways. Ultimately, the lands last settled were those with the least value for cultivation—the arid to semi-arid pastoral lands and the inhospitable forests that lay beyond the practical limits of human habitation. It is these residual lands, only lightly touched by human activity and distantly remote from the center of most human activity, that have remained sufficiently intact to become parks, refuges and forest reserves.

American public lands are a case in point. They are what remain of an arid West subjected to a half century of rapid settlement. Homesteading ranchers and farmers quickly occupied fertile valleys fed by mountain streams, leaving as open pastoral lands millions of acres of unwatered arid range. They settled next to forests where supplies of timber for fuel and building were abundant, but they rarely extended their occupation into the higher elevation forests where soils were shallow and acidic, and where the fury of high country winters ruled out year-long residence. These settlement preferences carved much of the West into ecological fragments. In places like Yellowstone and Rocky Mountain national parks, the fragments in public ownership continue to provide good summer habitat for many species, especially elk. In contrast, the adjacent fragments in private ownership are no longer capable of providing the same quality or quantity of winter habitat essential for those same species.

Towns, houses, crops and livestock have supplanted open, untrammeled spaces and occupied streamsides and valley bottoms.

Many of today's public lands in the American West suffer an ecological deficit; they are not intact ecosystems. The bulk of wetlands lie in private ownership, and a disproportionate share of critical winter range exists in private hands. Fortunately, most of these private spaces have so far escaped the degree of development that has transformed the northern boundary of Yellowstone and most of the eastern boundary of the Rocky Mountains. This gives hope that fortress island parks can reach out and unify the fragmented pieces of their once expansive ecosystems. But to do this, private lands must be given conservation standing equal to those of public protected areas, and incentives must be provided to the owners of those lands to enlist and engage their cooperation in landscape-level conservation of species and habitat.

In Africa, Amboseli National Park in southern Kenya faces many of the same habitat challenges common to America's parks and public lands. Once the summer and fall rains arrive, a large contingent of Amboseli's wildlife migrate to the greening, low elevation plains that surround the western and southern slopes of Mt. Kilimanjaro in Tanzania. These summer and early fall migrations are essential. They allow the plants of the Amboseli to recover from heavy grazing, and they provide a substantial alternative forage base to sustain an extravaganza of species and populations. But the southern wildlife migrations face increasing competition from growing numbers of people and their settlements on the mostly common-use lands that lie below the higher elevation Kilimanjaro National Park. Although people and wildlife still coexist in the Amboseli corridor, and beyond to the plains west of Kilimanjaro, the signs of habitat fragmentation are increasingly evident—and increasingly threatening to the wildlife of the region.

Besides their failure to encompass whole ecosystems, there is a much more profound reason for the failure of public protected areas to meet the full habitat needs of species. Public spaces are ultimately political spaces, subject to all of the intrusions, compromises and exploitations that political decision-making entails. In the United States, our public lands and national parks have long been buffeted by the machinations of congressional decision-makers. The track records of our national forests and public rangelands have already been mentioned. The track records of our national parks are no better. Grand Canyon National Park, for example, is forced to beg for foundation dollars to fund its natural resource and science programs. At the same time, a reelection-minded Congress spends tens of millions of dollars on the making of inconsequential parks such as Steamtown, a park devoted to maintaining a collection of mostly Canadian steam locomotives. And at the Presidio in San Francisco, a former military base, the U.S. Park Service is prepared to spend up to $40 million a year for that park's operating expenses alone—a sum just slightly greater than the operating budgets of Grand Canyon, Yosemite and Yellowstone combined.

Politics compromise international protected areas to an even greater extent. Although they have grown by 50 percent or more in many areas of the world in recent years, the discouraging fact is that over 85 percent of these protected areas are little more than paper creations.[2] They exist in law, they are listed in the ever-expanding repertoire of world parks and preserves, but their conservation status, particularly in regard to species and species habitat protection, is more fantasy than fact. In Indonesia, for example, 17 percent of its tropical forest park lands have been logged illegally. In Costa Rica's Corcovado National Park, gold miners invaded its interior, scarring parts of its landscape. In Thailand, national parks are being developed for golf courses, second homes and hotels. And in Chile's Alerce Andino National Park, ancient and towering coastal cypress trees, one of several signature species of the park, are being logged in public view.

Public spaces fall short of species needs on purely ecological grounds too. Even when they encompass the full gamut of habitat needs, be it summer and winter range in the Rockies or dry and wet season phases on the African savanna, the fact is that most public spaces are simply too small and too isolated to sustain healthy and continually reproducing populations of many species. In the early 1960s, biologists framed the theory of island biogeography based on observations of species diversity, richness and extinction rates on isolated islands. They noted that on smaller islands and on islands disconnected from larger land masses, species numbers were fewer and fluctuated greatly. Extrapolated to inland protected areas, the same scientists argued that small, isolated nature preserves would experience higher rates of species extinction than large preserves, particularly those connected to other protected areas by land corridors that allowed the free movement of species and the free flow of genetic material. Their reasoning was straightforward: small habitat areas were more vulnerable to natural disturbances and their collage of species more susceptible to catastrophic population crashes linked to genetic and environmental fluctuations.

Strong evidence for the theory of island biogeography came with the publication of a study of North American national parks by William Newmark in 1995.[3] Newmark documented the loss of mammal species in all but the largest North American park complexes. He also found that the rate of local species extinction in parks was inversely related to their size. His findings, and earlier decades of conservation research along similar lines, convinced a growing number of scientists that the strategy of creating fortress island protected areas did little to help plant and animal species on the edge of extinction. Instead, they argued that saving endangered species and protecting the natural heritage of biological diversity demanded a conservation strategy at odds with the dictum of John Muir. It required looking beyond the nominal five percent of the earth's surface that was public and protected and looking, instead, to the remaining 95 percent that was divided between various forms of private and communal ownership.

The urgent need to do just that—to look beyond public spaces to save plant and animal species—is universally evident in developing nations, in Europe and in the United States. In East-Central Africa, for example, over 70 percent of all large mammals now live beyond the boundaries of protected areas. Despite this fact, notes David Western, former director of the Kenya Wildlife Service, "conservationists have ignored the non-park areas in favor of saving nature by segregating it from humanity."[4] Recent setbacks in elephant and other large mammal conservation in Kenyan parks testifies to the increasing importance of nonpark lands, and to the vital need to address conservation issues on tribal lands where the bulk of wildlife reside.

Africa is not alone in learning the hard lessons of relying too heavily on island refuges for species protection. Europe's wildlife is at increasing risk as ecologically suitable habitat for many of its most sensitive species steadily and irreversibly contracts down to the borders of parks and other minuscule protected areas. This happened recently in southern Germany where political pressure forced a park to be carved out of surrounding pastoral hinterlands. The loss of traditional grazing lands, in turn, compelled farmers to sell their lands for summer home development on and near the park's boundary—a trend not unlike vacation home development around the periphery of major U.S. national parks. And like the U.S. experience, the cost of development is being paid for in the currency of diminished and, in some cases, lost wildlife populations. Today, Europe's large carnivores—lynxes, wolves, and brown bears—are endangered; protected areas are grossly inadequate and little if any attention is being devoted to how best to win over surrounding private lands and their owners to the cause of large mammal protection. Unless this changes, European wolves, bears and lynxes are doomed to extinction in the coming millennium.

Much the same scenario applies to the grizzly bear in the Selway-Bitterroot Mountains of western Montana. Despite the commanding force of the Endangered Species Act and its mandate to restore the grizzly bear to much of its former range, the brightest prospect for the bear's successful reintroduction into western Montana is a proposal that would give landowners and resource extractors a positive say in how the reintroduction is done. It would provide them a voice in setting the rules for grizzly reintroduction and in determining an equitable sharing of the costs linked to the bears' return.

Saving space for species requires a fundamental rethinking of the traditional role of public lands and a new vision for the untapped yet potential role of private and common-use lands. Non-government lands, irrespective of ownership, cannot and should not be relegated to an ecological status subservient to, or somehow less important than, public protected areas. Albeit politically pragmatic in some cases, it is ecologically arbitrary and biologically simplistic to cast, as a best case scenario, non-protected areas as buffer zones in service to so-called public "core" protected areas—or, at worst, to dismiss them as sacrifice areas by dint of their severe histories and possibly more severe current uses. These lands are often as ecologically vital and biologically rich as public parks and reserves. At the very least, they have the potential to assume past ecological roles and recapture past biological richness with conservation care and appropriate management. In either instance, these lands are essential to any blueprint for species protection, recovery or restoration.

Saving space for species on private and common-use lands demands that the command-and-control framework and the regulatory strategies used to protect public lands for biological diversity be set aside in favor of less invasive and more voluntaristic approaches. This is essential if non-governmental lands and landholders are to be enlisted in the crusade to conserve species. It means salvaging public policy from the outmoded mindset of the Endangered Species Act, which wrongly presumes that people can be told and, if necessary, coerced to do what is right for nature and its wild residents. History tells us, however, that coercion in the cause of conservation is a poor performer from Africa to Asia to the Americas. The people who live and work on private and common-use lands cannot be ordered—at least successfully— to do what is right, even if it is in the public's best interest. Human nature is almost always contrary to coercion, and coercion in the field of conservation has achieved relatively little when measured in the absolute acres saved for teetering species.

Southern Africa demonstrates this point with disturbing clarity. Having coexisted with a coterie of large herbivores and carnivores for centuries, black Africans found themselves by the mid-19th century estranged and at war with what was quickly becoming the white man's wildlife in the wake of European colonization. To counter the mounting slaughter of elephants and other key game species—in which, ironically, white settlers had taken the early lead—colonial governments simply outlawed traditional hunting and instituted West-ern-style game management founded on the twin pillars of state wildlife own-ership and centralized, command-and-control conservation.

In effect, white African states took wildlife from the historic control, and effective ownership, of self-governing tribal bodies and placed it inad-vertently into the cauldron of the open access commons. Their plan was to save dwindling African game by restricting its future harvest to paying hunt-ers and proscribing its traditional harvest by black tribesmen. It was an idea that had worked admirably in North America, but in the bush of southern Africa it backfired.

Now off-limits to hunting by native Africans, elephants and kindred spe-cies became what they had never been before: marauding pests with no re-deeming economic or social worth (except on the black market). Worse, na-tive Africans now saw wildlife as alienated property, stolen and expropriated by a state they had no role in making. Bereft of all legal access and claim to wildlife, Africans donned the only role left to them by their governors: they became outlaws. They resorted to poaching to stem wildlife destruction of their crops, to provide meat to their families, and to trade in skins, horns and ivory. And they assumed that role with a vengeance, stewarding it to perfec-tion during the wars of liberation in the 1960s and 1970s, when wildlife was not only the enemy but the symbol of hated white rule.

Scattered efforts in the United States show at least recognition, if not full understanding or grasp of the solution, of the problem of alienation be-tween private landholders and wildlife. New institutional arrangements, such as the network of land ownerships and organizations assembled under the umbrella of The Greater Yellowstone Ecosystem (GYE), make motions to-ward reconciling human and non-human interests. The Greater Yellowstone Coalition (GYC), for example, has facilitated communications between vari-ous land managing agencies, resource user groups and environmental inter-ests, providing input into the management of the GYE that was not there pre-viously. Because of GYC's insistence, lands beyond the island fortress park are now part of a larger administrative and planning unit, making management of Yellowstone National Park and its surrounding lands more rational and more ecologically sound.

Yet few areas in the world fit the parameters of the GYE model. More often than not, public lands are not as consolidated or dominant as those that comprise most of the GYE; instead, private and common-use lands fracture the continuity of public spaces and call for solutions that extend far beyond facilitating cooperation among a handful of government agencies. For those reasons, we must look at private and communal spaces anew—seeing them not as peripheral areas possibly helpful in, or ancillary to, species conservation, but as nontraditional core areas where the imprint of humankind is explicit and where the fate of species and their habitats rest in the balance.

Tapping the Wells of Private and Communal Spaces: The African Experience

Southern Africa took the first steps to put private and communal lands at the forefront of species and habitat conservation—and for good reason. Decades of unregulated hunting followed by unrestrained poaching, skyrocketing human population, and massive government subsidization of cattle ranching had reduced wildlife habitat in the region to a fraction of what it had once been. In the blink of a century, 90 percent of the bulk mass of all grazing animals in the green hills of Africa had shifted from rhino, elephant, kudu, sable, giraffe, zebra, roan, impala, wildebeest and gazelle to European-bred cattle.

By the early 1960s, big game numbers were at historic lows, and species such as elephants, crocodiles and leopards were perilously close to extinction. Moreover, prospects for the future of southern African wildlife were bleak, given the relentless advance of poaching, cattle ranching and human population. For all practical purposes, wildlife had become an ornament of the state, a luxury for camera-toting tourists and a handful of trophy hunters, yet a luxury that subsistence and commercial farmers—the very ones who controlled the bulk of its habitat—could ill-afford. Habitat critical for saving species was crumbling under the policies and legacies of the past, and except for a handful of wildlife parks and refuges, the wildness that was once Africa was succumbing. Fortress islands designated state protected areas were all that remained—fragmented landscapes sufficient to maintain a few living relics, but too small to sustain the fullness and richness of Africa's species heritage.

Finding new space for Africa's beleaguered wildlife started first on large private landholdings, owned, as the result of colonial rule, almost exclusively by European-Africans. It began with a simple idea: if people can benefit from wildlife, their attitudes and actions toward wildlife will improve. Starting in Namibia in 1967 and then extending to Zimbabwe in 1975, lawmakers put the idea into actions. Large landholders were allotted rights to wildlife—an idea totally alien to the European and U.S. traditions of exclusive state ownership. Wildlife now had a value, not only a value that could be captured and maximized by prudent private stewardship, but one which far exceeded its costs in terms of crop and livestock loss. White farmers, for the first time since the start of colonial rule, were free to make economically informed—and, as it turned out, ecologically desirable—market decisions on how best to use their land.

Wildlife was the clear winner. By 1990, 75 percent of all Zimbabwean ranchers in areas too dry to support crop production had shifted partly or entirely to wildlife ranching—an easy economic decision, given the near quadruple net profit per acre advantage held by wildlife over cattle. Groups of ranchers combined to form "conservancies" of five to 25 properties, each with common rules and objectives, and each with sufficient land base to reintroduce far-roaming yet economically valuable species such as elephant and cape buffalo.

Over the years, the benefits of private ownership and cooperative conservancies have accrued to a range of endangered species. Liberal game ranching laws now accommodate the lucrative business of crocodile farming. Crocodile eggs are collected in the wild, and the hatchlings are raised for domestic slaughter. A significant percentage, though, are returned to the wild to seed new populations. Once on the edge of extinction, crocodiles are now thriving in areas of southern Africa where their commercial exploitation is allowed.

The benefits of private enterprise have also spilled over to non-farmed wildlife. Black and white rhinos, for example, are flourishing on private ranches, and elephants are making dramatic comebacks. The Bubiana Conservancy of southwestern Zimbabwe, for example, contains the largest and fastest reproducing herd of black rhino in the world. Moreover, at a time when rhinos were being poached to extinction, it was the private space of Bubiana that provided critical refuge for the species survival—and, in effect, extended an umbrella of protection to less conspicuous and less marketable species. Most telling of all is the tale and status of leopards and cheetahs, species long viewed and treated as vermin by ranchers fearful for the well-being of their livestock. In Zimbabwe, leopards were removed from protected status, endowing them with high market value as trophies and pelts. Now that leopards are money-making assets, their numbers are on the upswing, and the use of dogs or traps to gratuitously kill them is blocked by social sanction and the economic incentive to sustain a flourishing population for lucrative hunts. In contrast, cheetahs, which were less numerous than leopards, were kept in protected status, suppressing whatever commercial value they might have had. They remain, for that reason, imperiled; they are, in ranchers' eyes, vermin with no redeeming value.

Although private solutions to species and habitat conservation have had dramatic results, their promise and application in post-colonial southern Africa is limited by the political power and cultural dominance of common-use or communal lands. First, communal lands are the enduring legacy of traditional tribal land tenure; the overwhelming majority of black Africans live and farm on them, and the prospect of changing that reality is slim. Second, communal lands were excluded from the wildlife reforms granted to the private sector; such lands remained open-access commons under state dominion, subject to the full gamut of national laws that have made wildlife more a burden than a benefit to rural Africans. Third, communal lands are generally the most marginal and least productive lands for agriculture and, for that reason, often the last intact and fully functional habitat for wildlife. Fourth, communal lands frequently surround park lands and protected areas; together, the two land systems form vital ecological units in which much of the biological richness and diversity of southern Africa resides.

From the outset, tribal lands posed a unique challenge to African conservationists who understood that saving the region's wildlife could not be done on public or private preserves alone; communal lands would have to be included in the strategy—a strategy that, for both cultural and political reasons, could not entail broad-based privatization. Moreover, they knew that any strategy to conserve wildlife on communal lands would have to have a compelling and enticing economic component. Unless conservation could be linked to economic development, it would have no more value to peasant farmers than a marauding elephant declared off-limits by the state.

Making conservation pay both for species and people started with a basic question: how could nonsustainable open access to wildlife be curtailed and individual incentives for wildlife conservation be created while communal ownership of land and communal harvest of wildlife was promoted and encouraged? One answer, advanced by Garret Hardin in his seminal essay,

"The Tragedy of the Commons," was that the problem as stated was unsolvable: Individuals tend to consume as much of the common resource as possible, without preserving it for future use, because they get all the benefits and bear only some of the costs.[5] Over time, this incentive to overconsume leads to permanently depleting land or killing off wildlife.

By all appearances, those conditions held sway on the communal lands of southern Africa. Harvest of key game species, from elephants to rhinos to buffalo, exceeded birth rates, and the benefits of slaughtering them made the prospect of their impending demise, and the bonanza of their free meat, skins, horns and ivory, net gains for a rural people plagued by the ever-present reality of hunger, disease and death. Yet appearances can be deceiving, for what made the "wildlife commons" tragic was not its lot as common property but rather its open-access status, created by the state's usurpation of village rights to wildlife and its eclipse of tribal institutions that had once governed the harvest of big game. That this would happen is partially explained in the writings of Fikret Berkes, Daniel Bromley and Elinor Ostrom[6]—scholars who have seen that communal institutions can govern common property resources, but only if their power to do so is not corrupted by state intrusion. Southern Africans took this lesson to heart, and in the wildlands of Zimbabwe the Communal Areas Management Programme for Indigenous Resources (CAMPFIRE) was born in 1986.

CAMPFIRE, a program of the Zimbabwe Department of National Parks and Wildlife, was designed to improve wildlife conservation on communal lands much the same way wildlife conservation had been improved a decade earlier on private lands by private ownership of wildlife. Its goal was to allocate rights to use communal big game to small rural communities, which could then sell those rights, mainly in the form of licenses for trophy hunters. The revenue earned— several thousand dollars for a buffalo and many times more for an elephant—would, supporters theorized, give villagers strong incentives to protect wildlife species by protecting their habitat from both poachers and the plow.

The goals of CAMPFIRE are simple: to secure community claims to wildlife and to engage local villagers in the sustainable harvest and economical marketing of wildlife products (primarily hunts)—to benefit, in a word, the very people who must pay, on a daily basis, the conservation price of not farming their lands for the sake of less-than-benign wild neighbors. The CAMPFIRE program works by devolving property rights in wildlife from the state to the lowest possible level, by making clusters of villages the focal point of communal self-governance and by making the body of villagers who can comfortably assemble in the shade of a meeting tree the arbiters of democracy and the marketers of safaris. So far, the results suggest a degree of success comparable to that attained earlier on private lands in Namibia and Zimbabwe. Poaching is down, cultivation of communal wildlands has virtually stopped, wildlife numbers and species are rebounding, and communities are reaping meaningful revenues. Moreover, the CAMPFIRE model is being emulated throughout southern and east-central Africa.

On the west slope of Kilimanjaro in the Munduli and Ol'Molog districts of northern Tanzania, the CAMPFIRE model is being taken to its logical conclusion on one million acres of Maasailand. There, the decades-long rule of Tanzanian socialism is coming to a speedy end. Where once poachers, paying hunters, and the government-run animal hide industry took turns decimating the region's wildlife, a new tribal authority is in the making that will bring local control and ownership to wildlife—and with it the means to protect rare species such as the lesser kudu and maintain adequate habitat for the migrating herds of elephants, wildebeests, gazelle and giraffe that move seasonally down from the Amboseli in southern Kenya.

Unable to manage and conserve wildlife with existing institutions that are either underfunded or simply corrupt, the Tanzanian government has agreed to a new set of policies that will 1) transfer ownership of the west Kilimanjaro lands to local Maasai villages, and 2) simultaneously transfer management and effective ownership of the wildlife of those lands to the same people. Working in tandem with several larger private lessees, the villagers of west Kilimanjaro are headed toward an unprecedented experiment in wildlife management. The Maasai, traditional livestock graziers, will for the first time in recent history have the power to make choices between raising cattle or setting aside habitat for economically profitable wildlife.

Already, the policies are in the first stages of implementation. Maasai elders are debating how best to use the wildlife resource that will now be theirs. As a first step, Maasai villages have joined with a safari operator to offer walking tours through the west Kilimanjaro bush. Revenues from these modest safaris have already had a significant impact on the Maasai's willingness to tolerate such troublesome species as elephant and lion—indeed, to tolerate them even after a recent killing of a villager by an elephant and the loss of several head of cattle to a newly arrived pride of lions. This is a fundamental change. Prior to the start of the program, elephants were rare, chased and preyed upon by people. Lions were almost nonexistent, hunted to local extinction by young Maasai braves anxious to prove their manhood. Since early 1998, elephants have returned to west Kilimanjaro, lion prides are beginning to move south from the Amboseli National Park in Kenya, and extremely rare species such as lesser kudu and gerenuk are on the upswing.

An even greater change, with far-reaching implications for species habitat in general and endangered species in particular, is the growing awareness among the local Maasai of the relationships and tradeoffs between domestic livestock and cattle. Although it is unlikely that wildlife incentives alone will persuade an ancient people like the Maasai to abandon a core element of their culture, which is cattle, it is likely that those incentives will influence how and where their livestock are grazed. Today, cattle are the primary grazers on west Kilimanjaro lands. Fewer livestock or improved grazing management could open up significant new habitat for wildlife and provide important protection for species on the edge of extinction. If these developments proceed as expected, the Maasai of Kilimanjaro will have taken the necessary steps to share, if not relinquish, their common-use lands for wildlife populations that are now constrained to insular and inadequate public protected areas.

Making Space at Home: Private Lands for Public Purposes

Parallels to southern Africa are now appearing on the U.S. landscape. After 150 years of centralized, command-and-control wildlife policy, capped-off by the Endangered Species Act, policy makers at the state level are beginning to take private lands seriously in the management of both ubiquitous and endangered species. Hints of evolving environmental policy are abundant. Markets are rapidly replacing prescriptive regulation in areas of water allocation, land preservation, conservation easements and saleable credits for wetland development and upland building on potential endangered species habitat. Experimental reintroductions of species, such as wolves, are now routine and provide a means by which the most onerous commands and controls of the Endangered Species Act can be lawfully sidestepped.

Greater reliance on incentives, in turn, is providing a powerful mechanism to win over private lands and their owners to the cause of saving more space for species. Livestock loss compensation programs run by Defenders of Wildlife have taken the bite out of wolves from Montana to New Mexico. At a very minimum, ranchers have the opportunity to be paid, by a private organization, for the cost—measured in lost livestock—of putting up with wolves.

Green marketing strategies promise even more benefits to ranchers who learn to live with predators. Facilitated and certified by environmental groups, green marketing labels for beef provide a powerful incentive for ranchers to put up with wolves and other predators, and to graze their lands in an ecologically sound manner. Consumers get predator- and land-friendly beef, a product they know has helped protect the environment, while ranchers get almost twice the price per pound of beef sold. Together, incentives and markets go a long way toward assuaging landowner fears of endangered species and making them amenable to setting aside habitat for species other than the domestic variety.

Markets and incentives work to the benefit of species and habitats in numerous ways, of course, though none exhibit more promise than the Colorado Ranching for Wildlife program—a private sector initiative pioneered by Malcolm Forbes as an economic surrogate for subdivision of his 150,000-acre Trinchera Ranch in southern Colorado. Done properly, Forbes believed, quality trophy hunting of elk, deer and bighorn sheep could generate sufficient revenues to justify keeping the ranch intact. Working with his managers, Erol and Ty Ryland, Forbes persuaded the Colorado Division of Wildlife (DOW) to start the Ranching for Wildlife Program in 1986.

Open to any substantial private landholding, the program offered a way for landowners to make environmental quality the focus of private land management, to make it pay big dollars, and to make it happen in an historic setting where the state of Colorado owned the wildlife, and where game ranching for private purposes was otherwise strictly forbidden. The program was and remains simple yet elegant.

In return for meeting the DOW's habitat management goals, a private landowner can control not only access to his property but also the number of hunters who can hunt there and the licenses that allow them to do so. Furthermore, once he and the DOW have agreed upon what kind of annual kills the big game herds can sustain, the owner can market the state-issued licenses in any way he pleases. The landowner also gets extended rifle seasons which allow him to spread hunters over a greater time period, enhancing the hunting experience and the price hunters are willing to pay for a quality hunt. Equally important, the landowner gets DOW help in policing poaching problems, since the state-owned animals must be free to roam at will onto or off the ranch. Finally, the state conducts a public lottery for 10 percent of the bull licenses, with a special break for locals. This means that for the price of a hunting license ($35 in Colorado), ordinary people get a shot at the same trophy bulls clients are paying up to $7500 to shoot. And to control animal numbers in a setting managed primarily for elk, the state also gets to allocate the cow elk licenses in a similar manner.

Since 1986, Ranching for Wildlife has spread throughout Colorado, in large part because both state agencies and hunters realize that it is an important tool in the battle to keep big pieces of wildlife habitat intact, regardless of ownership. This is especially true in Colorado, one of the fastest growing states. That growth, combined with an accelerating trend toward subdivision of large ranches and fragmentation of wildlife habitat, convinced Colorado conservationists to support the program. In supporting it, conservationists also learned an important lesson in the utility of property rights. Ranching for Wildlife is proving a dictum counter to John Muir's, namely that secure private property rights to intact ranch lands, and to resources (like elk habitat) that may yield significant economic revenue, are crucial weapons in the battle to save space for common and not-so-common species.

Ranching for Wildlife has proven a boon to the Forbes Ranch and to the other 29 landowners participating in the program. At Forbes, elk routinely go for about $7,500 a hunt, which includes first class accommodations and first class food and drink. With more than a hundred bull-elk licenses assigned to it under the program, Forbes earns an annual gross profit from elk approaching three-quarters of a million dollars. Adding icing to the cake is the annual sale of two bighorn sheep permits on the ranch at $50,000 apiece. So lucrative is the wildlife business that all plans for future subdivision of the ranch have been halted. Moreover, the Forbes family and the ranch manager are eyeing wolves and lynxes as potential species for reintroduction for both profit and sounder wildlife management. Now that wildlife is a paying partner on the Forbes ranch, the owners are eager to keep the ranch wild and open to the full array of native herbivores and carnivores. The end result is that 150,000 acres of ranchland that might have been bulldozed for homes is now safely set aside for species and habitat, thanks to markets and incentives.

Ranching for Wildlife shares many of the features of Zimbabwe's conservancies, save one. Apart from several ranchers who have entered into partnership in the program, most participants are individual landowners. Conservation of species and their habitat in Ranching for Wildlife lacks the associational and community-based face that distinguishes Zimbabwean efforts. Indeed, this is generally true of most market- and incentive-based wildlife programs in the U.S.: individual initiatives eclipse most cooperative endeavors. A notable exception to this is the Grass Bank run by the ranchers of the Malpais Association in the southwest boothill country of New Mexico. Spurred on by concerns over future development of local ranchlands for summer and retirement homes, and anxious to restore the ecological condition of historically overgrazed rangelands, the Malpais ranchers coalesced and agreed to a unique solution: they created a Grass Bank out of the half million-acre Gray Ranch operated by the Animas Foundation.

Every neighboring rancher was given the opportunity to buy into the Grass Bank. They could do so by depositing in the bank all future development rights to their ranches in exchange for a bank credit in grass. That credit, in turn, allowed participating ranchers to access forage on the Gray Ranch up to a quantity equal to the value of the development rights surrendered to the bank.

This did two things, both of which contributed to the long-term prospects of species and species habitat. First, it created a voluntary process by which communities of landowners could preserve their lands as open space in perpetuity and, in the process, reap significant benefits. Second, it gave landowners a powerful tool for restoring their lands to full ecological health. For the first time in the Malpais's history, ranchers had a safety-valve in case of drought. Rather than overgraze their rangelands in hard times, they could make grass withdrawals from the Grass Bank to keep their herds and their lands healthy. More importantly, it gave ranchers a proactive tool for restoring rangeland health in good times. With the security of a community grass bank behind them, they could now afford to rest their lands for extended periods or to burn their pastures to eliminate invasive brush and to stimulate grass growth.

The Grass Bank is one of many innovative ideas aimed at restoring private lands and making them—once again—a critical spatial link in the conservation, protection and restoration of plant and animals species. A small herd of desert bison, descended from a much larger but now extinct southwestern herd, makes the Malpais its home, thanks in part to the Grass Bank. The jaguar, long-extinct in the U.S., made its first return two years ago on the Gray Ranch, again a tribute to the changing attitudes on wildlife management forged by the Grass Bank. Further, versions of the grass bank are emerging across the West, all aimed at making ranching economically viable, environmentally friendly, and sufficiently stable to maintain the private spaces needed for the region's rich heritage of fauna and flora.

Ideas such as the Grass Bank provide fertile ground for the hybridization of African and American private and communal approaches to the saving of space for species. A prime example is the Resource Bank that is now materializing in the Sangre de Cristo Mountains of southern Colorado. This offspring of the Grass Bank is the product of both private and communal traditions, and is linked to a private conservation effort that Tom Wolf, a southwestern conservationist and environmental writer, has termed "The String of Pearls"—a series of contiguous private land ranches anchored to the south by Ted Turner's New Mexico Vermijo Park Ranch and continuing north along the Sangre de Cristo spine through the Forbes Trinchera Ranch and terminating at the 100,000 acre Baca Ranch, owned by Gary Boyce and bordering the Great Sand Dunes National Monument. In all, the String of Pearls includes a half-dozen ranches, stretches over 100 miles south to north, and embraces about 1.5 million acres.

The String of Pearls is both unique and important. It is unique because it is made up of exclusively private lands. It is important because it holds the habitat potential for restoring key carnivore species to the Sangre de Cristo ecosystem: the lynx and the wolf. Moreover, the landowners who hold title to the pearls are either exclusively in the wildlife business or moving in that direction. Elk, for example, is the bread and butter crop of both Turner's Vermijo Park Ranch and Forbes' Trinchera Ranch. In addition, both The Nature Conservancy and the Baca Ranch are setting aside their portions of the String of Pearls as private wildlife refuges. By a combination of historic accident and prudent foresight, the lower Colorado and upper New Mexico Sangre de Cristo Mountains constitute one of the largest effective wilderness areas in the lower 48 states—a wilderness area that is thoroughly private, committed to saving space for species, and successful at making money doing both. And the landscape it circumscribes embraces a nearly intact and fully functional ecosystem, one that is suitable for one of the most migratory of large carnivores, the gray wolf—or, more accurately, would be suitable save for one weak link in the String of Pearls: the Taylor Ranch.

The history of the Taylor Ranch is colorful and controversial. Wedged between the Turner Vermijo Park and Forbes Trinchera ranches, Taylor is one of the smaller pearls, less than 80,000 acres in size. Nonetheless, it may well be the most critical of the pearls, providing what amounts to a functional corridor for wildlife between the more massive ranches to the north and south. Its history—and its title—are clouded by claims and counter-claims as to who has legal and moral rights to its resources.

Like the Forbes Trinchera Ranch, the Taylor Ranch—known locally as La Sierra, or the mountain tract—was carved out of the Sangre de Cristo Land Grant in 1843. When finally sold to Jack Taylor in 1960, the title to the ranch was in immediate dispute between the new owner and the Hispanic residents of nearby San Luis, who claimed they held communal rights to the ranch's forage, water, wildlife and wood. Jack Taylor and his descendants have since fought community claims on ranch resources and have been victorious up to this day. Nonetheless, the barrage of lawsuits and ill-will that has arisen from the conflict has compromised the ecological integrity of the ranch and threatened its critical role as a connecting corridor between the much larger private ranches that lie to its north and south.

Much of the problem stems from the ranch's timber cutting policy and the acrimony—and misunderstanding—it has bred among neighbors. The owners of the Taylor Ranch are fearful that local opinion and mounting protests from environmentalists, all of whom are opposed to any logging on the ranch, may create a political environment that could shut down their multi-million-dollar timber program and severely erode the $20 million-dollar market value of their ranch. These concerns have caused them to accelerate their timber cuts (all select cuts aimed at removing the largest diameter trees)—but not without social and ecological ramifications. Local residents are enraged at the rate of timber cutting, fearing adverse effects to their summer irrigation waters, all of which originate on the Taylor Ranch. More significantly, the accelerated timber cuts have ruled out much needed post-harvest silvicultural treatments that could enhance water storage and improve wildlife habitat and wildlife movement along the Sangre de Cristo spine.

Making matters worse, the singular focus on logging by all sides in the dispute has encouraged lax to no management of cattle grazing at lower elevations on the ranch. Although the owners of the Taylor Ranch have never grazed domestic stock themselves, they do lease grazing privileges to adjacent farms in an effort to improve relations and to provide much needed summer range to small farms that are otherwise dependent on irrigated meadows. This has resulted in localized overgrazing of riparian areas, deterioration of some upland meadows, and heavy grazing on low elevation winter ranges that are essential for the ranch's trophy elk herd—and mandatory for the ranch's participation in Colorado's Ranching for Wildlife program. As a result, an almost invisible yet pervasive deterioration of the ranch is occurring, potentially.

Timber, water, range and wildlife issues on the Taylor Ranch have given rise to a bold plan that could transform the ranch into a model of private conservation throughout the West and, at the same time, give substance and form to the moral, if not legal, claims of San Luisans to a share of the forage, water, wood and wildlife resources of their adopted La Sierra. The plan—a hybrid of grass banks, grassroots conservation, conservationists working in tandem with Taylor Ranch, and a ranch ownership friendly toward innovation—would reconcile private property rights with historic communal uses and usufruct rights, and do so through the transforming power of the marketplace.

Similar in intent to the community-based conservation initiatives now under way in southern and east-central Africa, the plan would turn the Taylor Ranch into a resource bank for both its owners and its neighbors. The bank would provide a continuous flow of resource benefits to San Luisans. Those benefits would then contribute to the profit-making wildlife and timber ventures of the Taylor family, or whoever holds title to the ranch. Here is it how it would work.

The Ranching for Wildlife Program would be expanded, on a voluntary basis, to embrace the valley bottom farms that border the Taylor Ranch and that contain the unrealized though much needed elk winter range that could make the ranch a fully intact ecosystem. Currently, those farmlands grow grass to feed cattle in winter. Yet the value of those cattle when fed on that winter hay is only a fraction of the economic value of elk when raised on the same forage, uncut and unbaled. By adding small private parcels of former livestock haylands to the ranch's expansive summer upland ranges, the total number of available elk licenses in the ranch's Ranching for Wildlife contract would increase significantly. The Taylor family would earn more revenue, small Hispanic farmers would more than double their per-acre net profits from their valley meadows, and enough cash would be left over to buy local hay to sustain their displaced cattle for the winter.

During the summer, cattle grazing would continue on the Taylor Ranch, but with two big differences. One, there would no longer be an assessed grazing fee or, for that matter, a fixed stocking rate. The number of cows grazed each year would fluctuate to meet specific management needs. Two, in turn for free grass, community stockmen would assume responsibility for 1) protecting sensitive areas, such as wetlands, from adverse cattle impact; 2) stopping cattle trespass and associated overgrazing; 3) herding and holding their livestock in key areas to attain specified wildlife goals; and 4) conserving low elevation winter range for elk use. For example, community stockmen might be required, as a condition of their Resource Bank rights, to use cattle grazing as a way to rejuvenate overgrown meadows for fall elk use or to diversify the variety of plants in aspen stands for summer elk use. By hitching grazing to wildlife conservation, local graziers would not only gain the summer forage their stock demand, but they would contribute to the expansion of elk habitat and, in time, to the hunting revenues they would share with the Taylor family. At the same time, they would provide the very management needed to make the Taylor Ranching for Wildlife operation an economic and ecologic success.

It's too early to tell if the Resource Bank will work—or even if all the players in the ranch's future will embrace its benefits, its responsibilities and its challenge to the conventional thinking on species conservation. But the idea is, like its African siblings, an unequivocable declaration for the ecological merits of private and communal spaces. It sets a course for species conservation that straddles the fine line between private and communal ownership and that links the backbone of the Sangre de Cristo mountains to the conservancy and CAMPFIRE programs of Zimbabwe and to the western foothills of Tanzania's Mt. Kilimanjaro. It embodies a new way of thinking about saving species, about the processes of ecology, and about the meanings of wilderness, core zones, buffer areas and protected preserves. It blurs the divisions between all four and projects a more unified vision of man and nature, one where people assume responsibility for nature and where nature reciprocates with fair and equitable interest. Above all, it steers us toward a world where private and communal landholders embrace as their lodestar the self-evident truths of a firmly held and resolutely upheld land ethic.

Notes

1   John Muir, Our National Parks. 1970. (New York: AMS Press), p. 361.

2   McNeely, J.A., J. Harrison, and P. Dingwald, eds. 1994. Protecting Nature (Gland, Switzerland: IUCN).

3   Newmark, W.D. 1995. "Extinction of mammal populations in western North American National Parks," Conservation Biology 9:512-526.

4   Western, David and Mary Pearl. 1989. Conservation for the Twenty-First Century (New York: Oxford University Press), p. 158.

5   Hardin, Garrett. 1968. "The Tragedy of the Commons," Science 162:1243-1248.

6   See: Berkes, Fikret, ed. 1989. Common Property Resources: Ecology and Community-Based Sustainable Development (London: Belhaven Press); Bromley, Daniel W., ed. 1992. Making the Commons Work (San Francisco: ICS Press); and Ostrom, Elinor. 1991. Governing the Commons (London: Cambridge University Press).

2 Science and Values in Species Protection

JAMES L. HUFFMAN

.

Endangered species, even the small, slimy or ugly ones, are having an impact on American economics and politics which the early proponents of endangered species protection could not have imagined. The Endangered Species Act, which lay largely dormant for the first several years of its existence, has become one of the most powerful weapons in the armory of environmentalists. For many proponents of economic growth and resource development, the Act has come to symbolize what is wrong with America's environmental laws. As a result, the debate over the future of the Endangered Species Act has been, and will remain, at the forefront of environmental politics. All the more so because many proponents of species protection, like the Act's traditional opponents, believe the Act is in desperate need of amendment. While the traditional opponents of the Act seek to weaken its take-no-prisoners approach to the protection of individual species, advocates of biodiversity and ecosystem management seek to strengthen the Act by shifting its focus from species to ecosystem protection. In the face of this ongoing political debate, it will be useful to step back a bit and bring some perspective to this particularly contentious case of scarce resource allocation. No doubt some will object, already, to this way of describing the endangered species question. It will be argued that species and ecosystems are not "resources" to be analyzed in the amoral terms of economics. Indeed, it will be argued that such economic analysis is not just amoral, but immoral. Species and ecosystem protection, for some, is a moral imperative. To those of this perspective, I urge that you bear with me as I describe how morality influences both private and public decision makers. What follows is not a moral or a policy argument. Rather it is an effort to describe how decisions which impact on species are made in fact, and how those who seek influence might bring their values and objectives to bear on those decisions. Legislation like the Endangered Species Act and the regulations promulgated pursuant to such laws are part of a vast array of human initiatives meant to serve human welfare. Among the legal tools we have relied upon in environmental protection, command and control regulation has been our dominant approach, based upon a heavy reliance on science. I will argue that we should place greater reliance on market-based approaches to endangered species protection, and that we should recognize the limited role of science in choosing among policy alternatives.

The Instrumentalist Perspective

In his book Law and the Conditions of Freedom in the 19th Century United States,[1] Willard Hurst brought the insight to American legal history that the law of 19th century America was less the product of abstract ideas than of practical ambition. Hurst did not mean to say that ideas do not matter, but rather that they do matter, and that people are variously influenced by them in the pursuit of human purposes. For Hurst and most of his followers, legal history is the story of reliance on the law to achieve human objectives—a view which has come to be known as legal instrumentalism. Hurst's view that legal history can be best understood as a product of human ambition, and his focus on 19th century America, make his analysis particularly relevant to contemporary debates about the Endangered Species Act. Hurst brings two assumptions to his analysis of 19th century instrumentalism, both of which remain dominant in American thinking, even as we prepare to enter the new millennium.

First is the importance of individual liberty (including for private, voluntary associations which are themselves a product of individual liberty) to the improvement of human welfare. Second is the importance of state power to the improvement of human welfare. We remain legal instrumentalists, even those who seek to use the law to protect species ecosystems for their own sake, as we enter the 21st century. But we have lived through more than half a century during which individual liberty has been viewed by many as more of an obstacle to, than an instrument of, human welfare, and the power of the state has been the default method for achieving pursuit of the public good. In the environmental arena, the predisposition for reliance on the state is bolstered by the widely accepted view that most environmental degradation is a product of an unregulated market economy. The result has been heavy reliance on command and control environmental laws, of which the Endangered Species Act is an archetypal example.

In the 19th century described by Hurst, state power sought to improve human welfare by expanding liberty. In the 20th century, particularly since the New Deal, state power has been employed to improve human welfare by constraining liberty. Some might object that in the 20th century liberty has expanded in the form of universal participation in the democratic process, and that our regulatory approach to environmental protection is the product of liberty rather than a constraint on liberty. But this perspective misunderstands what Hurst and his 19th century subjects meant by liberty. Unlike late 20th century Americans, 19th century Americans did not conflate the public liberty of democratic government with the private liberty of individual enterprise. They understood that public liberty is not an end in itself, but a means to the achievement of a private liberty which is compatible with and contributes to, indeed is essential to, the public good.

Liberty, the Public Good and Species Protections

The 19th century instrumentalists, about whom Hurst writes, were explicitly concerned about the improvement of human welfare. No doubt many mainstream environmentalists of the late 20th century will read Hurst and conclude that therein lie the roots of the environmental problems which have focused our attention for the last three decades, particularly the problems of species and ecosystem loss. They will argue that, following in the steps of our 19th century predecessors, we have been concerned with private gain and short-term human welfare at the expense of the environment, and thus, unwittingly, at the expense of human welfare in the long run. Radical environmentalists would be even more condemning of Hurst's 19th century instrumentalists for their blatant anthropocentrism—their word, not mine. The term anthropocentrism is meant to be descriptive of a world view which assumes that human welfare is the central focus of law and policy. In radical environmentalist circles, and even among some mainstream environmentalists like Vice President Gore, it is also meant to convey disapproval, if not disdain. For Gore, anthropocentrism is the root cause of our "dysfunctional society;" biocentric thinking is the cure.[2] To state it in the moral reference of the Star Wars generation, Darth Vader would be an anthropocentrist; Luke Skywalker a biocentrist. But the reality is that we cannot escape our humanity, just as Luke cannot avoid that Vader is his father. We might cheer for Luke to rise above his lineage, but we should not be so anxious to abandon our western, liberal heritage. Of that we do have a choice, but we cannot supplant some set of human values with those of the forest or the meadow. The decisions we make are unavoidably based upon human values, and more than a millennia of intellectual history demonstrates that humans are better off for it. Humans have neither the capacity nor the moral authority to assess whether the planet and its species and ecosystems are worse or better off. Indeed, absent the presence of humans with their capacity for valuation and judgment, there is no other measure of "better." The human capacity for reason, while perhaps not unique to our species, is so far superior in humans that the rest of the natural world is chaos and randomness by comparison. Neither the bald eagle nor the ancient redwood can be said to value its circumstance. The nobility of the former and the grandeur of the latter are only expressions of human values, as is their place in an ecosystem which provides pleasure and sustenance to humans. Those values may be more or less concerned with environmental protection, but they are nonetheless human. The 19th century was not devoid of what, in today's unfortunate terminology, would be called biocentric thinkers. Thoreau,[3] Muir[4] and Marsh,[5] among others, made nature's case in their writings and sought to live their lives as an example for others. But they understood that it would take more than written and exemplary persuasion to alter the impacts of human development on nature. It would take legislation and private acts of resource protection, which meant that one needed to be able to influence the myriad decision makers whose actions affected nature. One not only had to persuade others of nature's worth, but also to devise legal and extralegal institutions which would create the incentives necessary to affect human behavior. In other words, 19th century conservationists and preservationists were among the instrumentalists about whom Hurst writes. The pitched battle between Gifford Pinchot and John Muir over Hetch Hetchy in the Yosemite Valley was not finally a moral argument. It was a disagreement about means as well as ends. Both men understood that to achieve their purposes, they had to prevail in a political contest. It has been Willard Hurst's greatest contribution to our understanding of our legal history to teach us that, while ideas matter, they do not, alone, win the day. Ideas and values give us reason to devise the legal and nonlegal tools necessary to achieving the results we seek. We may choose to call ourselves conservationists or environmentalists or biocentrists, but we are whistling in the wind unless we are also skilled instrumentalists. The successful instrumentalist is one who understands those whose behavior we seek to influence. Human history is replete with examples of governments commanding the results they seek. But such unsophisticated instrumentalism inevitably fails, while doing untold harm to affected humans. There is a reason we call it tyranny. It is not the American way, nor, as 20th century history demonstrates, is it an effective way. There may be a few individuals prepared to sacrifice their freedom and their very lives for species preservation, but the vast majority of people in this country, and I dare say in every country on the globe (including the aboriginal nations of our own continent), seek to satisfy a complex array of human values. One can easily be a martyr to the cause of nature, but with little impact on the realization of that end. The achievement of something more than martyrdom requires a commitment to influencing and affecting the behavior of one's fellow humans. Chaining oneself to trees and communing with nature's creatures just will not do it. People across the globe value liberty. They also value a safe and healthy community which, among other things, is essential to liberty. In the United States we govern ourselves under a Constitution designed by its framers to establish a government which would provide for the common good while promoting and protecting liberty. The common good and individual liberty were not understood to be in conflict. To the contrary, the common good would be served by the protection of liberty and visa versa. History confirms that the framers were correct in this understanding of the relationship between individual liberty and the common good. It will serve us well, whether we seek to preserve species or some other public good, to understand this fundamental premise of American constitutionalism. While the environment will sometimes benefit from the use of state power to limit individual liberty, it is also clear that private institutions founded on liberty can and do benefit the environment. This fact, combined with the recognition that liberty is a core value of our culture and constitution, and therefore sometimes in competition with environmental protection, should cause us to pursue a broad range of public and private approaches to species protection and ecosystem preservation. For too long in the environmental area, as in many other areas of public concern, our default position has been command and control regulation. We will serve our multiple purposes best if we are open to the whole range of legal and policy tools, and if we bring an understanding of human behavior to our selection among these tools. By no means do I mean to embrace a regime of social engineering, nor do I suggest that we have the capacity to govern our future with anything approaching precision. But if we are persuaded by Hurst's instrumentalist interpretation of legal development, we must accept that laws have consequences and that through the enactment and interpretation of those laws we have some capacity to influence those consequences. It is not that social engineering is necessarily a positive good, but rather that it is in the nature of the legal enterprise.

Law as Technology

The instrumentalist perspective suggests thinking about law as the technology of social existence. Human life is filled with uncertainties rooted in both nature and society. Life in the natural world is buffeted by weather, disease, earthquakes and an array of other influences which can disrupt the best laid plans and even threaten survival. The social existence inherent to humans is also filled with the uncertainties of human interaction. We have undertaken all manner of controls on the risks imposed by nature, some based on the simple strategy of avoidance and many others relying on technologies designed to keep us warm or cool, prevent disease, and reinforce our buildings against structural damage. Much of the earth was once scarcely habitable because of the risks imposed by nature. Today, technology permits permanent human settlement even in space. Some will contend that these technological fixes for expanded human settlement are increasingly threatening the earth's sustainability as a home for many species and even for humans. But my point is not that the technologies which have tamed the risks of nature are sustainable, rather that resorting to technology is part of human nature. It is also in human nature to seek control over the uncertainties of human society. We have devised various approaches to making social life safer and more productive by influencing individual and group behavior. Education, although we have not been very successful at it in recent years, is one important approach. We seek to educate people about the consequences of their actions. We also seek to influence their values and to appeal for modified behavior in light of those values, although such appeals seldom produce sustained changes in human behavior unless they become part of the core religious or community norms. Environmentalists have been strong advocates of education as a tool of environmental protection, but there is little evidence that appeals to voluntarism are very effective absent other incentives. Another approach is the public provision of services, facilities and benefits with the expectation that desired private actions will follow. Public works projects and other subsidies have had many desired effects, although usually with the inefficiencies inherent in public enterprise and with the inevitable institutionalization of pork barrel politics. They have also had many unintended effects, often environmentally harmful, as is the case of the extensive network of dams in the Columbia River which has resulted in serious risk to anadromous fish runs. An alternative to public works and subsidies paid for with tax dollars is regulation of private actions thought to be harmful or undesirable. This command

and control approach has dominated the first three decades of modern environmental protection with mixed results. Regulations can seldom account for the infinite variation in circumstances over time and space, and they inevitably have unintended consequences, often in the form of perverse incentives with resultant environmental harm. Finally, human behavior can be influenced by affecting the costs and benefits of human actions through the laws which can be accomplished through regulating private transactions and the laws which define the relationship between individuals and their government. This approach assumes that people have a significant degree of free will and that the incentives of costs and benefits will influence the choices they make. Thus, the law is a tool kit for influencing human conduct, both private and public, by creating and rearranging incentives. The tools include constitutions, contracts, property, crime, regulation and the whole panoply which is the bread and butter of every law school curriculum.

Environmental Law and the Allocation of Scare Resources

Much law is concerned with the allocation of scarce resources. Many advocates of environmental protection might prefer to think of environmental law in ethical terms, but even when the objective is species or ecosystem preservation, it is not inaccurate to describe the problem being addressed as one of scarce resource allocation. This view of environmental and species protection laws conflates them with what are commonly described as natural resources laws. It is a conflation offensive to some environmentalists, but essential to effective pursuit of environmental and species protection goals. The Endangered Species Act commands that threatened and endangered species receive prescribed levels of protection, a command which impinges on most aspects of our day-to-day lives. We cannot achieve the goals of the ESA in isolation from the wide array of choices about the allocation of other scarce resources. Endangered salmon runs in the Pacific Northwest illustrate the point as well as any prior experience under the ESA. Residents of the Columbia River Basin are advised by their state and local governments that they should expect their lives to be impacted in many ways by the recent listing of several runs of endangered salmon. Not only will hydroelectric management, commercial and sport fishing, timber harvesting and land use decisions be affected, but everything from lawn fertilizers to the hosing of one's driveway, we are told, will probably be subject to regulation. These and many other affected decisions are made in the context of laws and legal relationships which are unrelated to the ESA. Together these laws, regulations, contracts, property rights, and constitutional protections constitute a complex array of legal technology influencing the allocation of scarce resources. As much as we might like to focus on the specific problem of species protection, we will not succeed if we fail to understand the legal context and the many alternative legal tools we might employ in pursuit of our objective. Whether we are concerned with air quality, water pollution or species protection, we are dealing with resource scarcity problems. While some may argue that pollution of the air or water, or risk to a living organism, must be constrained, presumably for moral or ethical reasons, without regard to the availability of substitutes, the reality is that humans have not evidenced concern for environmental values matters absent competing demands for the resources in question. The reason is that there are opportunity costs to such constraints. The avoidance of air and water pollution, and the preservation of species and their habitat, are not free goods. Virtually every human activity affects air and water quality and species habitat. Even if these effects are insignificant in isolation, in aggregation they have consequences. Avoidance of the consequences requires modification or elimination of the affecting activities. In other words, there are tradeoffs for environmental and species protection. If we value them infinitely, we will be willing to trade our very existence for their achievement. But no one, save perhaps a handful of zealots, will volunteer their lives to environmental purity. For most people, environmental protection, like everything else, has its price. The point was made convincingly nearly three decades ago by William Baxter in People or Penguins: The Case for Optimal Pollution.[6] Baxter made clear that zero pollution will seldom if ever be optimal, which is to say it will probably never be the choice we make if we are faced with consideration of all of the tradeoffs. Baxter made the case for optimal pollution in the context of what we might call non-environmental tradeoffs—a sort of guns versus butter analysis. Less pollution means more expensive cars. Species protection means fewer board feet of lumber. But less air pollution also may mean more water pollution. And protection of one species may mean threat to another. In the context of pollution policy these tradeoffs were understood by those in the Bush Administration who advocated integrated pollution control. It is not clear that advocates of species protection at any cost have come to a similar understanding. In the Northwest it is widely held that we must save the salmon no matter the cost. Salmon, it is said, are nature's expression of the Northwest as a unique and special place. But we do not really mean to save the salmon at any cost. What if we breach the lower Snake River dams and the salmon are still in trouble? Will we breach the Columbia River dams, and the dams of the other tributaries? And what if the salmon are still in trouble? Will we curtail all timber harvesting and agriculture? Will we forbid the Indians to fish, notwithstanding their religion and their treaties? No, we will have our price at which we will conclude, although with great regret, that the salmon will have to make it or not on their own.

The Role of Science in Environmental Policy

Advances in the ecological and environmental sciences have been invaluable to the pursuit of environmental protection. We have come to understand many of the detrimental environmental consequences of past actions and to anticipate and avoid future environmental damage. But in our public policy making, we have often substituted science for the challenge of making hard choices. By looking to science for policy prescriptions, we have obscured that policy decisions are centrally and unavoidably about making tradeoffs in the allocation of scarce resources. Illustrative is the ongoing debate about salmon protection in the Columbia River Basin. Thirteen species and subspecies of salmon and trout have been listed by the Fish and Wildlife Service as threatened or endangered in Oregon alone. The implications of these listings are potentially enormous for the states of Washington, Oregon and Idaho. Under the Endangered Species Act, the fish and their habitat must be preserved at almost any cost. Those costs are certain to be very high, but they have no relevance to the prescribed scientific inquiry. While it is unlikely that anyone in Congress anticipated such region-wide impacts when the ESA was enacted, it is not a surprising result. It was only a matter of time until the mandatory nature of the Act would be utilized by environmental groups to pursue interests well beyond individual species and local habitat protection. But for most of the history of the ESA, the impacts have been local and therefore of little interest to Congress. The only notable exception was the very early Tellico Dam case which, because of its size and the general surprise that the Act applied to puny fish as well as grizzly bears, elicited a Congressional response. Not until the listing of the northern spotted owl was there an application of the Act that had extensive regional consequences. And in that case a presidential forest summit saved Congress from facing up to what it had wrought. What Congress has wrought is a species protection system which relies largely on science to resolve what are unavoidably political and economic issues. Section 1533(b)(1)(A) of the Endangered Species Act directs that listings of threatened and endangered species shall be made "solely on the basis of the best scientific and commercial data available." If the science indicates that the survival of a species is threatened or endangered, it is listed, and activities impacting on the species are prohibited or restricted without regard to economic or social consequences. While the Act provides for exemptions, it is a process almost never used and unlikely to be used given the thousands of existing and potential listings. It might be argued that Congress has made the political and economic choices in the adoption of the Act and that the only thing remaining for the agencies is the science. But it is implausible to assume, as we must if we accept this argument at face value, that Congress intended that we preserve every species without regard to cost. The potentially immense costs of species protection might be spent on education, health care or national defense. And while the good scientist will tell us that we cannot know for certain that some species can be safely sacrificed, there seems to be general agreement that some species are more important than others to maintenance and survival of ecosystems. Also, it seems that some ecosystems are more important than others to the general welfare of the planet. So unless we really mean to preserve every species without regard to cost, we cannot rely exclusively on scientists to set species protection policy. This is not a criticism of scientists as scientists. It is merely a recognition of the fact that scientists have nothing special to contribute on the subject of scarce resource allocation. What scientists can do, and what we must look to them to do, is provide decision makers with the best information possible. Whether we allocate scarce resources by political aggregation of individual preferences or by market aggregation of private choices, decision makers will benefit from good information about the costs and benefits of their actions. To the extent that resource use and development harms endangered species, it is important to understand the nature of the harm and how it might be mitigated. But that understanding, which scientists can provide, will be only one among many factors relevant to most resource allocation decisions. Recently some 200 scientists wrote to President Clinton urging the breaching of lower Snake River dams to save the endangered salmon. Like any other voters, scientists are certainly entitled to their opinions, but that was not the point of their letter. They did not write to say that 200 voters who happened to be scientists believed that it would be a good thing to breach the dams. Rather they asserted special standing as scientists, and they had every reason to believe their opinions as scientists might trump the competing opinions of mere citizens whose lives would be affected by breaching of the dams. Scientists have been asked repeatedly to save us from the difficult choices inherent in environmental regulation. It is all too tempting to ask the scientists to tell us what the science says we should do. This reliance on science is rooted in the progressivism of the early 20th century. It defined the founding of the Forest Service, our first real resource management agency, and has come to define virtually every federal agency with resource management jurisdiction, even the venerable Bureau of Land Management, which had its beginnings as the dispenser of real estate at bargain prices. All of the public lands management legislation since the 1960s, notwithstanding a romance with planning and public participation, looked finally to science to resolve what was always controversial in politics. The Endangered Species Act is the culmination of this belief in scientific management. It may be that the best thing to do is save the endangered salmon runs of the Pacific Northwest, no matter what the cost. But we will not get to that conclusion by reading a letter from 200 scientists who believe that the best prospect for saving the salmon is the breaching of the lower Snake River dams. Those very same scientists will be the first to say that there is no guarantee that dam breaching will save the fish. Presumably they might agree to some assessment of the probability of success, and they might also agree to some estimate of the probability that barging, a ban on fishing, or some other strategy will contribute to the desired result. But there are a multitude of other variables to be considered, some relating to alternative fish management strategies, and others relating to the vast array of other things which people in the Northwest care about. Scientists will be helpful to our understanding of many of these other variables. They can help us to assess the impact on agriculture of reduced water storage and on energy supplies of reduced hydropower generation. They can provide their best assessments of the effects on migratory waterfowl and other wildlife which might be affected by the loss of the artificial lakes now behind the dams to be breached. But finally the decisions to be made, whether public or private, will not be dictated by science. They will represent our best guess as to what mix of resource allocations will maximize net social and personal welfare.

Notes

1   Hurst, James Willard. 1967. Law and the Conditions of Freedom in the Nineteenth-Century United States.
2   Gore, Albert. 1992. Earth in the Balance: Ecology and the Human Spirit, 223.
3   Thoreau, Henry David. 1988. Natural History Essays.
4   Muir, John. 1997. Nature Writings.
5   Marsh, George Perkins. 1965. Man and Nature.
6   Baxter, William F. 1974. People or Penguins: The Case for Optimal Pollution.

3 Models or Muddles? Property Rights and the Endangered Species Act

MARK SAGOFF

"When landowners find an endangered animal on their property," Chuck Cushman says, "the best solution under current law is to 'shoot, shovel and shut up.'"[1] So The Arizona Republic newspaper reported the response of one landowner to the decision of the Supreme Court in Babbitt v. Sweet Home Chapter of Communities for a Great Oregon. At issue there was Section 9 of the Endangered Species Act (ESA), which makes it a crime to "take" an endangered or threatened species. The ESA defines "take" as "to harass, harm, pursue, hunt, shoot, wound, kill, trap, capture, or collect."[2] The Interior Department extended the definition of "harm" to include "significant habitat modification or degradation [that] actually kills or injures wildlife by significantly impairing essential behavioral patterns, including breeding, feeding, or sheltering."[3] In Sweet Home, the Supreme Court by a 6-3 majority upheld this extension of the meaning of "harm" in Section 9 of the Endangered Species Act. Cushman, executive director of the American Land Rights Association, based in Battle Ground, Washington, identified civil disobedience as a rational response to the Court's decision. He explained, "A private property owner is thinking to himself, 'I find a spotted owl on my property, I'm going to lose everything I've worked for all my life.'" A property owner may find immediate recourse in shooting and burying the bird before federal agents discover it. In Cushman's view, a more general remedy must be sought from Congress. "I think you're going to see an eruption in Congress. It's obvious to everyone now that the Endangered Species Act is broke and it's gotta be fixed."[4] Landowners like Chuck Cushman know how to deal with a statute they do not like. They bollix up the implementation process through legal and other maneuvers while they lobby the legislature to get the law changed. The Republican Party was able to gain control of Congress in 1994 in part because several of its candidates, for example, in Texas, we able to take advantage of citizen discontent with the way the ESA had been enforced. Republican members of Congress, in their Contract With America, promised to reassert the rights of private property against what they thought was a federal bureaucracy run amok. By softening its enforcement policy, the Clinton Administration managed to keep the ESA on the books.[5] But agency officials know or should know that property owners like Mr. Cushman, if properly organized and motivated, may do more that shoot, shovel, and shut up. If they associate politically, they may move Congress to eviscerate the Endangered Species Act and unfund the agencies charged with enforcing it.

The Thesis of the Essay

This essay agues that the extent to which species are to be protected—the extent to which the ESA should be enforced—is and ought to be a political question. This means that the nation should adopt whatever policy musters the most political support. In this respect, species protection is like education. No one opposes education, but people disagree about how much the public should pay for. How much education is worth the costs? What sort of programs work best for the money? Some people think society should pay, others think that individuals should pay, some people favor a mix. The political process decides how much education—or species protection—we should have and who should pay for it. This essay will argue for the plausible thesis that no better—or at least no other—basis exists on which to make this kind of decision. If environmentalists succeed in moving Congress to strengthen the enforcement of the ESA, then stricter enforcement is the correct policy. If their opponents succeed in moving Congress to eviscerate the Act, then less enforcement becomes the appropriate outcome. If the political process is open, responsive and fair, there is no basis on which anyone can second-guess its result. The proper amount of species protection, like the proper amount of education, given the costs, cannot be determined by scientific research, deduced from constitutional principles, or divined by policy analysis. It is simply a political question. The question is not whether species protection (like education) is a good thing. Let us assume it is a good thing. That having been said, one confronts the interesting and controversial question, which is, how much is it worth and who is to pay for it? The government or landowners? On this question, political opinion divides. Property-rights advocates argue that regulation may not diminish the value of property unless compensation (implicit or explicit) is paid. To suppose otherwise, on this view, is to remove any discipline or constraint from regulatory agencies. It is also to ignore the constitutional mandate that private property shall not be taken for public use without just compensation. Environmentalists, in the spirit of Aldo Leopold, in turn, argue that the land community forms an interconnected ecological whole, the functioning of which the government must protect. Statutes like the ESA, on this view, require no compensation in their enforcement because they simply protect biological systems on which the public depends and no one has a right to destroy. Each side has high hopes that the courts will vindicate its position. And each deplores the persistent refusal of the courts to recognize the obvious philosophical merit and scientific truth of its position. This essay does not take either side in this controversy. Rather it argues that both positions, though presented as the findings of science and reason, express ideological views better accommodated through the political process than vindicated in the courts. This essay starts from the assumption that courts should not attempt to adjudicate among citizens with opposing scientific, philosophical or metaphysical opinions. Rather, the courts should assure the openness and fairness of institutions through which those with opposing doctrines in science and philosophy can deal with each other without violence. On one side of the controversy environmentalists and, on the other, those who defend the rights of private property, each press visions of the scientific or philosophical truth, often confronting each other in futile stand-offs from which neither side has much to gain. Alternatively they can climb down from their theoretical or ideological high horses to solve particular problems on the ground, for example, by finding and agreeing upon methods to preserve specific endangered species cheaply and upon ways to allocate the costs. Each species in jeopardy may present a different opportunity for devising a clever cost-saving preservation plan. The philosophical and ideological disagreements that divide environmentalists and their adversaries may never be settled. These two groups might be able to agree on practical approaches to species protection, however, if they tried to find businesslike ways to solve problems rather than to press general theoretical concerns. This essay condemns as self-righteous and undemocratic the tendency of each side to appeal to theory—ecological or constitutional—to show it is right. It celebrates the political give-and-take that encourages property-owners and environmentalists to see that they can accomplish a lot more by working together to solve problems than by stalemating each other in order to vindicate the integrity of their positions.

The two sides engaged in debating the "taking" of property rights under the ESA appeal to a priori constitutional or scientific arguments which, as they hope, will sway the courts. Fortunately, the Supreme Court has refused to vindicate either side in this academic debate and has instead maintained a conservative course while respecting the priority of the political process. The public interest may now best be served not by those who engage in academic debate about property and ecological rights, but by those who solve the problems, case by case, involved in keeping threatened species intact. This requires leadership that can build constituencies and exploit practical opportunities for getting a particular job done at the lowest cost. Those who care about protecting species need to learn about the particular details of each plant or animal and about the places in which it may thrive. They must also earn the trust of landowners and others whose cooperation they have to secure. Theorizing has become a form of laziness; the particulars on the ground are what count.

The Two Sides to the Controversy

Advocates of property rights do not applaud the extinction of species. They do not suggest that protecting species is a bad idea—most agree it is a lovely idea—but they ask who should pay for it.[6] If the public wishes to protect a warbler, lousewort or toad, that is well and good, these commentators say, but the public should purchase the necessary habitat, acquiring it in the open market or by eminent domain.[7] These critics point with approval to Section 5 of the statute, which gives the government authority to buy critical habitat. They oppose the idea that the government may require private landowners to dedicate their property gratis to the purpose of maintaining habitat when they would rather develop their land in more profitable ways. Commentators of this persuasion often appeal to libertarian constitutional theory, particularly, to belief that all rights—civil rights, property rights and political rights—are interconnected so that a threat to one right is a threat to all. Any diminution of the prerogatives of property, therefore, must be prevented as a matter of constitutional law. On this view, the ESA, insofar as it diminishes the value of property, constitutes a "takings" for which compensation must be paid. If Congress is unwilling to compensate landowners, then it should abandon its pretense that it cares about protecting endangered species. Environmentalists often reply that the government rightly exercises its police powers when it prohibits individuals from using their property in ways that harm others. By compelling landowners to maintain habitat for endangered species, according to this argument, the ESA prevents a public harm or nuisance.[8] Professor Oliver A. Houck, for example, argues that endangered species are "indicators of the health of the ecosystems that they inhabit."[9] Houck says that "the protection of these species should trump private property rights in the same way that other indicators of pollution do..."[10] According to this view, a property owner who causes the extinction of a species by converting its habitat harms his or her neighbor or the public as a whole. Restrictions on habitat conversion imposed under the ESA, like regulations that control pollution, would therefore fall under the nuisance exception to the "takings" clause of the Fifth Amendment.[11] Accordingly, the government need not compensate landowners even when ESA restrictions deprive them of all economic use of their land.[12] The debate between these positions engages two fundamental—and fundamentally opposed—conceptions of property rights. The first conception, which describes property rights as natural rights, has been brilliantly, clearly and elegantly presented by many authors among whom Professor Richard Epstein is the most celebrated. In his words, "If rules are in accordance with the law of nature, the rights acquired in property are 'bottom up' rights derived from individual acts of acquisition, not 'top down' rights derived from the largess of the state."[13] According to Epstein's position, which finds an historical authority in the political theory of John Locke,[14] private property rights are created by private action, that is, by individuals who either produce objects or acquire them from the natural commons. Once property rights are thus defined by private production or acquisition, the role of the state is to protect them, for example, by enforcing conditions under which those rights may be consensually transferred.[15] If the government itself takes or restricts property rights of one person for any reason other than to protect the rights of another, it must pay just compensation. In other words, the government is bound by the same rules of acquisition and transfer that bind private landowners, except that the government, by exercising eminent domain, can purchase land the owner may not wish to sell. A softened and more flexible version of this insistence on the primacy of property rights in land is found in the tradition of legal analysis that descends from the utilitarian philosopher Jeremy Bentham to the writings and opinions of Justice Scalia.[16] This tradition differs from that of natural law by conceding that private property rights, far from preexisting society, are artificial creations of it.[17] This is not to say that property rights are arbitrary; on the contrary, they are central to the established customs and expectations that allow society to function.[18] To see why, one need only ask what is wrong with theft if there is no natural basis for property rights. The reason that Utilitarians such as Bentham condemned theft is that it contravened settled and established expectations and so destroyed the security on which the social order and therefore human happiness depends.[19] The opposing environmentalist position also invokes natural law or pre-existing conditions, but of a different kind. It appeals to laws or principles supposed to govern the functioning of ecosystems and to constitute land as a living community. According to this approach, the forms, functions and faculties of nature pre-exist and support the human economy. Landowners must conduct themselves consistently with these pre-existing systems and, if they put them in jeopardy, they threaten their neighbors and the public.[20] On this view, individuals do not acquire property rights to all uses or aspects of land when they remove certain of them from the commons; on the contrary, those resources they do not actually use or remove from the commons remain in nature where they were. If any of these functions of natural communities or systems becomes imperiled or scarce, then the government may declare that not even the owners of that property can acquire or dispose of those remaining natural uses of their land.[21] This limitation on land use may even be consistent with the doctrine of John Locke that one acquires a property right when one removes a resource from the state of nature and mixes one's labor with it "at least where there is enough, and as good left in common with others."[22] On this view, one can come too late to the commons; even the owner of a wetland, for example, who fails to dredge and fill it may lose the right to do so, if so many others of his neighbors have already filled their wetlands that a scarcity exists of whatever public good it is wetlands are supposed to provide. Several commentators draw an analogy, moreover, between wildlife and air and water, insofar as all belong to the public even when they flow over private property. It is an established principle of law that the government, in its sovereign capacity, may regulate the taking of wildlife "for the benefit of all the people,"[23] for otherwise wildlife "would be destroyed."[24] The analogy between wildlife and air and water suggests to some analysts that the public retains an interest in and, in some sense, public ownership of "nature" even with respect to privately owned land. Professor Eric Freyfogle makes this point as follows: "To the overflying hawk, human boundaries mean nothing. To the percolating groundwater, they mean no more."[25]

Natural Rights or Natural Systems?

To what extent may the government assert its interest in the natural functioning of land, including the well-being of wildlife, without so infringing on the rights of the landowner that it must pay him or her compensation? In answering this question, the two sides in this controversy both appeal to nature—whether natural rights or natural communities. In a political context, as one commentator has written, "'nature' and its cognates serve as metaphors for moral or religious truth. Saying that something is 'natural' is to assert both that it is desirable and that its virtues have a foundation in reality."[26] Each side also appeals to the interconnectedness of the "nature" it values—whether it is the integrity of person and property or the integrity of ecological systems. For those who agree with Epstein, liberty and property are inseparable. "A nation in which private property is protected contains independent, decentralized sources of power that can be used against the state, reducing thereby the possibility that any group will be able to seize control over the sources of information or the levers of political power."[27] Epstein summarizes: "Property is defensive, not exploitive."[28] In asserting that property rights are no less fundamental than other liberties, Epstein follows F.A. Hayek's view that "the system of private property is the most important guarantee of freedom, not only for those who own property, but scarcely less for those who do not."[29] From this it is supposed to follow as a matter of moral and constitutional principle that when the government—for any purpose other than to prevent a harm that would be considered a nuisance under common law—limits the use of private property, for example, to provide "wildlife habitat or some other 'public good,' compensation should be paid."[30] To be sure, the government has the power of eminent domain to dedicate private land to public uses, for example, to maintain a natural commons or a refuge for wildlife. In exercising this power, however, the government must compensate landowners for the economic loss they bear when they lose the right to develop their property in ways permitted under common law. Those who join Epstein in defending property rights may hold that the government, if it restricts those rights for any reason other than to prevent a nuisance cognizable in common law, must pay compensation, whether explicit or in kind. In ordinary instances of zoning, property owners receive implicit (in kind) compensation for their losses. For example, when a zoning ordinance imposes height limits and setbacks, each property owner arguably gains more from the restrictions imposed on others than he sacrifices from having to obey those restrictions himself or herself.[31] The nature of the regulation in question, then, "should determine whether or not compensation is due, not the level of devaluation experienced by the landowner."[32] On the other side, some environmentalists propose that because everything in the ecosystem is connected,[33] the destruction of habitat on private land injures the public, and thus regulations protecting habitat may be subsumed under the nuisance exemption to the "takings" clause. Michael Bean, a respected authority on wildlife law, suggests that "restrictions aimed at protecting endangered wildlife are designed to keep the exercise of one property right (the landowner's) from destroying another property right (the public's)."[34] The image of a chain often occurs in discussions of ecology. As one commentator declares: "Devastating chains of events within ecosystems can also be set in motion by seemingly minor causes, such as the elimination of a few insect or plant species. Thus, human-caused extinction of any organism is tantamount to a planetary game of ecological 'Russian Roulette.'"[35] In passages like these—analogizing species to cogs in the planetary machine or rivets in nature's wing—environmentalists explain with metaphors how landowners who destroy the habitat of threatened species harm the public, just as if they caused pollution or some other nuisance recognized by common law. The contention that the destruction of habitat constitutes a public harm or nuisance, however, may seem to concede Epstein's principled position that landowners would be owed compensation under ESA regulations if the extinction of the relevant species did not harm human beings in the sense of harm, injury or damage known to common law. Environmentalists and property-rights advocates may seem to agree, then, in restricting non-compensable regulation to the prevention of harms that would be actionable in common law. Plainly, environmentalists do not intend to endorse Epstein's idea that the government must compensate landowners for all losses they incur as a result of regulations that exceed those needed to prevent nuisance. Environmentalists are likely, indeed, to applaud the Supreme Court's assertion that the "common law of nuisance is too narrow a confine for the exercise of regulatory power in a complex and interdependent society."[36] Accordingly, the appeal environmentalists make to the principle of the police power, supported by the common law doctrine of nuisance, may not serve their interests in the long run.

Slippery Slopes

Both those who defend property rights and those who would use the ESA to restrict the use of private land rely on the same form of argument, namely, the "slippery slope."[37] Libertarians assert that all rights are interconnected, so that if the courts fail to protect even the smallest property right, they will undermine fundamental political and civil rights as well.[38] Environmentalists respond by describing all nature as interconnected, so that if society fails to protect the habitat of the least creature, the entire ecological system may collapse. Barry Commoner, in a popular book that appeared two years before the passage of the ESA, summarized this latter view of ecosystems as follows: "The more complex the ecosystem, the more successfully it can resist a stress. ...Like a net, in which each knot is connected to others by several strands, such a fabric can resist collapse better than a simple, unbranched circle of threads—which if cut anywhere breaks down as a whole."[39] Although the hypothesis that the stability of ecosystems depends on their diversity has been questioned, indeed, abandoned by many or most ecologists, it remains central to arguments favoring the strict implementation of the ESA. The Ecological Society of America recently reiterated the belief that "Ecosystem function depends on its structure, diversity and integrity."[40] In a recent and much-touted experiment, ecologists found a site in which the diversity of an ecosystem apparently correlates with its stability, at least on some scales of analysis.[41] Biologist Paul Ehrlich introduced this metaphor of species holding the wing of Nature's airplane, to which he and other environmentalists continue to appeal. Ecosystems, like well-made airplanes, tend to have redundant subsystems and other "design" features that permit them to continue functioning after absorbing a certain amount of abuse. A dozen rivets, or a dozen species, might never be missed. On the other hand, a thirteenth rivet popped from a wing flap, or the extinction of a key species involved in the cycling of nitrogen, could lead to a serious accident.[42] Events have not borne out the forebodings of either libertarians or of environmentalists. There is little evidence, for example, that Americans have lost their civil, personal and political rights because the courts have been less than zealous in applying the "takings" provision of the Fifth Amendment to environmental regulation.[43] On the contrary, the courts have severed "takings" jurisprudence from its common law moorings, but this has had no apparent effect on the personal or civil liberties American enjoy. The Supreme Court has experienced little difficulty in distinguishing property rights from fundamental civil and political freedoms[44] and attenuating one while augmenting the other.[45] The dire predictions of environmentalists, moreover, have not materialized. "It seems certain," Paul and Anne Ehrlich wrote in The End of Affluence (1974), "that energy shortages will be with us for the rest of the century, and that before 1985 mankind will enter a genuine age of scarcity in which many things besides energy will be in short supply." Ehrlich predicted that the world would run out of food in part because of growing population, in part because of ecosystem collapse. "Starvation among people will be accompanied by starvation of industries for the materials they require."[46] In fact, commodity prices have fallen continually since the 1970s, and raw materials—including food and energy—are generally more abundant and less expensive today than 20 years ago or, indeed, at any time in history. [47] The extinction of species has had no discernable effect on the economic growth of nations. There is no sign of ecological collapse on the farm. Farmers complain about the historically low prices they get for corn, wheat, soybeans and other crops, but this results from glut not scarcity.[48] No one can say, of course, that dire predictions will not turn out to be true someday. A slippery slope, because it is so slippery, gives one an easy ride until the bottom. Libertarians may dismiss the apparent evidence of the flourishing of personal liberty as obscuring the bitter truth that the authoritarian or totalitarian state is closing in. As Richard Epstein warns, the courts must protect property rights against uncompensated takings or sacrifice "the social function that private property serves as a constraint against centralized power in a system of limited government."[49] Big Brother may lurk around the corner. There is no way to disprove the argument that supposes current appearances to be deceiving—because these appearances are all we see. Environmentalists reject as delusional evidence (such as falling commodity prices) that suggest resources are becoming more plentiful as a result of substitution between materials flows and greater efficiencies. Paul Ehrlich in this way dismissed the bet he lost with optimist Julian Simon on whether the prices of certain commodities would increase. "The bet doesn't mean anything," Ehrlich scoffed. "Julian Simon is like the guy who jumps off the Empire State Building and says how great things are going so far as he passes the 10th floor." Ehrlich added, "It's true that we've kept up food production...but I have no doubt that sometime in the next century food will be scarce enough that prices are really going to be high even in the United States."[50] Each side in the debate over regulatory "takings" warns the courts must act to ward off disaster. Environmentalists warn that unless the courts force property owners to bear the costs of protecting endangered species, the nation risks ecological collapse. Advocates of property rights, in turn, warn that if the courts force landowners to bear these costs, the rights of property and with them all civil liberties may vanish. How are the courts to choose? In responding to these forebodings, courts confront a fundamental ideological decision akin to the crossroads Woody Allen described. "One path leads to despair and utter hopelessness. The other, to total extinction. Let us pray we have the wisdom to choose correctly."[51] The courts wisely leave this important choice to the two sides themselves to resolve through the political process. This essay proposes that the courts, rather than resolving controversies about the fundamental character of property, liberty, nature, ecology, and so on, appropriately limit themselves to reining in regulation at its frontier. As long as the Supreme Court threatens opposing positions equally with utter and devastating defeat—fanning fears that it may vindicate either the libertarian or the environmentalist extreme—it may succeed in restraining the ambitions of both property owners and regulators, who may then recognize they have more to lose from confrontation than from compromise and accommodation. The conviction that the freedom to wring the last speculative penny from one's land is of a piece with one's most fundamental civil, political and personal liberties seems to be grounded less on argument than on assumption. Likewise, the idea that there is such a thing as the "health" or "integrity" of ecosystems and that species are its indicators seems less a refutable proposition of empirical science than a first principle of a certain ecological faith. Society may adopt one principled theory or another in the way it regulates land use, but this determination must be a political and not a judicial one.[52] This analysis is consistent with the Supreme Court holding in Armstrong v. United States that the "takings" clause of the Fifth Amendment prevents "the government from forcing some people alone to bear public burdens which, in all fairness and justice, should be borne by the public as a whole."[53] One may infer from this doctrine that if political institutions and processes are open and impartial, prima facie grounds exist for thinking that the results will not unfairly disadvantage any politically powerful group.[54] By honing in on the fairness of the process and by protecting interests that are politically weak, the courts properly ride herd on legislatures and agencies on a case-by-case basis and keep well-organized groups from taking advantage of more vulnerable ones in the name of pieties about liberty or ecology. In applying the "takings" clause, the courts properly act to prevent particular forms of abuse of the weak by the powerful, for example, by making sure that governments do not regulate property in order to drive down its price before acquiring it through eminent domain.[55] They should not act generally, however, to vindicate one scientific, political, or other theory over another. Within its ad hoc jurisprudence, the Supreme Court has required compensation when a regulation affects politically powerless groups,[56] physically invades property,[57] defeats investment-backed expectations,[58] or deprives the owners of "all economically feasible use" of their land.[59] To go beyond these per se rules, however, may be to substitute judicial activism, based on one theory or another, whether libertarian, ecological or something else as compelling, for the outcome of an open and fair political process. Landowners hardly constitute an oppressed or insular minority; they can press their interests through political action, for example, by repealing or weakening the ESA, when its enforcement becomes too onerous.[60] Similarly, environmentalists are adept at cultivating and employing political power. These opposing ideological camps are used to doing political battle. They seem to enjoy it, and, when they do not—when political confrontation leads nowhere—environmentalists and landowners may find that cooperation offers better results than conflict. If the courts adopted a general theory—whether a theory that required compensation for all ESA "takings" or for none—they would remove the incentive for political bargaining and for stakeholder conflict resolution that the current happy state of uncertainty and confusion creates.[61] In a series of decisions, culminating in Lucas v. South Carolina Coastal Commission[62] and Dolan v. City of Tigard,[63] the Court has defined per se rules that establish that a regulation that is reasonably related to a valid public purpose will require compensation only under specific conditions, e.g., because it singles out a vulnerable minority, deprives the landowner of all viable use of his or her property, physically invades or occupies the property, and so on. Though under pressure from academic theorists, the Lucas court rightly refrained from augmenting this per se list with a more general jurisprudence.[64] Property owners and environmentalists will have to work out their differences on the local level through mutual accommodation and compromise. There is no one policy response to a thousand different situations, but it is often the case that a little goodwill and voluntary effort can go a long way to solving particular endangered species problems. When property rights advocates and environmentalists have worked together to find smart ways to deal with endangered species problems—planting lupine for the Karner blue butterfly is one example, transferring the American burying beetle from Oklahoma to Block Island was another—they generally get the job done at a trivial cost. (The cost of saving the American burying beetle, whose last known habitat stood in the path of a $100 million highway, amounted to about $10,000 to establish colonies elsewhere.)[65] The Supreme Court is correct to constrain land use policy at the margins while permitting the political process and private efforts to determine its overall direction.

A Nation of Zoo-Keepers

Writing a dissent in Sweet Home, Justice Scalia anticipated Mr. Cushman's response to the Court's decision. The majority's opinion, Scalia declared, "imposes unfairness to the point of financial ruin—not just upon the rich, but upon the simplest farmer who finds his land conscripted to national zoological use." Some academic authorities have reached the same conclusion. Professor Richard B. Stewart wrote that the Court "should have required a principle of clear statement, requiring firmer...evidence of a congressional determination to impose a sweeping, intrusive, counterproductive and inequitable system of federal land management on private property throughout the country."[66] How much of a federal land-grab may we expect in the wake of the Sweet Home decision? Professor Stewart, Justice Scalia and Chuck Cushman foresee the ruination of simple farmers, loggers and other fine Americans the Supreme Court has exposed to the sweeping, inequitable, intrusive, counterproductive, capricious, and confiscatory actions of the Fish and Wildlife Service (FWS), among other governmental agencies. Plainly, if the decision in Sweet Home gave federal authorities carte blanche to impose land use policies on property owners, it would be open to this sort of criticism. On the other hand, the decision could mean little in practice, if federal agents are constrained in other ways. To what extent has the decision in Sweet Home actually affected property rights? To what extent will aggrieved property owners—such as those who log for a living—appeal to the Fifth Amendment to force the government to pay for the land it conscripts for zoological use? The fate of the plaintiffs—there were eleven—who lost in Sweet Home may indicate how other landowners will fare as a result of that Supreme Court decision. What happened to the eleven yeomen loggers and farmers or to their land because they lost the case? The answer is, nothing. Since the FWS had neither initiated nor contemplated an enforcement action against any of the plaintiffs in Sweet Home, the outcome of the case did not affect them. The timber industry had engaged them to challenge the regulation simply on its face.[67] Typical of these plaintiffs, the Seattle Times points out, is Betty Orem, who inherited a "30-acre tract of forest land overlooking the pastoral valley of

Jimmycomelately Creek in the Olympic foothills south of Sequim," abutting a national forest. Orem knew why timber industry lawyers asked her to become a plaintiff. "The reason they chose me is I'm an old widow," she told a reporter. The outcome of the case had no effect on Orem's land. "It's been logged," the Seattle Times reported. "A year before Sweet Home had been decided, she received a state permit to cut it." Orem, like several other plaintiffs found that 'tis better to have logged and lost. "The federal owl-habitat guidelines remain in place," the Seattle Times concludes. "Orem is just one of many Washington timberland owners who have ignored them and logged their property anyway." How will the Sweet Home decision affect the nation's small loggers, farmers and other landowners? It will affect them, it seems, as it did the Widow Orem. In June 1995, the same month the Supreme Court announced its decision in Sweet Home, the FWS proposed to exempt nearly all small and residential land holders from its Section 9 requirements for protecting the habitat of threatened plants and animals.[68] Secretary of the Interior Bruce Babbitt greeted the Court's decision by announcing that: it makes all the more fundamentally important that we work to make this law more flexible and user-friendly for landowners...We will continue to aggressively pursue a variety of reforms to make the [Endangered Species] Act less onerous on private landowners.[69] Secretary Babbitt committed the FWS to an incentives-based rather than coercive approach in using Section 9 to conserve habitat. A "no surprises" policy ensures that once landowners agree to a habitat conservation strategy, they will be subject to no more ESA demands. Landowners who voluntarily enhance wildlife habitat on their lands would be immune from any further land use restrictions under the Act. In all, the FWS and the Department of Interior have taken great care to suggest that they will not exploit the Supreme Court decision but will carry on as if Sweet Home had been decided against them.[70] As a result, not a single case for inverse condemnation under Section 9 has been filed in Federal Claims Court.[71] In the Pacific Northwest, where the spotted owl controversy brought the ESA into greatest potential conflict with the logging of private lands, the FWS moved not to regulate but to reassure landowners. While designating 6.9 million acres of federal land as "critical habitat,"[72] it excluded all nonfederal lands from coverage under Section 9 guidelines regarding the habitat modification.[73] The political restraint the FWS has shown in the Pacific Northwest characterizes its practice in general. In 1993, A. Dan Tarlock, wrote that that "biodiversity protection...is becoming more decentralized and site-specific,"[74] and that "federal and state land use managers are extremely deferential to local concerns."[75] J. B. Ruhn observed in 1988 that "the local grip on land planning has remained tight" and "the federal role...has been largely passive."[76] Another commentator observed in 1991 that "the federal government, for the most part, has been reluctant to intrude on state and local land use decision-making authority."[77] Between 1985 and 1993, according to a 1994 U.S. General Accounting Office report, only eight landowners nationwide have been convicted of a crime for destroying the habitat of a species. That comes to one a year. This does not portend a large-scale confiscation of property.

Politics as Usual

The FWS showed the least political restraint—and learned the hardest lessons—in its efforts to protect two songbirds and some cave-dwelling invertebrates in central Texas in the late 1980s and early 1990s.[78] There, "the coercive nature of FWS's policies," as Ruhn reports, "eventually built pervasive resentment and distrust of FWS and the regional planning process within the regulated community."[79] This story has been told many times—brilliantly in a recent book by Charles Mann and Mark Plummer—and need not be recounted here.[80] Suffice it to say that agencies seeking to use ESA authority to protect the habitat of various species on private lands in central Texas in the early 1990s, and, most infamously, the habitat of the golden-cheeked warbler, accomplished little more than to organize effective local, state, and finally national resentment and resistance to the Act.[81] Voluntary efforts to protect and even care for the bird might have succeeded, had the FWS chosen to use carrots instead of sticks. In Texas, the FWS learned that it is no match for organized local opposition. With all the legal authority in the world, FWS officials appear nearly powerless when local groups organize and the political winds blow against federal intervention. And if the agency proceeds with less than complete political restraint and sensitivity to the concerns of landowners, it will only buttress the case of those working to eviscerate the ESA in Congress. A ham-fisted approach will also encourage the kind of civil disobedience and resistance that Mr. Cushman described at the outset of the essay. In its Texan debacle, the FWS learned that the legitimacy and effectiveness of regulations are established not so much through judicial review as by judicious application. User-friendly flexibility and responsiveness were sorely lacking in FWS practice in Texas in the early 1990s.[82] As a result, when the 1994 elections approached, candidates running for election in Texas defended the interests of their own citizens from the orders of the FWS, a federal bureaucracy. Candidates of each party competed in excoriating the feds. "Republicans embraced the issue for their political campaigns," the Bureau of National Affairs reports, "challenging Democratic rivals to choose sides with rural Texans or with Washington. One by one, the state's top Democratic officeholders—Lt. Gov. Bob Bullock, Attorney General Dan Morales, and Gov. Ann Richards—began lining up against the [FWS-initiated] plan."[83] In Washington, Secretary of the Interior Bruce Babbitt understood that administration support for FWS actions in Texas could only undermine the chances—already slim—of Democratic party victories in the 1994 congressional elections. In a letter to Texas Gov. Ann Richards, Babbitt said he had instructed Fish and Wildlife officials not to designate private lands as critical habitat and to work cooperatively rather than coercively to establish conservation plans for endangered species.[84] Aggressive efforts to enforce Section 9 requirements proved self-defeating in the field and in Washington. Habitat conservation plans will not succeed on private lands without public support, especially on the local level. Accordingly, the FWS will accomplish its mission more by earning the goodwill of citizens than by winning victories in court. One might argue that just a few horror stories, properly amplified and politicized, such as those associated with FWS policy in Texas, have done more than any Supreme Court could to influence the course of events. "There's nothing like a good anecdote," according to Stephen Meyer, a political scientist at MIT who studied FWS efforts to protect the golden cheek warbler in central Texas. "I've never seen a public policy debate so driven by stories."[85] A coercive approach can only undermine political support for the ESA and encourage the "shoot, shovel and shut up" reaction Mr. Cushman described. The Sweet Home decision, although welcomed by environmentalists, has made and is likely to make little if any difference in the way that Section 9 of the ESA is enforced. For environmentalists, the FWS, and the Clinton administration, the Sweet Home decision may seem like a Phyrric victory if the public will not sit still for the power over private property it gives to federal agents. If these agents use their power without sensitivity and self-restraint, moreover, public opinion may turn against anything more than a pretextual Endangered Species Act. (Senator Slade Gorton, for example, introduced into the Senate a bill to revise the ESA thoroughly, restricting the definition of "harm" to include only direct actions against protected species.)[86] In urging Congress not to enact Republican-sponsored ESA amendments, Secretary Babbitt promised to make the current Act "work better for private landowners." The FWS, for its part, has given up the idea that broad coercive policies can be anything but self-defeating. It is careful to acknowledge that a command and control approach would "actually generate disincentives for private landowner support for threatened species conservation."[87] Thus, rather than embolden the FWS, the Sweet Home decision may in fact have chastened it, leading it to emphasize voluntary and cooperative efforts to protect threatened species on private property.[88] A great distance, then, separates the cup of regulatory authority from the lip of enforcement. The Clinton administration effort to protect species—as signaled by a Memorandum of Understanding signed on September 27, 1994—more and more avoids interventions on private property and concentrates public actions on public lands.[89]

Leave "Takings" a Muddle

Those who have theories of judicial "takings" to offer deplore the "muddled," "ad hoc," or "chaotic" state of "takings" jurisprudence.[90] If we are to treat the differences among these theorists as more than academic interest, however, we must first understand why we need a theory of "takings" at all. Such a theory is not needed to make judicial outcomes predictable; the current per se or laundry-list approach does that tolerably well. One may predict that if a land use regulation suffers from none of the defects on that well-known list, the plaintiff will lose an action for inverse condemnation. Lawyers advising clients whose land has lost value as a result of regulation can give them guidance on the basis of this handful of per se rules, telling them, for example, that even in the absence of theory, "our constitutional culture" will require compensation when regulations eliminate all economically valuable use of land.[91] The mere fact that academic lawyers and other theoreticians disagree about the theoretical foundations of "takings" law hardly suggests that we face, as a result, a crisis of legitimacy in environmental policy and jurisprudence. Indeed, no one questions the legitimacy of legislatures to make laws protecting the natural environment, regulatory agencies to be flexible and sensible in applying those laws, individuals to organize to change those laws if they are too onerous, and judges to decide cases in which regulatory applications of those laws are challenged. Five hundred years of legal and political tradition and experience are sufficient to establish that kind of legitimacy, if anyone doubted it. The muddled state of "takings" jurisprudence reflects the political culture to which courts and agencies continually adjust. The need for a timeless theory based on first principles—economic or ecological—seems to be more an academic crochet than an institutional necessity. Property owners have demonstrated their power to protect themselves politically; for example, by confronting environmentalists during the ESA Reauthorization process.[92] Civil disobedience also remains a haunting prospect, since it may be nearly impossible to prosecute property owners who have eliminated endangered species before federal agents have discovered them on their land. Abusive regulatory actions may lead to stunning defeats in legislatures as in the courts even if—or especially if—"takings" jurisprudence remains a theoretical muddle.[93] Thus the kind of uncertainty that characterizes "takings" jurisprudence has a chastening—or at least a moderating—effect by restraining regulation at its borders. If citizens believe that the ESA is too onerous, let them go to Congress to weaken the statute or to provide funds for paying compensation in hardship cases. Let them go to the agencies to moderate its implementation, and, best, to one another to get the species taken care of in some private or negotiated arrangement that cuts down on costs. The mere threat that the Court could take a principled position one way or another, however, may dissuade both governmental agencies, such as the FWS, and landowners from pushing their luck, since a judicial decision could go badly against them. As long as "takings" jurisprudence remains a muddle, adversaries have a reason to cooperate rather than to litigate. It would be a mistake for the Court to move from its present path of ad hoc case-by-case review to a more principled, coherent or consistent doctrine.[94] There is no need for a clear theory of regulatory "takings."[95] Questions of environmental policy generally fall within the broad category of concerns that constitute matters of opinion, i.e., public opinion. The extent to which the demise of species will lead to general ecological collapse is a matter of opinion. Likewise, it is a matter of opinion how many of our cherished civil liberties will evaporate if the government regulates property use without always paying compensation. The founders of our republic established democratic political processes to work out ideological and religious differences—and environmental policy nearly always involves such differences—within the bounds of well-recognized civil and political rights. As a rule, environmental policy always has its basis in political choice because the intersection between environmental and constitutional law is so slight.[96] Those who care about the ESA, for or against, may best express themselves by organizing politically; for example, by making their views known in key congressional districts. It would be even better if they joined voluntarily in civil society to work out collaborative ways to maintain threatened species—often an easy enough task if undertaken in a cooperative spirit. Neither side should expect the courts to vindicate its theory of nature or of the state in defiance of the evolving political culture of the community.

Notes

1. The Arizona Republic, July 1, 1995, pg. B1 "Endangered Species Act 'Gotta Be Fixed,' Foe Says;" by Martin Van Der Werf.
2. 16 U.S.C. 1532(19) (1994).
3. 50 C.F.R. 17.3 (1994).
4. "Endangered Species Act 'Gotta Be Fixed,' Foe Says," pg. B1; see also, The Detroit News, June 30, 1995, Friday, Editorial; HEADLINE: Endangered Property Rights. "The U.S. Supreme Court in a 6-3 decision yesterday trampled property rights in granting federal regulators broad control of private land to protect endangered species. No worse environmental decision has come from the high court in two decades. The harm can only be undone by Congress, which must overhaul the Endangered Species Act (ESA)."
5. For discussion, see Ike C. Sugg, "Beware Interior's 'Greater Flexibility,'" Wall Street Journal (Sept. 16, 1996), A19, arguing that selective exemptions from regulation might be used "in an attempt to quell a grassroots property rights rebellion."
6. See, for example, Robert Meltz, Where the Wild Things Are: The Endangered Species Act and Private Property, 24 ENVTL. L. 369 (1994); Susan Shaheen, The Endangered Species Act: Inadequate Species Protection in the Wake of the Destruction of Private Property Rights, 55 OHIO ST. L.J. 453 (1994).
7. See, e.g., Susan Shaheen, "The Endangered Species Act: Inadequate Species Protection in the Wake of the Destruction of Property Rights," 55 Ohio State Law Journal 453 (1994); Ike C. Sugg, "Caught in the Act: Evaluating the Endangered Species Act: Its Effects on Man and Prospects for Reform," 24 Cumb. L. Rev. 1 (1994).
8. See, e.g., David B. Hunter, An Ecological Perspective on Property: A Call For Judicial Protection of the Public's Interest in Environmentally Critical Resources, 12 HARV. ENVTL. L. REV. 311, 323-24 (1988). The principle behind the nuisance exemption, as Professor Frank Michelman formulates it, "is that compensation is required when the public helps itself to good at private expense, but not when the public simply requires one of its members to stop making a nuisance of himself." Frank I. Michelman, Property, Utility, and Fairness: Comments on the Ethical Foundations of "Just Compensation" Law, 80 HARV. L. REV. 1165, 1196 (1967).
9. Oliver A. Houck, "Why Do We Protect Endangered Species, and What Does That Say About Whether Restrictions on Private Property to Protect Them Constitute 'Takings'? 80 Iowa L. Rev. (January 1995) 297, 302.
10. Oliver A. Houck, "Why Do We Protect Endangered Species, and What Does That Say About Whether Restrictions on Private Property to Protect Them Constitute 'Takings'? 80 Iowa L. Rev. (January 1995) 297, 302.
11. See, for example, Penn Central Transportation Co. v. New York City, 438 U.S. 104, 145 (1978) (Rehnquist, C.J., dissenting) (citing the nuisance exception). The Court has resisted extending the nuisance exception, however, beyond its moorings in common law, preferring to exempt regulations from the "takings" clause on other grounds. For discussion, see John A. Humbach, Evolving Thresholds of Nuisance and the Takings Clause, 18 Colum. J. Envtl. L. 1, 10 (1993) (arguing against the idea that nuisance law can provide a

suitable exogenous anchor for takings law.) The concept of nuisance has become so amorphous as to have little meaning outside of its most traditional applications. Law students encounter this warning in W. PAGE KEETON ET AL., PROSSER AND KEETON ON THE LAW OF TORTS @ 86, at 616-17 (5th ed. 1984) (" There is perhaps no more impenetrable jungle in the entire law than that which surrounds the word 'nuisance.' It has meant all things to all people, and...there is general agreement that it is incapable of any exact or comprehensive definition. Few terms have afforded so excellent an illustration of the familiar tendency...to seize upon a catchword as a substitute for any analysis of a problem.") Nevertheless, one could argue that if wildlife is owned by the public, then its destruction, even on private lands, could be considered a nuisance or harm; thus, arguably, regulations prohibiting the destruction of habitat might be subsumed under the "nuisance" exemption to the "takings" clause. For an example of this argument, see Sierra Club v. Department of Forestry & Fire Protection, 26 Cal. Rptr. 2d 338, 347 (Cal. Ct. App. 1993) (citing the public ownership of wildlife in upholding restrictions on logging on private land to protect the marbled murrelet and the spotted owl).

12   Lucas v. South Carolina Coastal Council, 112 S. Ct. at 2900 (stating that "regulations that prohibit all economically beneficial use of land...must inhere...in the restrictions that background principles of the state's law of property and nuisance already place upon land ownership.").

13   Richard A. Epstein, "Takings: Of Private Property and Common," AEI paper, March 7, 1996, p. 4.

14   Customary references to Locke, Nizick, others.

15   "The strength of a natural law theory is in its insistence that individual rights (and their correlative obligations) exist independent of agreement and prior to the formation of thre state." Epstein, TAKINGS, p. 334.

16   See. e.g., Antonin Scalia, Morality, Pragmatism and the Legal Order, 9 Harv. J.L. & Pub. Pol'y 123, 124 (1986) (dismissing libertarian principles to argue that "practical utility is what we are really discussing here") Fred Bosselman writes that a "student of early Scalia essays would recognize land as one of those 'well-defined and fully developed "existential" categories of legal activity' that are recognized by lawyers and judges, though not always by scholars, as a category of 'factually similar precedent' whose 'consistency among themselves' is more important than 'their reconcilability with the mass of decisions involving the general principle.'" Fred Bosselman, Four Land Ethics: Order, Reform, Responsibility, Opportunity, 24 Envtl. L. 1439, 1493 (1994), citing and quoting, Antonin Scalia, Sovereign Immunity and Nonstatutory Review of Federal Administrative Action, Some Conclusions from the Public Lands Cases, 68 Mich. L. Rev. 867, 882, 919, 920 (1970).

17   Jeremy Bentham, Theory of Legislation 111-12 (R. Hildreth, ed. 4th edn. 1882) ("Property is nothing but a basis of expectation: the expectation of deriving certain advantages from a thing we are said to possess, in consequence of the relation in which we stand towards it.").

18   Bentham wrote: The idea of property consists in an established expectation; in the persuasion of being able to draw such or such an advantage from the thing possessed...Now this expectation,...can only be the work of law. I cannot count upon the enjoyment of that which I regard as mine, except through the promise of the law which guarantees it to me ...Property and law are born together, and die together. JEREMY BENTHAM, THEORY OF LEGISLATION 112-13 (4th ed. 1882).

19   "The disutility caused by theft can only be explained by reference to the expectations of the owner, the expectation to retain possession indefinitely." Gerald J. Postema, Bentham and the Common Law Tradition 169 (1986). For a current summation of utilitarian views,

see Leonard G. Ratner, The Utilitarian Imperative: Autonomy, Reciprocity, and Evolution, 12 Hofstra L. Rev. 723 (1984).

20 See, for example, Barry Commoner, The Closing Circle ("all this results from a simple fact about ecosystems—[that] everything is connected to everything else; thesystem is stabilized by its dynamic self-compensating properties; that these same properties, if overstressed, can lead to a dramatic collapse; the complexity of the ecological network... determine[s] how much it can be stressed...without collapsing" pp. 34-35).

21 Professor Eric Freyfogle has stated this position: property law in the United States is slowly beginning to deal with the inexorable issue of carrying capacity—the reality that any type of human land use, however benign the use and however appropriate the location, can prove harmful when too many acres are devoted to it. At some point, in some manner, society must start drawing lines where the carrying capacity is reached and we can disturb the land no further...Will it mean, in the end, a fundamentally new way, an ecological way, of thinking about owning the land? Freyfogle, "The Owning and Taking of Sensitive Lands, 43 UCLA L. Rev. 77, 79 (1995).

22 Second Treatise, Sec. 27.

23 Barrett v. State, 220 N.Y. 423, 426, 116 N.E. 99, 100 (1917).

24 Id.

25 Eric Freyfogle, "The Construction of Ownership," U. Ill.Law Rev. 1996(1) 173, 175 (1996). Of course, the view encounters various problems. One involves the difference between "taking" wildlife by shooting, trapping, or otherwise hunting it and, on the other hand, by destroying wildlife as an incidental result of modifying its habitat. Second, while it is clear that polluting groundwater harms one's neighbors and thus creates a nuisance, it is not as clear that extinguishing a species harms anyone, especially rare species the existence of which may be known only to experts. The passenger pigeon was hunted into extinction largely because its existence was perceived as a nuisance. There seems no value-neutral or non-ideological way to determine whether the extinction of an endangered species constitutes a nuisance or harm except, perhaps, in very special cases. Otherwise, one must suppose that by providing habitat of species, landowners provide a benefit. In the face of this kind of controversy and confusion, the Lucas court rightly described the "benefit-harm" distinction as "difficult, if not impossible, to discern on an objective, value-free basis." 505 U.S. 1003 (1992).

26 Alston Chase, In a Dark Wood: The Fight Over Forests and the Rising Tyranny of Ecology," (New York: Houghton-Mifflin, 1995), p. 3.

27 Epstein, TAKINGS, p. 138.

28 Epstein, TAKINGS, p. 138.

29 F.A. Hayek, The Road to Serfdom (1944). pp. 103-104.

30 Johnathan H. Adler, "Property Rights, Regulatory Takings, And Environmental Protection." CEI Working Paper, April 1996, p. 12.

31 For a discussion of implicit compensation, see Richard Epstein, Takings: Private Property and the Power of Eminent Domain (1985), pp. 194-215. See also, Frank Michelman, "Property, Utility, and Fairness: Comments on the Ethical Foundations of 'Just Compensation' Law," 80 Havard L. Rev. 1165, 1225 (1967).

32 Adler, p. 12. Adler cites Richard Epstein, "Lucas v. South Carolina Coastal Council: A Tangled Web of Expectations," Stanford Law Review, May 1993, p. 389. Epstein writes: "Whatever land uses may be forbidden by neighbors under nuisance law without compensation may similarly be forbidden by the state without compensation. But the converse proposition...is critical. Whatever uses the neighbors could not prohibit without just compensation, the state cannot prohibit without compensation either."

33 Deep ecologists pressed the idea of interconnectedness in nature to the point of declaring

the equality of all its denizens. "If everything is dependent on everything else, they reasoned, then all living things are of equal worth, and the health of the whole—the ecosystem—takes precedence over the interests of individuals." Alston Chase, In a Dark Wood, p. 7. For the doctrine of biocentrism or biospherical egalitarianism, Chase cites Bill Devall and George Sessions, Deep Ecology 1985.

34   Michael J. Bean, Taking Stock: The Endangered Species Act in the Eye of a Growing Storm, 13 Pub. Land L. Rev. 77, 83 (1992). Mr. Bean adds: "To date, American courts have not embraced the view that the Fifth Amendment protects a private right to destroy a publicly owned resource, nor could they without abandoning long settled principles." Id. Oliver A. Houck, "Why Do We Protect Endangered Species, and What Does That Say About Whether Restrictions on Private Property to Protect Them Constitute 'Takings'?" 80 Iowa L. Rev. (January 1995) 297, 311, describes the legal basis of the assertion of public ownership rights in wildlife. He cites Supreme Court opinions that have characterized state "ownership" of wildlife as a "legal fiction" expressing the "importance to its people that a State have power to preserve and regulate the exploitation of an important resource." Douglas v. Seafood Prods., Inc. 431 U.S. 265, 284 (1976) (citing Toomer v. Witsel, 334 U.S. 385, 402 (1948)).

35   Daniel J. Rohlf, The Endangered Species Act: A Guide to Its Protections and Implementations 16 (1989). This approach, which mixes metaphysics and ecology, regards land "as part of the earth's surface, land as part of the ecological community,...created by natural forces" that have priority over private economic interests. Freyfogle, "The Construction of Ownership," 176. On this view, land and people form an ecological community the principles of which suggest limits the government may and should enforce without having to compensate landowners for every penny of profit they might have otherwise wrung out of their land.

36   Lucas, S. Ct. 2903 (Kennedy, J. concurring).

37   See, for example, Ellen Frankel Paul, Property Rights and Eminent Domain (1987) at 192 ("The slippery slope is real, and it is alarming. What scintilla of liberty might be left to the citizen if one's decisions where to build a house, a school for one's children,...can be acted on only at the sufferance of politicans?").

38   Epstein makes an argument for this proposition in TAKINGS, pp. 134-140.

39   B. Commoner, The Closing Circle: Nature, Man, and Technology 38 (1971). Interestingly, experimental findings led many ecologists to precisely the opposite conclusion, namely, that systems with few species are the most stable. See Fraser Smith, "Biological Diversity, Ecosystem Stability, and Economic Development, Ecological Economics 16(1996): 191-203 ("Coming from studies of food web models, the prevailing view in the 1970s and 1980s was that ecosystems with a high degree of internal connectivity (associations among species) tend to be dynamically unstable: an oscillation in the abundance of one species could lead to perturbations in the populations of many others. By contrast, ecosystems with low internal connectivity tend to be dynamically stable." Id at 195).

40   The Report of the Ecological Society of America Committee on the Scientific Basis for Ecosystem Management, December, 1995, from the ESA Web Page.

41   David Tilman, "Biodiversity and Ecosystem Functioning," in G. Daily, ed., Nature's Services: Societal Dependence on Natural Ecosystems (Island Press, Washington, D.C., 1997): pp. 93-112.

42   Id. at 276. Six years earlier, R.B. Craig had written: "The science of ecology has matured dramatically in the last few years. From what was primarily a descriptive science has developed a new, mathematically based, evolutionary ecology." Craig, Evolutionary Ecology (Book Review), 57 Ecology 212, 212 (1976) (reviewing E. Pianka, Evolutionary Ecology (1974)). Stenseth and Craig—along with virtually every other theoretical ecolo-

gist—agree that a "mathematically based, evolutionary ecology" is possible; they disagree whether it is actual. The problem, though, is that the thing is oxymoronic: evolution is an historical process, not a mathematical one. P.R. Ehrlich and A.H. Ehrlich, Extinction: The Causes and Consequences of the Disappearance of Species (New York: Random House 1981). This view remains popular. See, for example, David Farrier, Conserving Biodiversity on Private Land: Incentives for Management or Compensation for Lost Expectations? 19 Harv. Envtl. L. Rev. 303, 303(1995) ("Conventional economic wisdom advises us, in the absence of a certain date for collapse, to persist in behavior that involves dealing our life-support apparatus ever stronger blows. It is as if people are prying the rivets, one by one, from the wings of an airplane in which we all are riding. They refuse to stop unless we can prove that the removal of any given rivet will cause the wing to fail").

43   Nevertheless, Americans tend to think that the freedom to do as one likes with one's land is basic to other rights. See Richard Lazarus, Debunking Environmental Feudalism: Promoting the Individual Through the Collective Pursuit of Environmental Quality, 77 Iowa L. Rev. 1739, 1764 (1992) ("The public continues to associate private property rights in land with personal freedom." Lazarus, supra note 41, at 1764. See also, Carol Rose, The Guardian of Every Other Right: A Constitutional History of Property Rights, 10 Const. Commentary 238, 244 (1993) (book review) ("And in a very practical way, perhaps property's symbolic force animates the incredible touchiness that is still set off by the regulation of landed property—particularly physical invasions of land...").

44   Eisenstadt v. Baird, 405 U.S. 438, 453 (1972) (defending rights "fundamentally affecting a person," see also, e.g., Roe v. Wade, 410 U.S. 113, 152 (1973) (citing "personal rights that can be deemed fundamental").

45   For example, the Court has been attentive to the rights of privacy and "personhood." See, for example, Planned Parenthood v. Casey, 112 S. Ct. 2791, 2807 (1992) (describing privacy cases in terms of one's right to "define the attributes of personhood"). For discussion, see LAURENCE H. TRIBE, AMERICAN CONSTITUTIONAL LAW Chap. 15-1 to -3 (2d ed. 1988). At the same time, the Court has been unwilling or unable to articulate more than a per se jurisprudence concerning the compensation owed landowners for regulatory "takings." The last major decision of the Supreme Court on "takings" issues, Lucas v. South Carolina Coastal Council, distinguishes between rights in land and in personal property, suggesting that the former are more fundamental. Lucas v. South Carolina Coastal Council 112 S. Ct. 2886, 2899 (1992) ("In the case of personal property, [an owner] ought to be aware of the possibility that new regulation might even render his property economically worthless...") Various commentators have questioned the point of this distinction. See, for example, Daniel W. Bromley, Regulatory Takings: Coherent Concept or Logical Contradiction, 17 Vt. L. Rev. 647, 672, 676-78 (1993); William W. Fisher, III, The Trouble With Lucas, 45 Stan. L. Rev. 1393, 1400-01 (1993); John A. Humbach, Evolving Thresholds of Nuisance and the Takings Clause, 18 Colum. J. Envtl. L. 1, 2-3 (1993). Fred Bosselman, however, correctly solves the mystery by pointing to the strong Benthamite slant in Justice Scalia's reasoning—in particular, his view that settled expectations about the use of land underlie other expectations about property on which people rely. See Fred Bosselman, Four Land Ethics: Order, Reform, Responsibility, Opportunity 24 Envtl. L. 1439, 1486 (1994).

46   Paul R. Ehrlich and Anne H. Ehrlich, The End of Affluence (New York: Ballantine Books, 1974), p. 33.

47   "Over the course of the twentieth century, according to a careful study conducted by the World Bank and published in 1988, the relative price of food grains dropped by over 40 percent." For this and other supporting evidence, see Nicholas Eberstadt, "Population, Food, and Income: Global Trends in the Twentieth Century." Pages 7-47 in Ronald Baily,

ed., The True State of the Planet (New York: The Free Press, for the Competitive Enterprise Institute, 1995), esp. pp. 28-29.

48 An immense literature reviews the predictions environmental "Malthusians" or "Cassandras" voiced in the 1970s. See, for example, Nicholas Eberstadt, "Population, Food, and Income: Global Trends in the Twentieth Century." Pages 7-47 in Ronald Bailey, ed., The True State of the Planet (New York: The Free Press, for the Competitive Enterprise Institute, 1995), esp. pp. 28-29 (pointing out that global food production can meet demand but that too many people lack the money to buy food even at historically low prices); Stephen Moore, "The Coming Age of Abundance," in Ronald Bailey, ed., The True State of the Planet (New York: Free Press, 1995), ch. 4, pp. 110-139; Jesse Ausubel, "The Liberation of the Environment," in Jesse Ausubel, ed., The Liberation of the Environment, Daedalus 125(3)(Summer 1996), pp. 1-19; Roger A. Sedjo, "Forest Resources: Resilient and Serviceable," in Kenneth Frederick and Roger Sedjo eds., America's Renewable Resources (Washington, DC: Resources for the Future, 1991), pp. 81-120; and many others.

49 Richard A. Epstein, Takings: Descent and Resurrection, 1987 Supreme Court Review, p.25. See also Susan Rose-Ackerman, Against Ad Hocery: A Comment on Michelman, 88 Colum. L. Rev. 1697, 1706 (1988) ("The compensation requirement can be understood as a way to force public policymakers to consider the opportunity costs of their proposed actions.").

50 John Tierney, "Betting the Planet," New York Times Magazine, December 2, 1990, Sunday, Section 6; Page 52; Column 3. See also, Jack Smith, "Bully for Earth: It Takes a Licking But Keeps on Ticking," Los Angeles Times, August 7, 1991, Wednesday, Part E; Page 1; Column 2.

51 Woody Allen, "My Speech to the Graduates," in Side Effects (1980).

52 This is not to say that it is ever resolved. The political process is more often than not a way by which opposing sides in envionmental policy live together without resolving their conflicts but without resorting to violence, either. For discussion, see ROBERT V. PERCIVAL ET AL., ENVIRONMENTAL REGULATION—LAW, SCIENCE, AND POLICY 72 (1992) ("The diverse philosophies that animate environmental concerns and the immense uncertainties that confront policymakers provide ample opportunity for controversy. When regulatory policy is developed and implemented, tensions submerged in ambiguous statutory language often are resolved in ways that contribute further to the extraordinary complexity of environmental regulation.").

53 364 U.S. 40, 49 (1980).

54 This analysis is consistent with that put forward by John H. Ely, Democracy and Distrust (1980). Epstein criticizes this idea that property owners can defend their interests in general through the political process. See Epstein, TAKINGS, p. 214.

55 Alan W. Roddy, Note, Takings—Isn't There a Better Approach to Planned Condemnations?-Joint Ventures, Inc. v. Department of Transportation, 563 So. 2d 622 (Fla. 1990), 19 Fla. St. U. L. Rev. 1169, 1173 (1992) (noting cases limiting a state's power to aggressively regulate property prior to acquiring it).

56 This is a standard view in the literature and reflects John Hart Ely's "political process" approach to constitutional law. (See John Hart Ely, Democracy and Distrust (1980)). Richard Epstein is completely on target when he observes that this approach "accepts the modern framework of preferred freedoms and fundamental rights, which relegates the takings to the fringes of constitutional interpretation." (See Epstein, Takings, pp. 21-15). Epstein argues that a powerful link exists betwen "legislative breakdown and insufficient compensation" p. 215). I believe that this link holds only—or at least primarily—when a vulnerable minority has been singled out for disadvantage. Otherwise, when powerful

groups such as landowners bear burdens, it is hard to show the political process has broken down. William Fischel, Regulatory Takings: Law, Economics, and Politics (1995) argues for much the same view as is presented in this essay. He writes (at p. 7): I embrace John Hart Ely's "political process" theory of the Constitution, which discourages judges from taking an active role in reviewing the products of properly apportioned, pluralistic legislatures. Judges have a limited capacity to evaluate regulatory regimes and an undemocratic hold on their office. They should normally respect the substitute methods—economic exit and political voice—by which property can be protected by its owners and their allies.

57 Loretto v. Teleprompter Manhattan CATV Corp., 458 U.S. 419 (1982) (holding that permanent physical occupation of property constitutes a taking). The Loretto court explained how the per se rule concerning physical occupation fits into its larger ad hoc jurisprudence: The Court explained [in Penn Central] that resolving whether public action works a taking is ordinarily an ad hoc inquiry in which several factors are particularly significant—the economic impact of the regulation, the extent to which it interferes with investment-backed expectations, and the character of the government action...The opinion does not repudiate the rule that a permanent physical occupation is a government action of such a unique character that it is a taking without regard to other factors that a court might ordinarily examine. Id. at 432. See L. TRIBE, AMERICAN CONSTITUTIONAL LAW (2d ed. 1988)at Sections 9.4, 9.5 (observing that physical invasions of property constitute per se constitutional takings). See also Nollan v. California Coastal Comm'n, 483 U.S. 825, 836 (1987) (noting that property owners were required allow the public access to their property). See also Frank I. Michelman, "Property, Utility, and Fairness: Comments on the Ethical Foundations of 'Just Compensation' Law," 80 Harv. L. Rev. 1165, 1184 (1967)) at 1184 ("The modern significance of physical occupation is that courts, while they sometimes do hold nontrespassory injuries compensable, never deny compensation for a physical takeover.").

58 Pruneyard Shopping Center v. Robins, 447 U.S. 74, 83 (1980) (reviewing the economic impact of the challenged statute "and its interference with distinct investment-backed expectations"). Of course, legal decisions determine which investment-backed expectations are "reasonable," so there is a circularity in this analysis. Lucas, 112 S. Ct. at 2903 (Kennedy, J., concurring in the judgment) ("There is an inherent tendency towards circularity in this synthesis, of course; for if the owner's reasonable expectations are shaped by what courts allow as a proper exercise of governmental authority, property tends to become what courts say it is.").

59 Pennsylvania Coal Co. v. Mahon, 260 U.S. 393 (1992) at 414. See also, Keystone Bituminous Coal Ass'n v. DeBenedictus, 480 U.S. 470, 485 (1987) (inquiring whether property owners retained an economically viable use of their land); and Lucas, 112 S. Ct. at 2893-94.

60 For an excellent review of recent legislative initiatives seeking to weaken the ESA by requiring compensation for regulatory "takings," see David Coursen, "Property Rights Legislation: A Survey of Federal and State Assessment and Compensation Measures," Environmental Law Reporter, May 1996, 26 ELR 10239. For a popular account of the same phenomenon, see, e.g., Douglas H. Chadwick, Dead or Alive: The Endangered Species Act, National Geographic, March 1995, at 3. See also, Stephen M. Meyer, The Final Act, The New Republic, Aug. 15, 1994, at 24. According to Meyer: Ranchers, loggers, home builders, members of the grossly misnamed "wise-use" movement and others are moving in, like a pack of wolves, to tear it [the ESA] to shreds. The act, they charge, is a misguided effort to save maladapted, obscure and useless creatures. It shaves percentage points off the gross national product, costs tens of thousands of jobs, tramples private

property rights, wastes valuable public resources and clogs the courts with frivolous cases. The act's foes hope to restore "balance" to the legislation with a series of "people first" amendments.

61 The view argued here sets "takings" jurisprudence in the context of the famous footnote in United States v. Carolene Products, Co. that describes ordinary political processes as sufficient to protect ordinary commercial transactions from undesirable governmental interference. The courts must devote greater scrutiny to governmental actions that restrict access to the political process or that are directed against "discrete and insular monorities." 304 U.S. 144, 152 & n. 4 (1938).

62 112 S. Ct. 2886 (1992).

63 114 S. Ct. 2309 (1994).

64 In his concurring opinion, Justice Kennedy signalled how far the Court was from making common law nuisance a bright line test for compensable "takings." He wrote: "[t]he common law of nuisance is too narrow a confine for the exercise of regulatory power in a complex and interdependent society . . . Coastal property may present such unique concerns for a fragile land system that the State can go further . . . than the common law of nuisance might otherwise permit." Lucas at 2903 (Kennedy, J., concurring). Compare Justice Rehnquist's earlier statement that "[t]he nuisance exception to the taking guarantee is not coterminous with the police power itself." Penn Cent. Transp. Co. v. City of New York, 438 U.S. 104, 145 (1978).

65 For this happy story of a cheap and successful program to save a fascinating creature, see Les Line, "Microcosmic Captive Breeding Project Offers New Hope for Beleaguered Beetle,"The New York Times, September 17, 1996, Tuesday, Section C; Page 1; Column 5.

66 Richard B. Stewart, "The Endangered Species Act: A Case Study in Takings Incentives: Comments," paper presented at the AEI Conference March 7, 1996.

67 Babbitt v. Sweet Home 115 S. Ct. 2407, 2410 (1995).

68 See "Endangered and Threatened Plants: Proposed Rule Exempting Certain Small Landowners and Low-Impact Activities from Endangered Species Act Requirements for Threatened Species," 60 Fed. Reg. 37419 (June 14, 1995).

69 "Secretary Babbitt Welcomes 'Common Sense' Action of Supreme Court Species Ruling; Says It Will Not Alter His Flexibility Push," press release June 29, 1995, DOI, Office of the Secretary.

70 Landowner-friendly provisions supposed to govern FWS behavior are listed and explained in a Department of the Interior document titled, "Protecting America's Living Heritage: A Fair, Cooperative and Scientifically Sound Approach to Improving the Endangered Species Act," March 6, 1995.

71 See footnote above seeking confirmation from Brookshire.

72 See ESA Sec. 4(a)(3), 16 U.S.C. Sec. 1533 (a)(3)(1988).

73 Determination of Critical Habitat for the Northern Spotted, 57 Fed. Reg. 1796, 1810 (1992).

74 A. Dan Tarlock, Local Government Protection of Biodiversity: What Is Its Niche?, 60 U. CHI. L. REV. 555 (1993) at 557.

75 Id. at 557 n.10.

76 Ruhn, Interstate Pollution Control and Resource Development Planning: Outmoded Approaches or Outmoded Politics?, 28 NAT. RESOURCES J. 293, 309 (1988).

77 Holly Doremus, Patching the Ark: Improving Legal Protection of Biological Diversity, 18 ECOLOGY L.Q. 265, 289 (1991).

78 See Melinda E. Taylor, "Promoting Recovery or Hedging a Bet Against Extinction: Austin, Texas's Risky Approach to Ensuring Endangered Species' Survival in the Texas Hill Country," 24 Envtl. L. 581; Thornton, Searching for Consensus and Predictability: Habi-

tat Conservation Planning Under the Endangered Species Act of 1973, 21 Envtl. L. 605(1991; Kevin D. Batt, CASE COMMENT: ABOVE ALL, DO NO HARM: SWEET HOME AND SECTION NINE OF THE ENDANGERED SPECIES ACT 75 B.U.L. Rev. 1995, 1177, 1198.

79 J.B. Ruhl, BIODIVERSITY CONSERVATION AND THE EVER-EXPANDING WEB OF FEDERAL LAWS REGULATING NONFEDERAL LANDS: TIME FOR SOME- THING COMPLETELY DIFFERENT? 66 U. Colo. L. Rev. 1995, 555, 636.

80 Charles C. Mann & Mark L. Plummer, Noah's Choice: The Future of Endangered Species (1995), esp. pp. 190-211.

81 Landowners who considered themselves possible targets of FWS conservation orders or- ganized to bring political pressure against the agency. Politicians of both parties had no choice but to defend local property rights against "Washington." Then governor Ann Richards, whose bid for re-election would be decided against her a few months later, took every opportunity to express the view all Texas politicians had to espouse: Our recent experiences with federal agencies and their ham-handed approach causes me serious con- cern about taking action that increases their authority in local matters. The possibility of greater federal involvement in state or local management or interference with economic development is unacceptable. Frankly, the unilateral actions of federal agencies without consultation with state or local government impedes rather than facilitates progress and I have had enough. Members of Congress agree that their good intentions to protect the environment become an open door for agencies to run amuck. Letter from Ann Richards, Governor, State of Texas, to John Hall, Chairman, Texas Natural Resources Conservation Commission 1 (July 25, 1994) (quoted and cited in Ruhl, Biodiversity Conservation etc. cited supra, 555. Governor Richards similary wrote to Secretary of Interior Burce Babbitt: The Fish and Wildlife Service's approach to implementing the [Endangered Species] Act in Texas has become so overreaching that it undermines public support for protecting our wildlife. During the past decade, the agency's efforts to enforce the law and protect wild- life have created enormous problems for landowners. . . . The Department of Interior, with leadership from your office, should initiate a thorough review of the Fish and Wildlife Service's overall approach to implementing the Endangered Species Act in Texas. Letter from Ann Richards, Governor, State of Texas, to Bruce Babbitt, Secretary, United States Department of Interior (Sept. 12, 1994). As Texas sued the FWS as parens patriae for its citizens (Texas v. Babbitt, No. W-94-CA-271 (W.D. Tex. filed Sept. 30, 1994)) and the reuathorization of the ESA came into greater question, Secretary Babbitt restrained the agency.

82 See Plummer and Man, Noah's Choice.

83 BNA STATE ENVIRONMENT DAILY, Sept. 30, 1994, Texas, "Interior Secretary Scuttles Proposed 'Critical Habitat' Plan For Central Texas."

84 Babbitt's letter, dated Sept. 22 and released by the governor's re-election campaign office Sept. 27. See BNA document, previous note.

85 Chicago Tribune, May 29, 1995, Monday, "Environmental Act Endangered As Private Landowners Cry Foul."

86 Slade Gorton introduced his bill as an Amendment to the Department of the Interior and Related Agencies Appropriations Act, S. amend. 2904, 102d Cong. (1992). The amend- ment was defeated.

87 60 Fed. reg. at 37420.

88 For an argument that only a voluntary or incentive-based approach to enforcement will work, see John Charles Kunich, The Fallacy of Deathbed Conservation Under the Endan- gered Species Act, 24 ENVTL. L. 501, 574-78 (1994).

89 Twelve federal agencies together with the United States Fish and Wildlife Service (FWS)

and the National Marine Fisheries Service (NMFS) joined to assert their "common goal of conserving species listed as threatened or endangered under the [Endangered Species Act] by protecting and managing their populations and the ecosystems upon which those populations depend." Memorandum of Understanding Between Federal Agencies on Implementation of the Endangered Species Act Signed Sept. 28, 1994, [July-Dec.] Daily Env't Rep.(BNA) No. 188, at E-1 (Sept. 30, 1994). For a detailed account, analysis, and evaluation of this agreement, see J. B. Ruhl, "Section 7(a)(1) of the 'New' Endangered Species Act: Rediscovering and Redefining The Untapped Power of Federal Agencies' Duty To Conserve Species" 25 Envtl. L. 1107, 1109 (1995).

90   See, for example, Ellen Frankel Paul, Property Rights and Eminent Domain 1987 ("Virtually everyone admits that this area of the law is in a chaotic state. The time seems right to address the fundamental cause of this unfortunate state of affairs. Perhaps an alternative tradition to ad hoc, utilitarian decision-making might hold out some hope for resolving this 'muddle.' The tradition I have in mind is...that of natural rights." Id. at 188.) Paul is correct that virtually everyone regards "takings" jurisprudence as a muddle. Joseph Sax may have been the first to emphasize the point. Joseph L. Sax, Takings and the Police Power, 74 YALE L.J. 36, 37 (1964) ("a welter of confusing and apparently incompatible results"). See also, Charles R. Wise, The Changing Doctrine of Regulatory Taking and the Executive Branch: Will Takings Impact Analysis Enhance or Damage the Federal Government's Ability to Regulate?, 44 Admin. L. Rev. 403, 410 (1992) ("In doing their balancing act, the courts employ no clear standard in weighing the factors.") See also: Carol M. Rose, Mahon Reconstructed: Why the Takings Issue Is Still a Muddle, 57 S. Cal. L. Rev. 561 (1984). Another commentator describes "takings" jurisprudence as a "mess." Daniel A. Farber, Public Choice and Just Compensation, 9 Const.Commentary 279, 279 (1992); see similarly, Saul Levmore, Just Compensation and Just Politics, 22 Conn. L. Rev. 285, 287 (1990). For more of the same, see John A. Humbach, A Unifying Theory for the Just Compensation Cases, 34 RUTGERS L. REV. 243, 244 (1982) ("a farrago of fumblings which have suffered too long from a surfeit of deficient theories"); Van Alstyne, Taking or Damaging by Police Power: The Search for Inverse Condemnation Criteria, 44 S. CAL. L. REV. 1, 5-6 (1971) at 2 ("With some exception, the decisional law is largely characterized by confusing and incompatible results, often explained in conclusionary terminology, circular reasoning, and empty rhetoric.") and BRUCE A. ACKERMAN, PRIVATE PROPERTY AND THE CONSTITUTION 8 (1977) ("a chaos of confused argument"). Several commentators have tried to read Lucas as an attempt to base "takings" jurisprudence on a set of consistent philsophical principles. See, for example, Barry M. Hartman, Lucas v. South Carolina Coastal Council: The Takings Test Turns a Corner, 23 Envtl. L. Rep. (Envtl. L. Inst.) 10,003, 10,004-05 (Jan. 1993) (arguing the Lucas court has moved from a "policy-based," "ad hoc" standard to a more "objective, principled" approach).

91   Lucas, 112 S. Ct. 2886, 2899.

92   Legislative attempts to require compensation for regulatory "takings" under the ESA include S. 605, 104th Cong., 1st Sess. @ 404(a) (1995) (forbidding regulations likely to "require an uncompensated taking of private property"); id. @ 404(b)(1) (requiring agencies to structure regulations so as to "reduce such takings...to the maximum extent possible within existing statutory frameworks").

93   See Penn Central Transp. Co. v. City of New York, 438 U.S. 104, 123-124 (1978): "While this Court has recognized that the 'Fifth Amendment's guarantee . . .[is] designed to bar Government from forcing some people alone to bear public burdens which, in all fairness and justice, should be borne by the public as a whole,...this Court, quite simply, has been unable to develop any 'set formula' for determining when 'justice and fairness' require

that economic injuries caused by public action be compensated by the government, rather than remain disproportionately concentrated on a few persons.'" William A. Fischel, in Regulatory Takings: Law, Economics, and Politics (1995), notes (at p. 81) that "the Court has always been suspected of basing regulatory takings decisions on ad hoc factors, and Penn Central was a signed confession that the justices did not care to do better."

94   For views opposed to the one I advocate here, see, for example, Mandelker and Berger, A Plea to Allow the Federal Courts to Clarify the Law of Regulatory Takings, LAND USE LAW & ZONING DIGEST (Jan. 1990) and Peterson, Land Use Regulatory "Takings" Revisited: The Supreme Court Approaches, 39 HASTINGS L.J. 335, 338 (1988) (deploring the confusion in takings law).

95   To put this thesis in a more general framework: one can base property law either on first metaphysical principles or on the outcome of democratic political processes. To those for whom the true metaphysical principles are obvious—fundamentalists among libertarians and environmentalists, for example—democratic political processes are a constant impediment to rational or logical policy making. Libertarians, property-rights advocates, and others who regard environmentalism with a jaundiced eye may point to its political successes—the ESA would be an example—to show how confiscatory, costly, inefficient, bumbling, and ridiculous the results of democratic political processes often are. Environmentalists, in turn, may regard poltical processes with suspicion, since greedy multinational corporations, as they believe, may purchase or otherwise capture legislatures and regulatory agencies. Anyone who has metaphysical truth on his or her side can condemn democracy as prone to unprincipled, corrupt, and costly manipulation by powerful factions. Democracy is a horribly flawed political system, to be sure, and it often produces egregious outcomes. The only thing that can be said for democracy—and it is often said—is that every other system is even worse. There is nothing novel about this position. Justice Stevens, writing in dissent in Lucas, argued in this spirit that the Court should maintain "essentially an ad hoc, factual inquiry," since "fairness and justice" are often disserved by categorical rules." 112 S. Ct. at 2922. Michael Treanor forcefully argues a similar position that "courts should mandate compensation only in those classes of cases in which process failure is particularly likely today—when there has been singling out or in environmental racism cases, where there has been discrimination against discrete and insular minorities. Outside of this realm, the Takings Clause should serve an educative function, but should not lead to court enforcement." William Michael Treanor, "The Original Understanding of the Takings Clause and the Political Process," 95 Colum. L. Rev. 782, 784. See also, William Michael Treanor, Note, The Origins and Original Significance of the Just Compensation Clause of the Fifth Amendment, 94 Yale L.J. 694, 698 (1985). It seems clear that several Justices have shared with Justice Stevens' conviction that in settling "takings" cases ad hoc, balancing is better than a consistent jurisprudence based on a set of coherenct principles. See, for example, Loretto, 458 U.S. at 442 (Blackmun, J., dissenting) (calling on the Court to maintain its traditional ad hoc, balancing approach and to eschew a "rigid per se takings rule") and id. at 456 ("the solution of the problems precipitated by...technological advances and new ways of living cannot come about through the application of rigid constitutional restraints formulated and enforced by the courts." But see David Coursen, Lucas v. South Carolina Coastal Council: Indirection in the Evolution of Takings Law, 22 Envtl. L. Rep. (Envtl. L. Inst.) 10,778, 10,782 (Dec. 1992) (describing the Court's "impatience" with its per se approach and its "search for a bright-line rule."

96   Environmental and constitutional law intersect at only three points: 1) standing to sue; 2) federal preemption of state law; and 3) regulatory "takings" of the value of property. As for standing, a lively debate in the 1970s about philosophical and metaphysical matters went nowhere because those matters are irrelevant. Courts use doctrines about standing to

manage their dockets, e.g., to make sure that those who argue cases are in a good position to present them well, not to honor any metpahyiscal or philosophical commitment. At the same time, minor uncertainties about the relation between federal and state environmental laws were settled largely consensually and by statute. The present essay discusses the pointlessness of deep and general theories about regulatory "takings." In all, we should relish the irrelevance of constitutional doctrine to environmental policy and law. Environmental law is insteresting primarily because it is 100 percent political and thus a free expression of our democracy.

4 Surprise, Surprise: Who Should Bear Nature's Risk?

MARK L. PLUMMER

On October 4, 1995, Hurricane Opal made landfall along the Gulf Coast near Pensacola, Florida. With 125-mph winds and 20-foot storm surges, the hurricane smashed boats and buildings, cutting a swathe northward through Alabama. As it crossed the border into North Carolina, the storm finally dissipated. Twenty-seven people lost their lives, and the hurricane was responsible for nearly $2 billion in damages. Amid the human toll and property damage was a different sort of potential casualty. To the west of Pensacola, on the Fort Morgan peninsula in Alabama, the Aronov Realty Management Company owned 52 acres of beachfront. Bordering the Bon Secour National Wildlife Refuge, the property was a mixture of sand dunes and scrub vegetation. The refuge managers had put the property high on their priority list for future refuge acquisitions, but Aronov had other plans for the site. The company wanted to build a high-density, residential development, to be known as "Martinique on the Beach." Before construction could start, the company had to acquire a slew of government permits—including one that Hurricane Opal threatened to block. Sometimes called the "Mini-Yellowstone of Alabama," the Bon Secour refuge is home to a rich brew of biodiversity, with endangered species such as the bald eagle, red-cockaded woodpecker, and, of interest to Aronov, the Alabama beach mouse (Peromyscus polionotus ammobates). *P. p. ammobates* is one of several subspecies of beach mouse that inhabit the sand dunes of the Alabama and Florida coast. Developments like the Martinique had cut deeply into their habitat, enough to convince the U.S. Fish and Wildlife Service to place *P. p. ammobates* and four other subspecies of Peromyscus polionotus on the official endangered species list in the 1980s. The Bon Secour refuge and the surrounding area was important to the continued survival of the Alabama subspecies. The surrounding area, of course, included Aronov's property—which brought the company into the bailiwick of the Fish and Wildlife Service, under the auspices of the Endangered Species Act. The ESA pro-

68

hibited Aronov from "taking" the beach mouse, which included adversely disturbing its habitat, a difficult hurdle for any developer. Alternatively, the company could strike a deal with the service. Aronov would fashion a proposal, known as a habitat conservation plan, or HCP, for mitigating any damage to the mouse's habitat caused by its development. In return, the service would grant the company an incidental take permit for harming the species, effectively allowing construction to go forward. In the spring of 1995, Aronov applied for such a permit, offering a number of mitigation measures in its HCP: "establishment of a walkover structure across that scrub dune, a prohibition against housing or keeping pet cats, [Alabama beach mouse] competitor control and monitoring measures, scavenger-proof garbage containers, restoration of dune systems impacted by the construction, and the minimization and control of outdoor lighting."[1] The service was considering Aronov's application when Hurricane Opal struck. The storm hit the Bon Secour refuge hard, washing away a good chunk of the mouse's local habitat. Biologists immediately worried that the species was now at even greater risk. If so, swift action might be needed to counteract the hurricane's effects. But who should take that action? Should the service shelve Aronov's plan, demanding a new one with more expansive protection or denying the permit altogether? Or should the service accept the plan and increase its own efforts to protect the mouse? Agreeing that a species such as *P. p. ammobates* deserves a strong protective effort does not automatically mean that a particular party should be the one to bear the costs (or enjoy the benefits) of providing that protection. A severe hurricane season, a sudden appearance of a disease, an unlucky reproductive season—should the effort to protect biodiversity place the burden for responding to these natural "disasters" on the shoulders of private and other non-federal landowners, or should the federal government be the one to respond? In short, who should bear nature's risk? As it turned out, the population of *P. p. ammobates* on the Fort Morgan peninsula was hit hard, but not hard enough to convince the service to reject the company's plan.[2] The case illustrates a problem, however, that has come to the fore of our efforts to conserve biodiversity. The federal government recently adopted a policy—the "no surprises" rule—that addresses the allocation of nature's risk. Several environmental and scientific groups have attacked this policy, arguing that it flies in the face of ecological reality. Addressing these concerns requires a deeper understanding of the role nature's risk plays in both the ecological and economic world. Risk and uncertainty have only recently been embraced by ecology, and although the history of its treatment in economics goes back considerably further, few treatises consider how nature's risk affects economic be-havior. Rather than present a formal treatise of my own, I will endeavor to illustrate the issue of nature's risk and the "no surprises" rule using a few simple examples.

The Nature of Nature's Risk[3]

Conserving endangered species is often presented as an either-or situation: Either a species is endangered or it is not. The Endangered Species Act re-flects this dichotomy, the law either affording a species the full protection of the law or not.[4] This view has its roots in what is sometimes called the "equi-librium" paradigm of ecology, reflected in the popular "balance of nature" metaphor. In this way of thinking, species have a natural, unendangered state; the influence of humans invariably knocks an ecological system out of bal-ance, thereby endangering its non-human inhabitants. Remove the human in-fluence, and nature has a chance to recover. The equilibrium paradigm has held a powerful sway over biodiversity policy for decades. In the process of considering the Endangered Species Act of 1973, for example, Congress noted that consideration of [the] need to protect endangered species goes beyond the aesthetic. . . . [M]any of these animals perform vital biological services to maintain a "balance of nature" within their realms.[5] The metaphor has been routinely translated into dire warnings and admonitions: All of us are passen-gers on a very large spacecraft—one on which we have no choice but to fly. And, frighteningly, it is swarming with rivet poppers ...[6] If the biota, in the course of aeons, has built something we like but do not understand, then who but a fool would discard seemingly useless parts? To keep every cog and wheel is the first precaution of intelligent tinkering.[7] The importance of wild species goes far beyond their direct use by humans. As more species become extinct, the living fabric of our planet is becoming tattered, endangering whole natural systems and putting us all at risk.[8] The message in these warnings is clear: Nature's risk is a catastrophic one, stemming from the possibility of total collapse. Pop one too many rivets, toss out one too many cogs, or snip one too many strands in the web, and human civilization will come to an end. While these warnings continue to surface in the popular media, ecologists have recognized severe limitations of the "balance-of-nature" view. They have moved away from the equilibrium paradigm, replacing it with one that fo-cuses on ecological processes, not delicate states of the world. Rather than a fragile balance, according to this new paradigm, nature is in flux.[9] An example is *P. p. ammobates*. The ecosystem it inhabits is made possible in part by the constant disturbance of waves and winds. As the primary dunes closest to the sea are washed away or built up, the mouse's population ebbs and flows accordingly, sometimes taking refuge in the secondary dunes further inland. A hurricane can have a severe effect on local populations, even wiping them out entirely. But over the broader landscape, *P. p. ammobates* survives because not all of its local populations are in one dune area. If a disaster wipes out one local population, the mouse can recolonize the depopulated area from other, extant locations. In this dynamic ecological world, the fortunes of populations and even species wax and wane—they are always at some risk of extinction (local or even global), although the natural risk may be (and usually is) vanishingly small. Human influence can raise the risk appreciably by lowering population numbers directly or by displacing the species from its habitat. In the case of the beach mouse, development has reduced the extent of the dune landscape, chopping it into disconnected fragments, thereby diminishing the species's ability to recolonize empty areas. Once a major but not disastrous event, a hurricane like Opal now has the potential to deal a serious blow to the mouse's chances of survival. Protecting species under the ESA may therefore call for strong action, strong enough to lower the risk of extinction appreciably, but that action will never take the form of saving a species unequivocally. As Scott et al. (1995) note, the choice of a conservation goal—what risk of extinction over what period of time—"may be guided by science but [is] essentially rooted in society's values."[10] Acknowledging the nature of nature's risk means accepting a discomforting fact: There is no bright line—save a species or don't save a species—that makes our choices easy.

Responding to Nature's Risk

Nature's risk is something any farmer, hiker or beachgoer learns to endure. Variability in weather, for example, can affect these people and their chosen activities, and so has given rise to weather forecasting, cloud seeding, and bustling markets in raincoats and umbrellas. In general, variation in nature encourages us to acquire better information, reduce that variation, and find ways to adapt to it. These activities are not costless, and the tradeoffs between the benefits and costs determine how much variation there will be and how the remaining risk will be borne. One way to look at nature's risk, then, is from an economic point of view. To keep matters simple, consider the case of a single person facing nature's risk: Daniel Defoe's Robinson Crusoe. By Defoe's account, the risks Crusoe faced were not, at first glance, overwhelming: I had no want of food, and of that which was very good too; especially these three sorts, viz., goats, pidgeons, and turtle or tortoise; which, added to my grapes, Leaden-hall Market could not have furnished a table better than I, in proportion to the company. And tho' my case was deplorable enough, yet I had great cause for thankfulness, that I was not driven to any extremities for food; but rather plenty, even to dainties.[11] Crusoe appears to have been ship-wrecked on the best of all possible islands, a primordial world devoid of rivet poppers, cog tossers and strand snippers. With so little human influence, Crusoe's island must have been a paradise. Not quite, as Defoe related, for nature's risk was still of major concern to Crusoe. One of the first tasks he took up, for example, was to learn to predict the weather patterns that affected his island. Crusoe's interest in this information stemmed from his desire to plant corn, but his effort was not without mishap: The rainy season and the dry season began to appear regular to me, and I learned to divide them, so as to provide for them accordingly. But I bought all my experience before I had it; and this I am going to relate, was one of the most discouraging experiments that I had made at all. I have mentioned that I had saved the few ears of barley and rice, which I had so surprizingly found spring up, as I thought, of them-selves, and believe there was about thirty stalks of rice, and about twenty of barley; and now I thought it a proper time to sow it after the rains, the sun being in its southern position, going from me. Accordingly I dug up a piece of ground as well as I could with my wooden spade, and dividing it into two parts, I sowed my grain; but as I was sowing, it casually occurred to my thoughts that I would not sow it all at first, because I did not know when was the proper time for it; so I sowed about two-thirds of the seed, leaving about a handful of each.[12] Unfortunately, Crusoe planted his corn at the beginning of the dry sea-son, and "not one grain of that I sowed this time came to any thing." With the remaining grain, he sought out moister ground and periodically planted a small crop, in case the rainy season would come during the next short while. "By this experiment I was made master of my business, and knew exactly when the proper season was to sow; and that I might expect two seed times and two harvests every year."[13] Predicting the weather was still an inexact science, however, and so Crusoe learned to accommodate the more inclement times: The rainy season sometimes held longer or shorter, as the winds happened to blow...After I had found by experience the ill consequences of being abroad in the rain, I took care to furnish myself with provisions before hand, that I might not be obliged to go out; and I sat within doors as much as possible during the wet months.[14] Crusoe also sought to reduce another form of nature's risk, the variation in time and space of some of the island's wildlife. As his supply of gun powder ran low, he undertook the task of domesticating some goats: I went to the three kids, and taking them one by one, tyed them with strings together, and with some difficulty brought them all home. It was a good while before they wou'd feed, but throwing them some sweet corn, it tempted them, and they began to be tame; and now I found that if I expected to supply myself with goat-flesh when I had no powder or shot left, breeding some up tame was my only way, when perhaps I might have them about my house like a flock of sheep.[15] Recognizing that keeping all his flock in a single location might court disaster, Crusoe reduced this risk by spreading them out in a "metapopulation":[16] I had a great concern upon me for my little herd of goats; they were not only a present supply to me upon every occasion, and began to be sufficient to me without the expense of powder and shot, but also without the fatigue of hunting after the wild ones, and I was loth to lose the advantage of them, and to have them all to nurse up over again. To this purpose, after long consideration, I could think of but two ways to preserve them; one was to find another convenient place to dig a cave under-ground, and to drive them into it every night; and the other was to enclose two or three little bits of land remote from one another and as much concealed as I could, where I might keep about half a dozen young goats in each place: so that if any disaster happened to the flock in general, I might be able to raise them again with little trouble and time: and this, tho' it would require a great deal of time and labour, I thought was the most rational design.[17] Crusoe's ecological efforts illustrate the possibilities for responding to nature's risk and, more importantly, the tradeoffs in doing so. Because he was alone during this part of his stay on the island, Crusoe bore all the benefits and costs of his actions.[18] As a result, he acted in ways that he, and he alone, believed were the "best." Still, his responses fell short of "perfect." He gathered weather information only to the point where he could predict a monthly pattern, not the high and low temperatures or the likelihood of rain for a particular day. He domesticated goats but not pigeons, which were both less valuable and more costly to tame: "I endeavored to breed them up tame, and did so; but when they grew older they flew all away..."[19] And when he divided his flock of goats, he placed them in two locations, not three or more. In each case, the "most rational" course of action involved a balance between the benefits and costs of responding to nature's risk, not a strict adherence to an ecological plan laid out by a team of conservation biologists. Inevitably, some risk remained because the costs of eliminating it altogether were prohibitively high, and just as inevitably, letting nature's risk take its course was unpalatable because the human costs of doing so were too high relative to the benefits of altering nature in some way. Crusoe may have faced "no want of food," but he did so largely by his own hand, and he still chose to get wet every once and awhile.

Hiding Behind Nature's Risk

Let us now travel to another island, whose inhabitants faced a similar set of risk-management decisions: the island inhabited by the castaways of the S.S. Minnow, otherwise known as Gilligan's island. If they had desired solitude and independence, the castaways could have divided the island into seven separate domains, each living as a modern Robinson Crusoe. Choosing instead to live and work together created social and economic opportunities not available to Crusoe. For example, rather than fish alone, the castaways of Gilligan's island could undertake a joint, cooperative fishing effort: Fashion a large net, and then cast and retrieve it together. Similarly, they could gather coconuts cooperatively, say, by stabilizing a tall ladder through the efforts of two or more people while someone scales it to pick the fruit. Human nature being what it is, the opportunities created through joint efforts include the possibility of shirking one's duties, as the case of Gilligan amply demonstrates. In some cases, shirking can be detected easily. If Gilligan is assigned the task of gathering coconuts, for example, his presence on the beach, sunning himself on a beach towel, would be a strong indicator of shirking behavior. But if he is part of a group casting and retrieving a net, whether or not he is giving his fullest effort would be harder to detect. And if the Professor is assigned the task of inventing a better ladder or net, his presence on the beach could be an indicator that he is either hard at work, thinking, or merely emulating Gilligan. Exacerbating this problem is nature's risk, which introduces variation into the productivity of the castaways' environmental enterprises. If the natural world is unvarying, a fish harvest that falls short is a clear signal that someone was shirking, even though the identity of the shirker may be difficult to ascertain. Natural variation in fish populations muddies this signal: If the harvest is low, was someone goofing off or was the fish population just naturally low this time? In an uncertain world, the castaways have additional opportunities for shirking by hiding behind nature's risk. One response to this problem is suggested by a supposed, not-so-old Chinese fable.[20] A visitor to China, the fable goes, came upon a group of large, hard-working men, pulling a barge through a canal from along the shore. Accompanying the laborers was an even larger man brandishing a whip, which he showed no hesitation in using. What an outrage, the visitor remarked to his guide, the man with the whip is so cruel. The guide was puzzled by this remark and replied, "But the men hired him to do that!" The castaways, in other words, could appoint one of their own number to be a taskmaster. This person would monitor the tasks assigned to each castaway, and have the authority to discipline anyone caught shirking. Policing the individual efforts of a joint venture in this way, however, creates its own problem: Who will monitor and discipline the taskmaster? Keeping tabs on six other castaways is hard work, and so the taskmaster will inevitably be tempted to shirk. But having the other castaways directly monitor the taskmaster's effort means double-checking everyone else's efforts, defeating the purpose of creating such a role. How will the other castaways have any faith that the taskmaster is doing the job? Among the many ways of answering this question is an appeal to what economists call the "residual claimant."[21] A residual claimant is the party (or parties) that has the contractual right to whatever remains after the other parties in a joint effort have been paid. If a taskmaster accepts the role of residual claimant, this can help instill faith in the other parties that the taskmaster will earn his or her pay. To show how this comes about, suppose the castaway who takes on the job of taskmaster agrees to pay each of the other castaways a certain amount of fish per week in exchange for their fishing effort.[22] Once the harvest is in and the other castaways have been paid, the taskmaster receives whatever fish are left over (the residual). If the taskmaster is lazy, any laborer who shirks is not likely to be caught but will still receive the agreed-upon wage (but with less exertion). The taskmaster, on the other hand, will end up with a relatively low residual, because shirking will reduce the fish harvest. Like Robinson Crusoe, being lazy therefore generates costs that redound to the taskmaster. By accepting responsibility for any shortfall, then, a taskmaster who desires a full stomach has an incentive to prevent shirking by others as well as by him or herself. Nature's risk complicates the work of a taskmaster, as noted above, because it makes the detection of shirking problematic. Nature may unexpectedly provide a bountiful harvest, masking any shirking by the laborers; or a shortfall in the harvest actually caused by shirking can be blamed on unlucky natural conditions. Distinguishing the effects of ecological nature from those of human nature is therefore a valuable skill when nature's risk is a major source of variation. The castaways of Gilligan's island are fortunate to have someone in their midst who is available to help in this way: the Professor. By applying his expertise to the island's ecosystems, the Professor is capable of producing a better understanding of the fishery. With this knowledge, the taskmaster could predict the likely size of the next harvest, find better ways to manage the fishery, or invest in reducing the fishery's natural variability or increasing its future viability. These efforts could both increase the harvest available to all and make the taskmaster's job more efficient by making it easier to detect shirking. Reflecting the vagaries of nature, the scientific enterprise is an uncertain one, and the worth of the Professor's advice may be difficult for others to judge. If the taskmaster hires the Professor to estimate the level of harvest that the island's fishery can support indefinitely, the accuracy of his estimate may not be revealed for some time. And checking the Professor's predictions through duplication will be very difficult (and wasteful) for the other castaways. For the castaways on Gilligan's island, one solution to this problem is straightforward: Put the Professor in charge. By combining the roles of scientist and taskmaster, and adding the rights and responsibilities of residual claimant, the castaways reduce the problem of shirking and increase productivity for their joint, "scientific" efforts in the following way. The cost of monitoring will be lowest when the person whose contribution is the hardest to evaluate monitors him- or herself.[23] As long as the other castaways perform simple, labor-intensive tasks, the Professor's contribution—his scientific predictions and recommendations—will likely be the most difficult to evaluate. Thus, he has an advantage over the other castaways in monitoring the joint effort, because any other arrangement would involve checking up on the Professor. Agreeing to be the residual claimant cements the arrangement, because it effectively creates incentives for the Professor to perform more efficiently both as scientist and taskmaster. As scientist/residual claimant, he has the incentive to balance the benefits and costs of responding to nature's risk. Scientific accuracy acquires a premium, as do cost-efficient ways of enhancing the fishery's viability. Another strong candidate for consideration is building a safety margin into the weekly harvest to guard against extinction, but again, the Professor-cum-residual-claimant has the incentive to find the "right" safety margin, balancing the long-run viability of the fishery against the short-run cost of going hungry. And as taskmaster/residual claimant, he has an incentive to police himself, for a sloppy job of monitoring the others' efforts may produce an unlucky string of shortfalls. Putting the

Professor in charge is no panacea. Gilligan will still find opportunities to goof off, and the Professor's predictions will sometimes lead the castaways' efforts astray. But when nature's risk is an important factor in a joint enterprise, the ability to forecast, manipulate and propose adaptations to that risk is an important skill, but one that is hard to evaluate. By offering to accept responsibility for his monitoring and scientific errors, the Professor relieves the other castaways of the need to constantly check his diligence as well as his math. The savings may just be enough to tide them over until their rescuers arrive.

The "No Surprises" Policy and Nature's Risk

The effort to conserve an endangered species is almost always a joint effort, like those on Gilligan's island, rather than a solo one, like those on Crusoe's island. Species are rarely endemic to one piece of property, instead being spread across several landowners. Although cooperation need not take place, it will undoubtedly enhance any conservation efforts directed at that species. Using Gilligan's island as our model, then, the Professor's role as residual claimant illustrates the logic of the "no surprises" rule. If the conditions supporting the fishery population on Gilligan's island unexpectedly deteriorated, the Professor would still owe the other castaways their weekly wage. He did not have the right to declare any shortfall their responsibility and lower their wages accordingly. Instead, being the residual claimant meant adherence to a "no surprises" rule: the Professor agreed to bear nature's risk. By doing so, he created incentives that helped ensure his own efforts, both as taskmaster and as scientist. In February of 1998, the U.S. Fish and Wildlife Service and the National Marine Fisheries Service (NMFS) announced their intention to fill a role similar to the Professor's: the residual claimant for this nation's endangered species. Can the "no surprises" rule play a role similar to the one it played on Gilligan's island? Or does it reject ecological reality, as some groups have charged? And are the two services, both federal government agencies, good fits for the role of residual claimant? The essence of the "no surprises" rule is straightforward: Once an HCP permit has been issued and its terms and conditions are being fully complied with, the permittee may remain secure regarding the agreed-upon cost of conservation and mitigation. If the status of a species addressed under an HCP unexpectedly worsens because of unforeseen circumstances, the primary obligation for implementing additional conservation measures would be the responsibility of the federal government, other government agencies, or other non-federal landowners who have not yet developed an HCP.[24] The rule's finer details allow the services to modify existing HCPs should circumstances change, but those modifications cannot "impose new restrictions [on the permittee's activities] or require additional financial compensation...."[25] For example, if an HCP's operating conservation program originally included a mixture of predator depredation control and captive breeding, but subsequent research or information demonstrated that one of these was considerably more effective than the other, the Services would be able to request an adjustment in the proportionate use of these tools, provided that such an adjustment did not increase the overall costs to the HCP permittee.[26] Finally, should circumstances change and the risk faced by a listed species increase, the government (or any other party) can act to reduce that risk: Nothing in this rule will be construed to limit or constrain the Services, any federal, state, local, or tribal government agency, or a private entity, from taking additional actions at its own expense to protect or conserve a species included in a conservation plan.[27]

The "no surprises" rule has generated vigorous opposition from environmental and scientific groups. The latter's opposition is often stated in terms of the unscientific nature of the rule: In a nutshell, [the no surprises rule] does not reflect ecological reality and rejects the best scientific knowledge and judgment of our era. It proposes a world of certainty that does not, has not, and will never exist....Because we will always be surprised by ecological systems, the proposed "no surprises" amendment flies in the face of scientifically based ecological knowledge, and in fact rejects that knowledge.[28]

A "no surprises" policy is troubling to scientists because it runs counter to the natural world, which is full of surprises. Nature frequently produces surprises, such as new diseases, droughts, storms, floods and fire. The inherent dynamic complexity of natural biological systems precludes accurate, specific predictions in most situations; human activities greatly add to and compound this complexity. Surprises will occur in the future; it is only the nature and timing of surprises that are unpredictable.[29] These comments have helped fuel considerable opposition to this policy. Does "ecological reality" have any bearing on the wisdom of the "no surprises" rule? The ubiquitous presence of nature's risk strongly suggests that parties to an HCP would be wise to cover a range of possibilities, and the "no surprises" rule encourages this. The rule goes to great lengths to describe the sections of an HCP that should cover circumstances that might change, or that were unforeseen when the plan was approved. As the future is realized, the plan might turn out to be inadequate, and so HCPs frequently contain adaptive management provisions that dictate certain actions for certain contingencies. An HCP that contains provisions such as these will have greater potential value to the parties because wrangling over matters left out of the agreement will then be avoided. The "no surprises" rule adds a similar type of value. It ties up loose ends, by assigning the responsibility for nature's risk—natural events that fall outside the scope of the HCP—to the federal government. "Ecological reality" is compatible with these provisions, because an HCP that contains them acknowledges the uncertainty of the natural world. The question of who should act through adaptive management or who should bear nature's risk, however, is decided by the parties to the HCP, not by any scientific deductions or inferences from ecology or conservation biology.[30] Ecologists and conservation biologists may have their own preferences about these provisions, but there is no obvious reason to give their preferences ascendancy over the arrangements chosen by the HCP parties themselves. If any group of scientists should be bothered by the "no surprises" rule, it is economists. Whenever a public entity assumes a role commonly filled by a private party, economists worry that the incentives to perform that role efficiently will be muted, if not absent altogether. Does this mean that the "no surprises" rule assigns nature's risk to the wrong party? Swallowing hard, I believe the answer to this question is a (heavily) qualified "No." Suppose the "no surprises" rule did not exist, and the parties seeking an incidental take permit were required to bear nature's risk. At first glance, this situation would give those parties incentives to learn more about that risk, adapt to it, and reduce it, none of which is substantially different from the incentives of a normal residual claimant. The absence of a "no surprises" rule, however, would not shift the risk altogether. As long as the government retained the right to any ecological windfalls, the risk would be split between the two parties. This appears to be the case: If a species's situation changes for the better (short of being delisted), nothing in the ESA gives non-federal parties the right to scale back their conservation efforts unilaterally. Thus, without a "no surprises" rule, HCP parties gain nothing from an ecological windfall, but must bear any shortfall. This asymmetry creates a set of perverse incentives, as Heyne (1997) notes: Only short-range projects will be undertaken. Fewer resources will be invested in research. Innovative projects will be explored less often. Problems that could have been avoided through better foresight will be encountered more frequently. Coordination failures will occur more often as individuals try to reduce their private risks.[31] Moreover, there is one way to reduce the risk to near zero: Avoid or even remove the conditions that make an HCP necessary.[32] If an endangered species is not present on a piece of property, or can be persuaded to depart, no permit is required and nature's risk is the government's tough luck. Given that splitting the risk is unwise, why not give it all to the non-federal party? The reason stems from the frequent mismatch between ecological and legal boundaries. Consider the case in which a single property contains the entire habitat—past, present, and potential—of a species. The owner of that property has complete control over the species, and, like Crusoe, bears the benefits and costs of actions that affect the species's risk of extinction.[33] Given the commandments of the ESA, the property owner, again like Crusoe, is well-suited to bear nature's risk. In this case, a "no surprises" rule would likely be misplaced. Now consider the more prevalent case, in which a species's habitat is spread across many landowners. In this case, a joint effort to conserve the species is likely to be more productive than separate, individual efforts. To give a simple illustration of this, suppose a population of a species exists on each of several properties. As it was for the S.S. Minnow castaways, each landowner could manage the species in isolation from the other landowners. Managing the populations together as a true metapopulation, however, would increase the overall viability of the species. Thus, there are definite potential gains from some form of joint conservation. One way to achieve those gains is to create a market for species exchange among the landowners.[34] If one population falls to a dangerously low level, that landowner could purchase individuals from other populations; similarly, occasional purchases could take place to enhance genetic diversity. Unfortunately, the market approach presumes a degree of control over natural populations that rarely exists. For a market to be viable, an individual landowner must be able to prevent other landowners from "consuming" the species without paying for it. If the landscapes and therefore the populations are linked naturally, this control will be difficult to assert. Indeed, the natural connectedness of the landscape is a valuable, ecological asset, owned jointly by the landowners. Taking the market approach would require extensive monitoring efforts at the least, or the destruction of that asset at the extreme (for example, through domestication). Moreover, to set prices rationally, landowners must understand how changes in population numbers and genetic diversity affect the viability of the species. If each landowner invests resources to make this determination individually, the efforts will be duplicative. An alternative that preserves the landscape's ecological capital and reduces the duplication of scientific effort is to undertake a joint effort to conserve biodiversity. This approach encounters the same problems found on Gilligan's island, however. Evaluating scientific information tion generic to the species will be wasteful if the evaluation involves duplicating the research,[35] and a particular landowner may have opportunities to shirk on whatever share of the joint effort that landowner has been assigned. Other landowners may notice that their populations are faring less well, but they may not be able to distinguish the effects of their neighbor's shirking from a bad "natural" year. Again assuming that a mandate to protect the species exists, such a group of landowners could solve their joint problem by emulating the seven castaways: Hire a "biodiversity taskmaster." This party would take on two sets of tasks: conduct research or collect information (of a generic sort) on the species, and monitor the performance of the individual landowners in their effort to protect the species. The advantages of a biodiversity taskmaster are manifold: duplicative research would not take place; the taskmaster would have an incentive to conduct accurate science and the right amount of science; and it would be in a position to create and coordinate conservation plans across all landowners, with an eye toward cumulative effects and other factors that affect the overall viability of the species. The taskmaster's performance could be ensured, in part, by making that party the residual claimant. In short, if the FWS or NMFS did not exist, private landowners operating under a mandate to preserve endangered species might choose to hire such an agency! And a "no surprises" rule, a likely part of the agreement covering the duties of the residual claimant, would help ensure (but not guarantee, of course) that the agency performed its tasks efficiently. Note the important difference between the actual government agencies and our hypothetical agency, however: No one hired them to enforce the ESA. The Fish and Wildlife Service and the National Marine Fisheries Service have been directed to administer the ESA by Congress, not by the many landowners with an endangered species on their properties. More importantly, the two agencies are beset by the usual host of distorted incentives that plague all government agencies. Hence, the economists' distress. However imperfect the incentives facing the federal government may be, removing its agencies from the management of endangered species conservation is unlikely to occur anytime soon. The ESA is here to stay, at least for the foreseeable future. The choice is therefore between an Endangered Species Act with or without a "no surprises" rule. The latter creates a set of perverse incentives because only half of nature's risk is shifted. As strange as it seems, giving the federal government the role of residual claimant through a "no surprises" rule is likely to be the more efficient alternative.[36]

Conclusion

Despite the problems introduced by a government agency acting as residual claimant, the idea of a "no surprises" rule hardly "runs counter to the natural world," as some in the scientific community have charged. At the very least, the rule potentially increases the efficiency of our conservation efforts. By doing so, the rule can create more opportunities for saving endangered species within the existing framework of the ESA. Whether we take advantage of these opportunities, and thereby improve the chances of survival for listed species, remains to be seen. In any case, the objections of environmental and scientific groups have little force: Ecological, economic, or any other type of reality gladly embraces a "no surprises" rule.

Notes

1   60 Federal Register 32161 (20 June 1995), at 32162.
2   In April 1997, a coalition of environmental groups challenged this decision, along with another HCP also covering the Alabama beach mouse, in federal court. In Fort Morgan Civic Association v. Babbitt (97-CV-773, D.D.C.; case transferred to Alabama, 97-691, S.D. Ala.), the groups charged the FWS with not considering the cumulative impacts of coastal development on P. p. ammobates. The lawsuit, decided in favor of the plaintiffs in August 1998, did not address the effects of Hurricane Opal.
3   Throughout this essay, I use the term "risk" a bit loosely. In the economic world, risk is usually distinguished from uncertainty, following Frank Knight (Risk, Uncertainty, and Profit, 1921). The former refers to future variability that is quantifiable, and therefore potentially subject to contracting, while the latter refers to variability that is not quantifiable. Here, the term "nature's risk" refers to future variability introduced by environmental forces. In some cases, nature's risk can be quantified, while in other cases it cannot.
4   Technically, the law has two categories of protection: endangered and threatened. The latter category does not automatically receive the law's full protection, but since early in the act's history, threatened species have routinely been granted the same level of protection as endangered species.
5   Endangered Species Act of 1973, U.S. Congress, Senate Report 93-307, 1 July 1973, at 2.
6   Anne Ehrlich and Paul Ehrlich, Extinction (New York: Ballantine Books, 1981), at xii.
7   Aldo Leopold, Round River (Oxford: Oxford University Press, 1993), at 146-147.
8   G. Jon Roush, "The Disintegrating Web," The Nature Conservancy Magazine, November/December 1989, at 3.
9   See, e.g., S. T. A. Pickett, V. T. Parker, and P. L. Fiedler, "The New Paradigm in Ecology: Implications for Conservation above the Species Level," in Conservation Biology, P. L. Fiedler and S. K. Jain, eds. (New York: Chapman and Hall, 1992), pp. 65-88.
10 J. M. Scott, T. H. Tear, and L. S. Mills, "Socioeconomics and the Recovery of Endangered Species: Biological Assessment in a Political World," Conservation Biology, 9 (February 1995): 214-216, at 215.

11 D. Defoe, The Life and Adventures of Robinson Crusoe (London: Penguin Books, 1965), at 122.

12 Id., at 117-118.

13 Id., at 118.

14 Id., at 120.

15 Id., at 155.

16 A metapopulation is a set of subpopulations that may be subject to local extinctions but in general are connected so that risk of extinction for the entire population is low. Conservation Biology, P. L. Fiedler and S. K. Jain, eds. (New York: Chapman and Hall, 1992), definition at 490. Crusoe's separate flocks would be a true metapopulation only if he allowed (occasional) interbreeding among them.

17 Id., at 169-170.

18 Strictly speaking, this might not be quite accurate. Suppose a species of grape turned out to be endemic (found only on that island). If other humans acquired knowledge of that species and valued it for its existence, Crusoe's decisions affecting that species would have consequences borne by others.

19 Id., at 93.

20 Or at least one of my graduate school professors, Steven N.S. Cheung, claimed it was a fable.

21 See P. Heyne, The Economic Way of Thinking, 8th edition (Upper Saddle River, New Jersey: Prentice Hall, 1997), at 265-270, and Y. Barzel, "The Entrepreneur's Reward for Self-Policing," Economic Inquiry, 25 (January 1987): 103-116, for two good introductions to this concept.

22 The determination of the wage rate on Gilligan's island is problematic, as is the competitive return for taskmasters, because the normal forces of competition are absent. I shall take the usual approach of economists and assume these minor difficulties away.

23 "[T]he person whose contribution to common effort is the most difficult to measure will assume the position of entrepreneur, employing and supervising the other persons. By becoming the residual claimant who bears most of the risk of variable outcome, his incentive to gain at the expense of his partners is curtailed." (Barzel (1987), at 103.) When scientific expertise is combined with simple labor, the former is arguably the hardest contribution to measure.

24 Id., at 8867.

25 Id., at 8868.

26 Id., at 8868-8869.

27 Id., at 8869.

28 Gary K. Meffe et al., "Revisions of the Endangered Species Act: A Letter to Senator John Chaffee and Congressman James Saxton," 23 July 1996.

29 "A Statement on Proposed Private Lands Initiatives and Reauthorization of the Endangered Species Act from the Meeting of Scientists at Stanford University," 31 March 1997, reproduced in R. F. Noss, M. A. O'Connell, and D. D. Murphy, eds., The Science of Conservation Planning (Washington, D.C.: Island Press, 1997), pp. 214-219, at 215.

30 In fairness to the authors of the statements quoted in the text, they acknowledge this point. This makes their objections seem somewhat disingenuous, however, because the scientific credentials they frequently trumpet are in fact irrelevant to that question.

31 Heyne (1997), at 274.

32 This incentive exists even with a "no surprises" rule, but the absence of a "no surprises" rule exacerbates it.

33 Again, if existence values are present, this will not be the case unless the property owner can somehow capture those values, which seems unlikely.

34 Another way would be to consolidate the species's populations by having one landowner buy out all the others. If the values generated by the species are the only ones under consideration, this option is probably the most efficient, but for that reason it is also the most likely to emerge out of private contracting. If other values dominate, consolidation may not be a viable option.

35 Gathering information on a particular piece of property will still have value to an individual landowner, but not to that landowner's neighbors. Generic information about the species can be used by all landowners, and it is therefore inefficient for more than one party to produce this type of information.

36 An interesting reform to the ESA would be to allow multiple-landowner HCPs, in which the parties agree to be bound and monitored by a private biodiversity taskmaster. Certain HCPs in California have elements of this proposal, but the central agency is invariably a local or county agency, with permitting authority over private land use decisions.

Part II

Specific Cases

5 The Single Species: The Efficient Focus for Biodiversity Protection

MICHAEL GILPIN

In this essay, I review the stages of conservation biology analysis that have been used to consider threatened and endangered species. Basically, there have been three general categories of consideration: case-by-case biology, population viability analysis (PVA), and multispecies habitat conservation planning. This last mode of analysis has led to the spate of Habitat Conservation Plans (HCPs) recently, and most controversially, accepted by the United States Fish and Wildlife Service as meeting requirements mandated by the Endangered Species Act. I argue that we have prematurely abandoned a single-species approach of population viability analysis, an approach that had the proper focus, and an approach that was rapidly proving its worth. This PVA approach has largely been replaced by a vague, feel-good process with essentially no scientific content. The focus of this third approach is the entire community of species. It is variously labeled as habitat conservation planning, natural community conservation planning (NCCP), or, sometimes, just ecosystem health.

This third approach won't work. It can't work. In the short run, it won't protect species. In the intermediate run, its scientific inadequacies will cause debilitating controversy, perhaps to the point of undermining the entire Endangered Species Act (ESA). Ultimately, no one will be happy with this multispecies approach. Yet different groups support it for different reasons. In this essay, I recount some of the dissatisfactions that have lead to this change of focus, but I go on to challenge its supposed scientific underpinnings. My recommendation is that we should prevent this shift to multispecies systems and constrain any future revision of the ESA to its present form: an act that targets individual species and manages for their long-term viability.

To help the non-ecologist reader, I preview with an analogy. We live in a troubled society. Among other pathologies, we must contend with dysfunctional people. One holistic approach to public health is to provide psycho-analysis to all of these dysfunctional people, to treat the root causes of their problems in the psychic fullness of their individual histories. Alternatively, we could dispense lithium or some other case-specific drug. The psychoana-lytic approach sounds humanistic but has inherent problems: which therapy— Freudian, Jungian or Addlerian? And it takes forever. And it is very expen-sive. Objectively, it rarely works. The drugs, however, quiet down the prob-lem cases, and these treated people can live with themselves, and we with them. Even though we lack a fully developed theory of how the drugs act to produce the observed effect, we can objectively demonstrate success. It took decades of bitter argument for us to reach this point in our approach to public health, but it is clearly where we are today. We treat the symptoms with rela-tively inexpensive therapeutics of demonstrated efficaciousness.   Similarly, we understand a lot about the population dynamics of single species. We have a good understanding of how our intentional or unintentional manipulations and disruptions of the environment affect the distribution and abundance of individual species. We know how optimally to harvest single species, and we have general approaches to restoring them into habitats and locals where they have been extirpated. That is, we have the empirically based knowledge and understanding to deal with biodiversity loss one species at a time. With fol-low-up monitoring and proper case-study review, the science of conservation biology will doubtless develop a standard set of treatments that will protect against the loss of biodiversity at the single-species level. By proving itself efficacious, this single species approach has the possibility to win wide public support, a result not possible today (as argued by other contributors to this volume).

The community or ecosystems approach suffers fatal epistemological difficulties. We don't have an agreed-upon theory of how such systems work, and we have precious little success in managing natural ecosystems to attain pre-defined goals.

Yes, most of us would like to live on a planet composed of harmonious, stress-free natural ecosystems, of full member species communities. But mod-ern man is disrupting wide and deep, and what we are in for is ecological discontent, as far into the future as we can see. We should approach this situ-ation with an understanding of the scientific and financial limits.

The single-species viability approach publicly foundered with the north-ern spotted owl, a case that Secretary of the Interior Bruce Babbitt has repeat-edly called "a national train wreck." This (sub)species has caused a decade of economic and political troubles for the states of Oregon and Washington. Politicians did not like the frontal confrontation between ecology and economics. It was jobs versus birds. Rural communities were threatened with extinction. Federal judges froze logging plans. Opportunity costs were excessive. Babbitt's agency, the United States Fish and Wildlife Service (USFWS), did not want to deal with an endless series of such emotion-charged biodiversity battles. It has sought, since about 1992, to prefer a process that focuses on smaller ownership-based landscape units and all species resident thereon. And, given the number of such accepted plans, this approach seems to be successful.

The USFWS carries this out, somewhat incorrectly in my view, under Section 10A of the Endangered Species Act (ESA). This section was added in the 1983 rewrite of the Act. Basically, this Section gives to private parties the same rights federal agencies have always enjoyed under Section 7 of the Act. If a federal project, after consultation with the USFWS, is seen incidentally to have adverse impact on a federally listed species (i.e., to jeopardize it), the federal proponents of the project can develop mitigation to balance the project's incidental take of the endangered species. If the USFWS accepts this mitigation, the project can move forward. There are no rigid standards for this mitigation, and, almost invariably, this process of consultation does allow the completion of such federal projects.

Section 10A gives to non-federal entities, e.g., regional governments or private property owners, similar access to a consultative approach to the mitigation of incidental take of a listed species. When a local or private project risks harming an endangered species, the proponents may propose mitigation with a Habitat Conservation Plan (HCP) for the listed species. The features and components of an HCP are not spelled out in any great detail in the Act. However, one common requirement is that the mitigation must be better than a do-nothing approach. On private lands, a do-nothing approach is generally unsatisfactory, since doing nothing is what may have led to the endangered status in the first place. A variety of approaches have been taken in such HCPs, but most involve the dedication of private lands for some form of publicly owned reserve. The point I wish to emphasize, however, is that the focus of such a Section 10A HCP is a single species.

I discuss several HCPs below. The first dozen HCPs targeted listed species, invariably covering all of the present range of the species, or at least the full range of a distinct population segment (DSP) of the species. The practice that today is popularly referred to as "HCP" is quite different. Of this new type of HCPs, there have been many hundreds. They customarily involve a particular landscape unit, e.g., a town, a valley, a large block of private property. Such spatial units contain at least one listed species, for without this, no private land owner would wish to deal with the USFWS. But often many other species are of concern or candidates for listing. Rarely, however, does the landscape unit contain all of the geographic range of any of these species. That is, this new approach is wider along the biodiversity axis, but narrower in spatial dimension. The group planning the action on this spatial unit wants to consult with the USFWS, and they want to take care of all of their species problems with a single mitigation plan.

Since this new HCP approach has a broader focus at the species level, such an accepted HCP can be viewed as solving all the endangered species problems associated with the project and the landscape unit that it affects. In consequence, the USFWS grants to the land-owning proponents of the project long-term immunity from further intrusions into their management affairs. This immunity is termed a "no surprises" policy. Without such guarantees, the project proponents would have no incentive to bear the costs of the mitigation. It sounds fair and rational.

A major problem confronting this multispecies approach is that it is not actually formalized in the current ESA. (It is, however, a key part in some of the drafts of reform versions of the ESA, such as the 1998 Kempthorn-Chaffey bill.) Some consider the USFWS to be acting beyond their authority when taking this approach. Fights are brewing on many fronts.

Based on the current status of conservation biology science, I argue that we are better off correcting the flaws in our single species approach to biodiversity conservation. I reject the alternative of taking a path with no objective standards, (or not even the possibility for standards), and where the spatial and temporal scales of any "answer" are entirely inappropriate to the fundamental questions of conservation. I am not against a "no surprises" policy or other such policies that make the ESA work better on private property. A no-surprises policy is quite rational when the chance of surprise has been minimized by sound reserve design and population-level mitigation. But the current multispecies practice violates sound reserve design (necessarily a top-down approach), and insults conservation science with a calculated refusal to monitor and thus adjust based on experience.

I am a scientist with early training in theoretical physics and operations research. I have a strong bent towards theory and modeling. Before 1982, my research in population biology dealt entirely with such standard academic challenges as population dynamics, community structure, and island biogeographic theory and metapopulation dynamics. In 1982, with my colleague Michael Soule, the founding father of the science of conservation biology, I turned to issues of population viability analysis (PVA) and reserve design. We first did conceptual analysis but soon became deeply enmeshed in actual case-study decision-making. Because I am suited by training and experience to handle the computational side of science, I have had the good fortune to work on a number of important endangered species problems.

I have been a member of two USFWS recovery teams (one successful [the desert tortoise in the western Mojave Desert] and the other an utter failure [we lost our species, the Morro Bay kangaroo rat]), and a conservation biology advisor to the USFWS, the United States Forest Service (USFS), two state governments, the World Wildlife Fund and The Wilderness Society. I have observed for decades the progress, or lack thereof, in the handling of a number of celebrated endangered species, e.g., the desert tortoise, the California condor, Yellowstone grizzly bears, Stephens kangaroo rats, the California gnatcatcher, the squawfish in the Upper Basin of the Colorado River, and the westslope cutthroat in Montana, among others.

I have been teamed with intelligent, experienced, and dedicated scientists in each of these projects. We have, under many and various constraints, carried out "best science," as mandated by the ESA. And in many ways we can be proud of our accomplishments. However, I do feel that some of the wording of the Act is weak and vague and even misleading. Yet the Act, written some 25 years ago, was formulated a decade earlier than the creation of the science of conservation biology. It is this science that attempts to give logical definitions to the long series of key terms set out in the ESA: endangered, critical habitat, distinct population segment, and so forth. But these definitions can be perfected out in time; their initial vagueness is not something that justifies abandoning the single species approach.

In the early 1970s, the drafters of the original ESA were largely thinking of grizzly bears, bald eagles, whales and the like—species being hunted and poisoned to the brink of extinction. For such species, the idea was to label them as endangered or threatened, and thereby to prohibit the human activities driving them to extinction. The ban on DDT has lead to a remarkable recovery of the bald eagle. And, less dramatically, the grizzly bear has held its population numbers steady around a thousand since being listed and seems actually to fill the habitat in its two bastions, Glacier National Park and Yellowstone National Park. Some whale species have made dramatic recoveries. All of these species could come off the list.

Today's challenges for the ESA come with the lizards, the drab song-birds, the butterflies, and the less colorful flies and beetles. These are species that typically have small geographic ranges and that have, largely unnoticed by us, irrevocably lost habitat due to human encroachment. Since their plight is usually recognized very late, these species are often driven to such a parlous state that a prohibitive, hands-off policy will not lead to their recovery. Positive action must be taken. Such positive actions typically involve the increase in the quality and/or quantity of their necessary habitat. Saving these species involves hundreds of millions of dollars of habitat acquisition. And even doing nothing can cost tens of millions of dollars of opportunity costs if hospitals are not built and roads not completed. The "genius" of the multispecies approach is that these problems can sometimes be swept under the table, to the relief of developers and resource management agencies alike. Whether the public and non-government conservation organizations will long tolerate this is a different question. And ultimately, of course, the real answers will come in the public policy arena.

Sticking with the science, I first review the intellectual underpinnings of viability analysis, and then explore two important case studies. From this base, I then criticize the multispecies approach to conservation.

Minimum Viable Populations

The National Forest Management Act of 1976, adopted three years after the ESA, contains better wording of the concept of species viability. In this document, each national forest supervisor is mandated to maintain "minimum viable populations of all vertebrate species." At about the same time (1979-1981) some early papers in conservation biology suggested 10, or 50, or 500 as minimal population size thresholds for species survival. But which was the right number, and how exactly do academic ideas relate to the practical management for minimal viability? In 1982, Hal Salwasser, then deputy chief of the USFS, assembled a small meeting of academics, me among them, to answer these questions. We focused on the northern spotted owl, then a species of concern for the states of Oregon and Washington. Initially, the USFS tried by itself to manage the northern spotted owl under this MVP concept, but the stakes were too high. Lawsuits finally forced the USFWS to list the northern spotted owl and to become the lead agency in its recovery planning. This tale has been told in many places, but invariably becomes a case of the blind men and the elephant. Even Alston Chase's In a Dark Wood falls well short of a proper scientific understanding.

Quite unappreciated, however, is how scattered, episodic and contentious has been the scientific analysis pertaining to the northern spotted owl. Between 1982-1992, the "best science" used to assess the viability of the northern spotted owl has been all over the biological map. Initially the concern was genetic: below what size would the species suffer irreversible loss of genetically based adaptability. Studies from fruit flies suggest a size, usually denoted by the variable N, of 500. But a "fudge factor" of 4 (based on the concept of genetic effective population size) was further required, bring the N to 2000. Soon, however, scientists noted that worrying about genetics when the population was demographically collapsing towards extinction was like fiddling while Rome burned. Quickly after this, focus was placed on the fragmentation and metapopulation dynamics of the species. Unfortunately, it is impossible to do manipulative science on endangered species. Thus it was impossible to do the experimental treatments that would offer clear support for one or the other of these approaches. The lack of a single voice from the conservation biology community exacerbated the political conflict resolution. The difficulties with the northern spotted owl have stimulated considerable conservation biology research on model systems that are experimentally more tractable, and today our understanding of the complex biological issues surrounding such a fragmented system are better understood.

Population Viability Analysis (PVA)

Prompted mainly by the USFS's need for a better mode of analysis for the decision-making and management of the northern spotted owl, Michael Soule and I[1] proposed an integrative approach to species viability analysis, which we dubbed PVA. The focus was on the species: its genetics, demography and spatial structure and how environmental perturbations drives each of these and produces interactions amongst them. That is, the data for this approach come mainly from the distribution in time and space of the individuals of the endangered species. It was implicitly assumed that the habitat relationships were represented in the population-level data. The approach, while based on historical and current information, was forward-looking and probabilistic in character. Viability was assessed as a probability, given some conditions for the population, of the species surviving to a distant time in the future—say,

100 or 500 years. Each species case involved a unique blend of its spatial, temporal, genetic and demographic data with the PVA models. Therefore, there were no magic numbers (e.g., a population size of 500) that allowed for rule-of-thumb decision-making. Nonetheless, PVA did offer the possibility of some closure within pre-specified probability limits. After 1986, PVA became a preferred mode of analysis for endangered species decision-making, both for listing and for evaluating recovery.

The Early HCPs

Section 10 of the ESA, added in 1983, allowed private landowners to take (i.e., destroy) endangered species incidental to otherwise lawful activity (e.g., real estate development) if they produced an acceptable HCP that did a reasonable job of mitigating the damage of their project on the endangered species. Two of the very first HCPs—the Mount San Bruno checkerspot butterfly, and the Coachella Valley fringe-toed lizard, both carried out in the mid-1980s—were pure habitat plans, with no formal viability analysis. After 1986, the standards changed. Thus, two of the important HCPs in the late 1980s— the Clark County, Nevada, desert tortoise and the Stephens kangaroo rat in western Riverside County, California—did include in the HCP explicit PVAs of the focal species. I was the lead conservation biology modeler for each of these analyses. For both species, map-based information on genetics, demography and population dynamics was translated into a set of statements about the spatial locations and configurations of a minimal reserve system. The development of these models was done publicly. There was extensive "buy-in" to the assumptions of the models by the various stakeholders. Each case took about three years to complete. These HCPs and associated PVAs were accepted by the USFWS as a basis for sound reserve design. For a few years it looked as if a PVA would be required in any HCP. But with the development of the multispecies approach, the PVA requirement began to fade, and PVAs are now almost entirely absent from the HCPs that are routinely accepted by Secretary of the Interior Bruce Babbitt's agency, the U.S. Fish and Wildlife Service (USFWS).

To set the time frame and context for the demise of PVA, I discuss two cases studies on which I performed PVA modeling. Both are kangaroo rats (K-rats) in the state of California. K-rats are attractive, big-eyed animals that hop about at night on their hind legs, seeking out grass seeds, which they pack into their cheek pouches and cache underground in their burrows. There are about 20 full species of K-rats in California. They inhabit the sandy soiled bottoms of valleys, between which movement is difficult. In fact, lifetime movement averages about 50 meters. Without the exchange of genes, populations can genetically diverge, ultimately leading to speciation. This may occur even in the absence of any functional change. Occupying small species ranges and being confronted by the massive landscape modifications that have been visited on the state of California, it is not surprising that a number of these species would end up as federally listed. Both of my K-rat stories can be viewed as failures, and the second of two, the Stephens kangaroo rat, led directly to the multispecies approach we have today.

The Rat Too Late

The Morro Bay K-rat was listed under the Act in 1982. Its former range was the several-mile-wide valley that runs 15 miles from San Luis Obispo to Morro Bay, California. In 1960, there were approximately 10,000 of these rodents. When I joined the USFWS recovery team in 1992, there were believed to be 50 of the animals still living. These K-rats had the misfortune to live in a beautiful locale into which humans were expanding, building houses, schools, businesses. They certainly lost land to this development, but fire suppression (to protect the development) might have been a bigger source of habitat loss. The Morro Bay K-rat, like others, requires open, grassy areas where they nocturnally gather grass seeds. Such open habitat is maintained by fire. With fire suppression, this habitat is successionally lost to brush encroachment. Domestic cats, some of which learn to feed on K-rats, are another problem. In 1960 the K-rats had been present on state lands. But the state of California saw all of its K-rats go extinct. The final 50 K-rats were resident on a single, privately owned 20-acre parcel of land adjacent to a subdivision of half-million dollar homes. A single, unfortunate landowner held possession of the entire species. Needless to say, he was not allowed to develop his property. He was forced to wait for something to happen or to be done. His reaction to this situation was: no trespass, no research, keep off. He was not going to be guilty of take. He doubtless knew that a do-nothing approach would probably lead to the timely extinction of the species and the elimination of his problem. However, he told the USFWS that if it wanted to trap out all of these Morro Bay kangaroo rats for transplant to a different, public location or removal to captive breeding, it could have them, which would relieve the landowner of any future responsibility. The landowner cannot be criticized for such tactics in this matter.

Transplantation from one habitat to another habitat of an entire population is fraught with difficulties. Managers have but one chance to do it right. The recovery team was loath to take such a gamble. The establishment of a captive population is much safer. This is a kind of halfway house approach. If a stable reproducing captive population can be established, scientists are offered the chance to learn restoration by doing; that is, with a growing captive population, it is possible repeatedly to return animals to the wild (e.g., the California condor, which is being released into the Grand Canyon as the zoo populations fill), and to find out the habitat requirements. But captive rearing, which the recovery team did, in fact, recommended, is labor-intensive and expensive. Did the USFWS really want to commit itself to an open-ended project that would cost at least $100,000 per year? Our recommendation fell on deaf ears. No action was taken. I will not comment on the USFWS' motives for this lack of action, but needless to say, we on the recovery team felt a little abused and betrayed. These K-rats, in the absence of any positive action, are now thought extinct.

This is a horrible story, with blame to share on all sides. There are lessons in this about finance and timing. However, I take it mainly as a failure of political will, a failure, early on, to ask the public to pay the price for effective conservation. The situation was dramatically different with the Stephens kangaroo rats (SKRs), different to the tune of $100 million dollars.

The Rat Too Early

The SKR was listed as endangered in 1989. It is a species largely contained in a wide valley (roughly 30 miles square) south of Riverside, California. At the time of listing, the SKR had suffered extensive habitat loss and habitat fragmentation, but there were tens of thousands of the animals extant. This large population, still distributed over most of its historic range, gave planners flexibility in their approaches to its conservation. The political leaders of the county were familiar with the HCP process, as the fringe-toed lizard HCP had earlier been carried out within their political jurisdiction. Thus, they sought a Section 10A permit from the USFWS. To finance the science and the habitat acquisition, they courageously voted for the entire affected area a $2,000/acre development assessment for K-rat protection. The projection was that at build-out, roughly $100 million would be provided for reserve acquisition and reserve management. A team of scientists (both from academe and from the consulting arena) was provided roughly $2 million to produce an acceptable plan. I was the lead modeler for this enterprise, which took three years to reach a consensus approach. We were successful. The SKR is a solved problem in species conservation. I look back on this intense undertaking with pride. We proved that good data and good PVA modeling could fashion a reserve system for an endangered species that would be judged as acceptable by the overwhelming majority of the stakeholders. I thought this case study would be the model for all future PVA-based conservation efforts. What I thought would be the launch point of the PVA approach proved in retrospect to be its apogee. PVA and the kind of data-rich, academically based modeling that we performed with the SKR crashed into oblivion almost immediately.

Why did this happen? Because there was a second endangered species in the same system—a bird, the California gnatcatcher. As we in the SKR project were toiling away, our eyes to the ground, spending our tens of millions of dollars for habitat acquisition, this second species was flying overhead inexorably on its way toward listing. We were not entirely unaware of this, but we saw the two cases as independent. We assumed that the politicians and local developers would be happy to give us another $100 million, given our obvious success with the first problem species. The politicians, who had gone out on the expensive SKR limb, were less thrilled with this new listing. They felt blind-sided: "When does it end?" they asked. "Well," we answered, "we've got a horned toad, a cactus wren, a whip-tailed lizard, some fairy shrimp, some substrate-specific dudlei plants...." All this in Riverside County alone.

The listing of the California gnatcatcher raised the embarrassing question: would it have been possible to have purchased with the first $100 million a reserve system that would not only have accommodated the SKR, but might also have fulfilled the needs of the gnatcatcher, which can often share some of the same habitats? Indeed, it was clear in retrospect that we could have done better. We should have stacked our PVAs in Geographic Information System (GIS) layers and selected a reserve system that optimally and efficiently served multiple species clients.

It is a huge economic watershed that a species crosses in going from unlisted (and unprotected) to listed. The USFWS needed to coordinate its decision making regarding listing, so as to keep politicians, developers and the public off an endless conveyor belt of bad news on the biodiversity front. Many people recognized this, and some scientific initiatives were started, but for the most part they have had slow going, as I will detail later.

Looking back, the SKR effort in Riverside County will be the last example wherein politicians raised the money before the solution was forthcoming.

A Fork in the Road

The listing of the California gnatcatcher in 1992 was much more profound than the listing of the SKR. The gnatcatcher population was in worse shape: some thought that there were but 1,200 pairs of the birds in all of southern California, principally Orange, Riverside and San Diego counties. The species was limited to coastal sage scrub habitat (this is different from what the SKR requires, but the two habitat types often intermix on a relatively fine scale, thus a particular piece of property might often contain both habitat types). With fewer animals remaining, there would seemingly be less flexibility in fashioning a solution. It was going to be expensive. Where one acre could hold maybe 50 SKRs, the situation was reversed for the gnatcatcher: one pair on 50 acres. And the gnatcatcher preferred coastal real estate, an extremely valuable commodity.

The California politicians could see the problems coming. It threatened to be worse than the northern spotted owl. In consultation with some members of the conservation biology community, members of California Governor Pete Wilson's administration proposed a state-controlled process called NCCP—Natural Community Conservation Planning. The USFWS soon accepted this approach under a Section 4D ruling connected to the listing of the gnatcatcher, whereby all the species of concern, approximately 80, would be saved by sub-regional HCPs. Among other things, they initially established a Science Review Panel (SRP) of five conservation biologists, of which I was one, to advise them as to how to proceed.

The press was full of praise for our forward-looking approach. Secretary of the Interior Bruce Babbitt visited the region many times, lauding the merits of the plan, and early on even contributing $5 million towards a land purchase. The wheels of commerce in southern California did not grind to a halt. For example, I live 30 miles north of the city of San Diego. Since the gnatcatcher was listed, I've seen tens of thousands of acres of pristine gnatcatcher habitat bladed into terraced subdivisions. And even though, in the housing boom of 1998, there are the routine complaints of "environmentalists" being responsible for the high cost of housing, the building industry is happy with the NCCP approach and staunchly supports it in all public discussion.

There were two paths to follow after the gnatcatcher listing. One path would have been to impose some sort of targeted building moratorium (as was done with the SKR) and to provide, up front, legislation for a billion dollar development assessment. Then, during an interim period of perhaps five to 10 years, conservation biologists would do the PVAs and the reserve design necessary to protect the tatters of native habitat remaining in southern California. We would not have to analyze all of the 80 species, for it would almost certainly be the case that, given the hierarchical structure of ecological systems and landscapes, a few of the species would "umbrella" all the others. But we shall never know, for this top-down, region-wide approach was not the path taken.

The actual operation of the NCCP has been piecemeal, bottom-up, and the associated HCPs have caused surprisingly little pain for developers and politicians, and surprisingly little gain for the science of conservation biology. Small- to medium-sized projects have developed their own HCPs, almost invariable using "science" from the consulting community. The project developers customarily provided some form of habitat mitigate (open space) on their project site or off site at a locale mutually agreed upon with the USFWS. Ribbons are cut before 100-acre preserves. The politicians have maximal opportunity for photo ops.

Because this piecemeal approach was garnering praise, the politicians had only to talk about the possible future need for a special bond issue to provide additional open space for these species. And the public gets the impression that the problem is being solved for free.

The NCCP science review panel on which I served was not funded to do science, nor were we provided data. We make a few vague pontifications and were disbanded after two years. There has been very little money spent on "research," and most of it was by the project proponents, as carried out by their consultants. There is no over-arching design philosophy employed in this approach to the problem, no attention to the region-wide needs of the endangered species. Looked at disinterestedly from a space station, the actual transformation of the landscape could accurately and legitimately be called "continued fragmentation."

The multispecies NCP process in southern California is vacuous and phony. When other local and private parties saw that Babbitt's USFWS was signing on to this charade, the great HCP land-rush commenced across the rest of the US landscape.

Note

1   Gilpin and Soule. 1986. "Viable Populations for Species Conservation" in Michael Soule, editor, Conservation Biology: the Sciences of Scarcity and Diversity, Sinauer Associates, Sunderland, MA.

6 With or Without the ESA, Can America Make a Place for the Grizzly Bear?

TODD WILKINSON

When we as a nation decide to recover isolated populations of imperiled species, inevitably we are confronted with the question: "How much is enough?" How many animals? How much habitat? How much money should we, and can we, spend to get the job done? How much are we willing to sacrifice? How much time do we have to act before these questions are no longer relevant? I'm not referring merely to the growing number of plants and animals threatened with extirpation in the United States and around the world, nor to the economic and social costs of mounting perpetual rescue attempts. Instead, I'm asking more precisely, what is our legal mandate in saving individual species? Is our responsibility just to stabilize a population living on the edge or, using the Endangered Species Act as a tool, is it to take bolder steps to ensure long-term persistence as a hedge against recurring crises? More fundamentally, are there some species that simply must remain federally protected forever because threats to their survival will always be present, assuming, of course, that shifts in human attitudes and patterns of development do not occur? Given this Sisyphean context, we must consider how the need, and responsibility for, habitat protection across the span of human generations can be reconciled with the more immediate values of politics, short attention spans and bureaucratic planning where four years, for some, is considered an eternity. Consider the case of the Yellowstone grizzly bear, representing the most famous population of wild bruins in the world which was cast into a downward spiral in the 1970s and required listing as a threatened species in 1975. We as a society have spent more money trying to keep viable grizzly populations alive in the lower 48 states—with mixed success—than we have spent on any other species. In the decades ahead, government agencies estimate that we will spend at least another $26 million. At present, those funds are being directed at roughly 1,000 grizzlies clustered in the Greater

Yellowstone Ecosystem, located at the intersection of northwest Wyoming, southwest Montana and eastern Idaho; the Northern Continental Divide Ecosystem, which includes Glacier National Park and the Bob Marshall-Scapegoat wilderness areas in northern Montana; the Cabinet-Yaak region along the Canada-Montana border; the Northern Cascade Mountains in Washington state; and possibly, with proposed reintroduction, the Selway-Bitterroot wilderness of western Montana and central Idaho. Grizzly recovery efforts are focused in the northern Rockies because elsewhere there are neither the relatively untrammeled tracts of sufficient wildlands to support them, nor low enough human populations to tolerate them. How many animals must exist for the species to survive? Although wildlife demographers assert that the number 500 represents the minimum threshold necessary to maintain genetic viability, genetics is far from the only factor in determining survival prospects. Formulas, after all, do not take place in a vacuum. Theories advanced on paper do not always hold up when tested in the reality of the field. Some prominent landscape ecologists studying grizzlies say that a minimum of 2,000 bears—or a doubling of the current total population—must exist in the lower 48 states, with their scattered island populations connected by "migratory corridors." In the Yellowstone Ecosystem alone, some conservation biologists assert that genetic viability requires 2,000 bears, or roughly four times the number of grizzlies that are estimated by the federal government to roam in the region today. That brings us to the questions of "How much land?" Where federal protection of imperiled species pertains to large, nomadic carnivores such as the grizzly—in which individual bruins inhabit home ranges measuring hundreds of square miles, we must probe deeper: How much habitat is enough to sustain the required numbers, and how does quality of habitat relate to long-term persistence? Unequivocally, grizzlies challenge the human resolve to share real estate with a species whose existence value is often discounted in the face of arguments made for jobs, personal economic wealth and safety. Brawny (weighing an average of 250 to 400 pounds), nomadic and dangerous (even Lewis and Clark complained of the bears' aggressiveness in their journals), grizzlies test human tolerance. Besides the rather daunting fact that grizzlies are fearsome and have been known, on occasion, to eat people, the management challenges of perpetuating them in the Yellowstone ecosystem revolve around their need for solitude.

Grizzlies require places where individual bears can find adequate supplies of high-energy natural foods and yet be buffered from human activities that cause bear deaths, namely hunting, developments in the middle of prime habitat, highways and poaching.

As an icon species, the grizzly represents more than merely a test for the adequacy of the ESA. The Great Bear, symbolically, is America's African lion, its Komodo dragon, its Bengal tiger, and Siberian snow leopard rolled into one. If the United States, the richest nation on earth, cannot develop a strategy which guarantees survival of this bellwether bruin for more than say, 50 years, conservationists rightly ask what hope there is for large predators in Third World nations where wildlife is viewed alternately as cash cows or expendable sources of human subsistence? What I would like to advance is an argument against the ongoing federal and state proposals to remove the Yellowstone grizzly population—e.g., to "delist" the bruins—from the federal list of threatened species, a subsection of the Endangered Species Act. Rather than making this argument on a set of personal political beliefs, I assert that while the Yellowstone grizzly is the most studied bruin in the world, there still is too much uncertainty about the government's ability to protect habitat. Few independent population biologists believe that removing the grizzly from federal protection will benefit the bear. Further, the public itself has become increasingly skeptical of the motives of bear managers who have been accused of suppressing scientists who challenge their assumptions, and holding closed door meetings in which their case for delisting has been placed beyond public scrutiny. But first, let us ponder the big picture of what a grizzly might encounter from the perspective of Chuck Schwartz, leader of the Yellowstone Interagency Grizzly Bear Study Team, the research arm of grizzly bear monitoring in Yellowstone and the adjacent public lands. Schwartz moved to the northern Rockies in 1998 after spending 21 years studying bears in Alaska. Thus, he is less impressed with the size of the greater Yellowstone region—comprised of seven national forests, two national parks, three national wildlife refuges, and roughly two million acres of private land—that together equal the combined area of Vermont and New Hampshire. He views the region differently than others in the lower 48 states. Schwartz also has attempted to encourage more public involvement in bear management issues. "In lots of areas where I've worked in Alaska, you can fly for hours looking out an aircraft window and never see a sign of human beings on the landscape," Schwartz says. "On the contrary, when you fly in the Yellowstone region, as large and wild as it is comparatively to other areas in the lower 48, I don't think you can look out the window in any direction without seeing some kind of human activity." The reality in greater Yellowstone, Schwartz says, is that very few bears can live their entire lives without getting into trouble, whether by stumbling onto an elk hunter, confronting livestock, happening upon a logging road where they are vulnerable to poachers, or becoming habituated to human food. "Those temptations are prominent in the ecosystem," he notes. "If we as a society want to have bears, the number one issue is providing them with secure habitat. If we do that, the numbers will take care of themselves."

The question is, will the imperative of habitat protection on these lands take priority over the politically driven push for accommodating traditional resource extraction (logging, mining, cattle grazing, and the new industry, tourism) as well as dramatic influx of people moving into the region.

Over the past 20 years, the locations where bears die during encounters with humans has shifted. Throughout the 1970s into the early 1980s, the vast majority of bear mortality was recorded inside the park and on the fringes of park gateway communities. Today, 95 percent of all grizzly deaths are occurring on forest service and private land outside the park, with most deaths caused by run-ins with hunters and recreationists. Outside the sanctified borders of Yellowstone Park, Chuck Schwartz says, is where the battle to protect grizzlies will ultimately be won or lost. Can the forest service be trusted to protect bears now when its track record of protecting bear habitat, even when it was mandated to do so by the Endangered Species Act, was dubious at best? On private land, where rural agriculture is being fast transformed by the imprint of suburbia, how will bears be affected by the lack of progressive land use planning and the destruction of not only bear habitat, but habitat for the animals and plants that bears eat? With this in mind, we return to the fundamental question of whether it's time to remove the grizzly from federal protection. Only a quarter of a century ago, when the Yellowstone ecosystem grizzly population was declared threatened, and drastic measures were taken to prevent its imminent extinction, talk of one day delisting the famous bruins might have been considered unthinkable. Today, it is U.S. Senator Craig Thomas's controversial position that the grizzly has "recovered" from its biological free fall, a position advanced not only by Wyoming politicians but by the U.S. Fish and Wildlife Service. These assertions have sparked a flurry of philosophical debate central to the very essence of the ESA. Certainly, Senator Thomas is no biologist, but this senior U.S. senator from Wyoming is pushing for federal action that would result in the federal government handing management of grizzlies over to the states of Wyoming, Montana and Idaho. Strangely, Thomas has cultivated sympathy from assistant U.S. Secretary of the Interior Don Berry—an advisor to Interior Secretary Bruce Babbitt—who has largely ignored concerns raised by independent scientists and conservationists about the government's use of science in grizzly bear management. It is unclear what political capital that Berry, an appointee for a Democratic presidential administration, would stand to gain from accommodating a Republican senator with allies in the Wise Use Movement. While Interior Secretary Babbitt has positioned himself as a reformer of failed land management and a fierce defender of the ESA, many independent scientists argue that removing the grizzly from federal protection would be a regressive maneuver. A prominent issue is whether the ESA, as it was initially crafted by Congress and signed into law by Richard Nixon in 1973, is intended merely to stabilize imperiled animal and plant populations, or to ensure their long-term viability. Recent federal court rulings, including one setback for the government's Grizzly Bear Recovery Plan, suggest the latter. U.S. District Court Judge Paul Friedman ruled in a lawsuit brought by the Fund for Animals and the National Audubon Society that the recovery plan was deeply flawed. Friedman called the plan's methodology "arbitrary and capricious" and ordered the Fish and Wildlife Service to write a new plan based on measurable habitat protection criteria. Until then, the IGBC did not address the issue of long-term habitat protection as a cornerstone of true recovery. "Judge Friedman noted that when the grizzly was listed as threatened, one primary reason was loss of habitat and he essentially asked the Fish and Wildlife Service how they could have something that parades as a recovery plan without identifying how much habitat a viable population of bears needs or what condition it needs to be in," said Doug Honnold, an attorney for Earthjustice Legal Defense Fund who helped litigate the case. "Somewhere along the line, the Fish and Wildlife Service needs to bite the bullet and say 'this is what we need for bears,' not 'how can we offend the least amount of politicians and wise use groups.'" A related question, one that has opened a fault line of heated disagreement in both the scientific and conservation communities, is farther reaching: Should a species like the grizzly bear, already reduced to less than two percent of its historic range in the lower 48, be removed from federal protection if its short-term status appears positive, but its middle to long-term prospects for survival appear bleak? Behind the scenes of public discourse, the topic of delisting the grizzly has ignited a contentious international debate. But it has also placed the methods of U.S. government science on trial, amid charges of political suppression of valid scientific dissent. In a pair of letters sent in 1998 to Jamie Rappaport Clark, the Fish and Wildlife Service's national director, Senator Thomas makes his desire clear. Implying that any hesitation to delist might jeopardize Congressional reauthorization of the ESA, Thomas suggests that a failure to declare victory with grizzlies could affect the listing of other species. "Further delay in delisting the grizzly only serves to strengthen the fears of folks who believe the Fish and Wildlife Service never intended to remove these animals from the endangered list once they had received this classification."

Senator Thomas has contended in the press that his constituents in the Cowboy State—who include the powerful oil and gas industry, timber companies, cattle ranchers and big game sportsmen (who hope to hunt grizzlies)—have suffered long enough with land use restrictions implemented to protect bear habitat: "As you know, the grizzly bear recovery effort has been highly successful in the Yellowstone region," he wrote. "By any reasonable measure, the grizzly bears in and around Yellowstone have reached the goals established under the recovery plan and the delisting process should begin." Bear managers in the greater Yellowstone region have taken heroic action to clean up garbage problems in Yellowstone Park gateway communities which lead to bears becoming habituated to human food and ultimately removed from the ecosystem. Compared to the challenge of protecting wild bear habitat, adding bear-proof trash dumpsters has been a largely cosmetic management action and relatively easy to accomplish. Indeed, Senator Thomas's analysis is correct that grizzly bears appear to meet most recovery criteria laid out by the Fish and Wildlife Service and the Interagency Grizzly Bear Committee, which has shepherded grizzly conservation since the early 1980s. Dr. Christopher Servheen, the national grizzly bear recovery coordinator for the Fish and Wildlife Service and author of the government's Grizzly Bear Recovery Plan has been at the forefront of bear conservation for two decades. A defender of delisting, he has been severely criticized for attacking those who question his optimism, including renowned bear biologist David Mattson, formerly a member of the Yellowstone Interagency Grizzly Bear Study Team. While researching my book, Science Under Siege: The Politicians' War on Nature and Truth (Johnson Books, 1998), I interviewed biologists from every state and federal land management agency in the greater Yellowstone ecosystem who said science pertaining to grizzlies was suppressed and scientists who questioned the government's positions were met with harassment. Some say they were asked to change the findings of reports, others were intimidated by colleagues in league with resource extractionists, and all were reminded their careers with government relied upon them "going along to get along." What does the lack of tolerance for dissent say about management of the grizzly and the integrity of science? At face value and by its own definition of a "recovered" bear population, the government's case for delisting might seem convincing. The Interagency Grizzly Bear Committee (IGBC), comprised of members from several federal and state agencies and lead by Servheen, argues that the number of breeding female bears with cubs—a key barometer for assessing population health—is up significantly over the early 1980s.

The committee also asserts that based upon increased sightings of bears in far flung corners of the ecosystem, a healthy grizzly population is rapidly expanding; and it cites as a hopeful sign the fact that far fewer bears are having to be physically relocated because of run-ins with people. Geographically, locales where bear sightings have occurred are hundreds of miles apart. "From our perspective in Yellowstone National Park, the trend in the near future for bears looks very positive," says John Varley, director of the Yellowstone research office. "We have a lot more bears than we did a decade ago. That's the good news, but considering the patterns of human encroachment into grizzly habitat beyond our borders, I would have to say the long-term prognosis is fairly negative."

Varley counts himself a proponent of turning bear management back to the states. Yet a growing, vocal body of respected scientists and conservation leaders claim that not only is divesting authority for bear protection premature, but a significant toll of bear deaths caused by clashes with hunters over the last four years offers an omen for what lies ahead if the bear is delisted. They argue that the delisting process is driven by politics to create a conservation success story as a gambit to salvage the ESA from the Congressional chopping block, even though it could doom the bear to extinction a century from now. "The Fish and Wildlife Service has endorsed a strategy which amounts to a biological crap shoot," says Louisa Willcox, who oversees the Sierra Club's Grizzly Bear Ecosystems Project. "In this case, the government is gambling on long odds that the grizzly will survive after delisting occurs, all in the face of threats to its habitat which are unprecedented and cause for alarm." Whether one agrees or disagrees with delisting or the views of Willcox, few people dispute the fact that there appears to be more bears alive today in Yellowstone than in the early 1980s. A quarter century ago, after bear managers initiated a bold strategy of closing trash dumps to wean bears off of unnatural foods, the population crashed to perhaps fewer than 200 bears. (An estimated 140 largely habituated bears associated with the Yogi and Booboo era of roadside begging bears died). Recovery strategies, including the end to grizzly hunting, combined with efforts to improve the storage of garbage in the park and surrounding gateway communities, radically reduced the number of deaths and allowed the bear population to grow. Various sources estimate the current bear population at somewhere between 300 and 600.

Nonscientists may be surprised at the uncertainty in counts, but calculating the number of bears in the region is an inexact undertaking; it's hard to count bears reliably in the field. At present, the count is based on repeated aerial overflights and extrapolations from limited sightings. To illustrate the importance of reliable arithmetic in these extrapolations, biologist Lee Metzger reviewed data collected by the Montana Department of Fish, Wildlife and Parks, which projected that the grizzly population in the Bob Marshall Wilderness was "tenuously stable." Yet after uncovering a calculation error of just one decimal point, Metzger discovered that, in fact, the Bob Marshall grizzly population is on a slight downward trajectory. Now ponder the data provided by the IGBC. According to Servheen, the Yellowstone bear population is growing at an annual rate of five percent. He asserts that the number of breeding female bears with cubs is between 90 and 100, resulting in the production of 60 cubs a year for three consecutive years. However, the Fish and Wildlife Service also says that in order for the bear population to remain healthy, acceptable mortality cannot exceed four percent, and for at least half of the decade in the 1990s, bear deaths have surpassed that threshold. What is the future mortality trend for bears due to hunting, pressures from extractive industry in remote grizzly habitat, and clashes with humans in the face of expanding recreation and suburbanization of the ecosystem? Bear managers don't know. Nevertheless, Servheen, again, estimates that there may be as many as 600 grizzlies in the Yellowstone ecosystem and he is convinced the bear population should be delisted. Paradoxically, the number of bears is both revealing and virtually meaningless, according to scientists. What matters, ecologists say, is having enough secured habitat to support a viable population of grizzlies indefinitely. Numbers are important, statistically, in that they allow the Fish and Wildlife Service to show there are more bears today than a quarter century ago. And, on that claim, grizzlies appear to have met nearly all recovery objectives—except for the number of bears dying in confrontations with humans. The converse argument is that bear numbers, in the absence of vast, secured, roadless habitat, provide only an ephemeral snapshot of current conditions. Biologist David Mattson, who for over a decade was considered the star scientist on the Yellowstone Interagency Grizzly Bear Study Team, published more peer-reviewed research involving the Yellowstone grizzly than any other scientist. But in retaliation for disagreeing with the government's agenda to delist, and for sharing years of public grizzly bear data with outside researchers, Mattson was exiled from the study team. Servheen has continually blocked efforts to bring Mattson back into the fold and sought to have him punished for talking with reporters asking questions about grizzly bear management. Mattson cites a population "lag effect"—presented in a paper published by biologist Dan Doak in the scientific journal Conservation Biology—in which bear numbers today are a reflection of habitat conditions in years past. Similarly, he believes the effects of eroding habitat today may not be detectable until well into the next century. "The number of bears you see now is a reflection of yesterday's habitat conditions," Mattson says. "What ostensibly could look like a large number of bears might be deceiving because the stuff that drives a short-term increase might have deteriorated significantly and you might not see that reflected for a decade or more. By the time you recognize it, it could be too late. The point is, we don't know what the numbers mean." He notes that the formula for calculating the number of grizzlies is, at best, imprecise because, as mentioned earlier, bears are difficult to count accurately. Until recently, the census method included tallying the number of radio-collared bears (which represents only a small fraction of the estimated population), actual sightings of bears with cubs, the known mortality for a given year, then extrapolating across the whole of grizzly range to estimate the rest of the bears were not seen. But does an unseen bear mean that it exists or does not exist? Not only is this arithmetic highly subjective, but over the last 20 years the data accounting formulas have changed so much that it is extremely difficult to pinpoint numerical trends. Accounting methods used by the Yellowstone Interagency Grizzly Bear Study Team have not always been consistent, transects have changed, and so has the quality of habitat in the landscape. Acknowledging the margin for error, the Fish and Wildlife Service states in both its habitat conservation strategy—required as part of the Judge Friedman ruling— and grizzly bear "white paper" that it aims to narrow the realm of uncertainty. It has recruited independent wildlife population demographer Mark Boyce to make a more reliable assessment of female bears with cubs. Curbing mortality is another matter, and this brings us back to habitat protection. Whereas in the old, Wild West, the human remedy for conflict was simply to pull the trigger, thus extirpating the grizzly from all but two primary ecosystems, making room for bears at the end of the 20th century involves a conscious effort on the part of land managers working in concert with private property owners. The payoffs extend well beyond bears, however. Safeguarding habitat for bears imparts benefits to a whole suite of secretive species, from pine marten and wolverine to goshawks and wolves, that require an untrammeled landscape largely free of human development. In the revised bear recovery plan authored by Servheen, the primary bear recovery zone—which is to say the area in which bears are afforded primacy over land uses traditionally hazardous to bears—has expanded little. That zone is still largely comprised of Yellowstone National Park at its core and surrounding national forest wilderness areas. Little room has been afforded bruins to safely roam beyond the arbitrarily circumscribed recovery zone into prime bear habitat deliberately left out because of grazing livestock and interest from timber companies and energy developers. Similarly, no guarantees have been made by the state of Wyoming, where most of the best bear habitat lies, that it will accommodate bears other than to make them available in sport hunts. Although Servheen notes as justification for delisting that bears are colonizing other reaches of the ecosystem, the recovery plan treats them as being, more or less, expendable. In Wyoming after delisting, wandering grizzlies would be subjected to a two-strikes policy where after a second run-in with people or livestock, they would be either euthanized or sent to zoos. Yet, even in the core of the recovery zone, Wyoming and the forest service have been reluctant to remove or relocate some cattle grazing allotments on public lands that officials know cause trouble for bears. Thus, state and federal agencies have done little to engender confidence that habitat will be protected. In Conservation Biology, biologist Doak wrote that not only could the optimistic conclusions of those pressing delisting be wrong but the apparent boom in bear numbers could be short lived and actually masking a downward trajectory for the quality of habitat. The optimism of bear managers is contravened by a cloud of negative trends gathering on the horizon, notes wildlife attorney Honnold with Earthjustice Legal Defense Fund, which sued the federal government over the grizzly bear recovery plan. As grizzlies push out from Yellowstone National Park and recolonize historic range, a record tide of humans is pressing in. The greater Yellowstone region has one of the fastest growing human populations in the West, and new residential subdivisions are platted in bear habitat nearly every month. In the Bridger-Teton and Shoshone national forests, more than half a million acres are being considered for oil and gas exploration. If commercial quantities of those fuels are found, full field development and extensive road building could extirpate bears from key habitat. Along the western front of bear range in the Targhee National Forest, the effects of removal of a billion board feet of timber already logged from the landscape can be seen from satellites. The clearcutting and construction of logging roads has caused bears to flee two government bear management units used as mea-suring sticks for gauging the health of the ecosystem bear population. While the fragmentation of bear habitat can be measured and quantified, the poten-tial loss of natural foods that sustain bears is alarming and uncertain. Bears are confronted with declining food resources, from pine nuts to bison car-casses. Inside Yellowstone, whitebark pine nuts—a vital, high-nutrition food that grizzlies seek out before their winter slumber—have declined both from the 1988 forest fires which killed 25 percent of the park's whitebark pine trees, and from the spread of an arboreal disease known as blister rust.

Mattson wrote in the Journal of Wildlife Management in 1992 that years when the crop of whitebark pine nuts is low correlate to a spike in the number of bear fatalities, because hungry grizzlies flee the mountain pinestands for lower elevations in a desperate search for food, and in turn, come into more conflict with humans. Since it takes whitebark pine trees a century to reach nut-bearing maturity, scientists believe the loss of more trees to fire and dis-ease could be disastrous. And with global warming changing the climate at high elevations where whitebark pine grows, there is fear the conifers could disappear altogether. The loss of whitebark pine is not the only negative omen involving the bears' natural food. The illicit introduction of lake trout to Yellowstone Lake in the park's interior has begun to threaten the indigenous population of cutthroat trout upon which dozens of bears feed during the spring spawn. Lake trout, which are an exotic species, are voracious predators and eat cutthroat trout. In numerous lakes across the West where lake trout have been introduced, native fish populations have suffered. Cutthroat trout are shallow water spawners and available to grizzlies, while lake trout, preferring deeper water, are not accessible to bears. The threat to natural foods doesn't end here. In the Absaroka mountains, a large concentration of bears feast on aggregations of army cutworm moths, but the insects face an uncertain future as their tundra food sources—the nectar in mountain flowers— are threatened by global warming and the moths themselves fall victim to pesticide spraying in the valleys below. Further, government programs that artificially reduce and tightly control park bison herds as a means of reducing bison interactions with domestic cattle outside the park threaten to reduce another food source. Studies by Mattson and Charles Robbins at Washington State University show that Yellowstone grizzlies are one of the most meat-dependent bear popula-tions in North America. "Between the proliferation of private land home sites and development, which represent land mines for grizzlies; and increasing numbers of recreationists displacing or having negative contacts with bears;

and the gloomy outlook for key natural food sources; and the high annual mortality from hunters, the Yellowstone grizzly faces tenuous prospects even under the best of circumstances," argues Louisa Willcox of the Sierra Club. "We already know what the future of the bear looks like in the absence of strict habitat protection. All we have to do is look to the Sierra Nevada and the San Juans of southern Colorado where there are no bears. Without sustained vigilance to preserve habitat and reduce conflicts, the Yellowstone grizzly is fated to become a footnote in history." Indeed, bears might already be feeling the pressure. As Mattson points out, a possible plausible explanation for bear dispersal—and thus increasing sightings—could be poor natural food years in the park, which force grizzlies to roam wider distances to scavenge. "It doesn't matter if you have 500 bears or 2,000 bears or 10,000," Mattson says. "Really it doesn't take long to kill 500 bears or even 2,000. If the long-term trajectory is negative, the population is going to go extinct. The most dramatic proof is that we eradicated almost 100,000 grizzly bears in the western U.S. between 1850 and 1920. What determines the trajectory is the status of habitat—undisturbed habitat where bears are not likely to get into trouble. A big part of this is cultural values and I've seen little evidence that the states who say they will take care of bears have convinced more people to tolerate bears." Indicative of the growing conflicts, Mattson says, is an incident that occurred in the fall of 1997 in the Teton Wilderness northeast of Jackson Hole where a party of elk hunters opened fire on a mother bear and her three cubs, killing the bruin quartet. The hunters claimed they were swarmed by aggressive bears, but some biologists and seasoned wildlife law enforcement specialists have reacted with incredulity. Those bears were among seven killed in a single week inside the Bridger-Teton National Forest. Although the government's "official" estimate for bear deaths in 1997 is eight bears, a government expert said privately that as many as 20 bears may have died (not even including grizzlies that were poached), yielding one of the highest number of bear fatalities in more than a decade. Another sobering anecdote about human-bear relations is that field observations suggest some bears no longer associate the sound of gun fire with danger, interpreting it instead as a dinner bell. Bears have learned that rifle shots equate with fresh elk meat, and this puts them on a potentially volatile collision course with hunters. Since the early 1990s alone, at least five dozen bears and a fairly high percentage of breeding-age females with cubs—the bedrock of the population—are known to have died, many in conflicts with hunters. One revealing statement is buried in the 1995 Yellowstone Interagency Grizzly Bear Study Team's annual report: "Relaxation of concerns about population size and trend probably will lead to an increase in bear mortalities, because it is much easier to destroy a bear than to manage sources of human-bear conflict."

Concern that bear fatalities will increase under state management is a "red herring," claims Wyoming Game and Fish Director John Baughman. He believes that Wyoming will do a better job of protecting habitat than the federal government. For Wyoming officials, including Senator Thomas, the grizzly bear has become a symbol of state's rights. Pioneering Yellowstone bear biologist John Craighead, who today oversees the Craighead Wildlife-Wildlands Institute in Missoula, Montana, says the logic underlying the delisting criteria is highly suspect. "I think delisting is the worst thing they could possibly do," Craighead says. "The Wyoming Game and Fish Department claims that because bears are moving back into their old historic habitat, there are more bears and the population is doing well, but that argument has no basis in fact." Bears are moving out of the national park into surrounding national forests and private land because they need secured and multiple sources of food. "Yellowstone Park is not big enough by itself to support a viable population. The only motivation to delist the bear is so it can be hunted and management of the public lands can go back to business as usual, which is why we came close to losing the bear in the first place," notes Craighead. Some of the best bear habitat in greater Yellowstone is found in the lower elevation valleys inhabited by historic ranches, and increasingly of late, residential subdivisions in counties that view land use planning as anathema to personal liberty. The ski resort community of Big Sky, Montana, for example, is only three decades old and yet its sprawl stretches across the entire Madison mountain range from the Gallatin River to the Madison Valley, essentially preventing bears from reaching prime habitat in the south with range to the north. Bears that try to negotiate the gauntlet embark on a perilous journey. One member of the IGBC's Yellowstone subcommittee, who asked not to be identified, admitted to me that private lands essentially have been "written off" because progressive land use planning and zoning is not in place to protect them. Then there's Hank Fischer, the northern Rockies regional representative for Defenders of Wildlife, who says the outlook for bears on private lands is "hopeful" because incentives, such as conservation easements, exist for property owners to keep their tracts in open space. Even so, he agrees that development is far outpacing the ability of conservationists to strategically protect crucial habitat tracts. For Mattson and other biologists, this means public land, namely the millions of acres under Forest Service control, is exponentially more valuable because it offers the only prospect of providing adequate refugia outside Yellowstone National Park. However, as the IGBC's habitat conservation strategy has evolved, some national forest supervisors have fiercely resisted any attempt to hold individual forests accountable for protecting bear habitat. They want requirements to be "voluntary" while other agencies lead by Servheen say that delisting can only proceed if the Forest Service legally commits itself to safeguarding roadless areas and limiting resource development. The reason for their foot-dragging is obvious. Forest supervisors, graded for job performance on their ability to meet timber targets and other aspects of the agency's "multiple use" mandate, know these uses clash with grizzly bear conservation and they do not want to be held personally accountable. Since the 1970s, the best example of Forest Service officials defiantly ignoring grizzly habitat requirements and thus the Endangered Species Act, has occurred in the Targhee National Forest. Timber cutting and road building has extensively fragmented the Targhee, yet these activities attracted little or no public condemnation from Servheen, who said he did not want to alienate a sister agency. Chuck Lobdell, a senior biologist with the Fish and Wildlife Service, became so frustrated by the lack of attention to habitat needs that he threatened to sue employees on the Targhee not only for logging but refusing to close logging roads after the cuts. He blames Servheen for not being more forceful in his civil service role as the citizens' designated bear advocate. Similar habitat fragmentation was occurring throughout the ecosystem with the Gallatin and Shoshone Forests regularly building roads at densities recognized as damaging to grizzlies. "I think Fish and Wildlife would consider the IGBC a raging success," Lobdell told the Casper Star-Tribune. "I think it's a disaster, because we've compromised our way out of recovery." He called the IGBC's level of vigilance "piss poor." Chris Wood, a senior aide to Forest Service Chief Mike Dombeck, says the Washington, D.C. office is "well aware" of the conflict and assures that his agency will not shirk its obligation to protect habitat. "We've had knock down, drag out meetings over this very subject," says Jay Gore, the Forest Service's national grizzly bear spokesman, who admits the agency has had problems with "rogue" forest supervisors who demonstrated little respect for the ESA. Despite past problems with monitoring the effects of resource development on wildlife, Gore advocates delisting. "It wasn't just the Forest Service. Quite frankly, Wyoming and Montana were killing the shit out of bears without knowing how many were dying and how many were replacing them," Gore says. "That will not happen again. I'm a Pollyanna kind of guy. I have confidence in the state agencies whom I believe are up to the task. I think we owe the states a chance to prove they can manage bears." Despite such promises from the Fish and Wildlife Service to re-list the Yellowstone grizzly should the number of bears again take a plunge, conservationists know it would involve an uphill political battle against members of Congress who receive large campaign contributions from resource extraction interests. A greater concern for scientists is that in the absence of protection under the Endangered Species Act, habitat loss may accelerate, leaving land managers with fewer creative options to sustain the population—even if they do show unprecedented integrity in managing for bear survival. Pam Lichtman, a public lands policy expert with the Jackson Hole Conservation Alliance, points to the paradox of Wyoming's lobbying to take over control of grizzly management from the federal government. During the mid 1990s, the Wyoming Game and Fish Department complained about the $600,000 to $800,000 a year it spent to manage bears, yet if grizzlies are delisted, Wyoming will face even higher costs and receive little or no federal assistance. If dollars are scarce now, she asks, where will the money come from later? The fear is that Wyoming will underwrite grizzly management by sanctioning a sport hunt of "problem" bears that get into trouble with people. Cynical biologists say that a sure way to guarantee a steady supply of huntable bears is to be lax on habitat protection, which would result in more bears wandering into human environs and thus a greater need to kill menacing bruins. Proponents of delisting, including Servheen, say that if the bear is taken off the threatened list, it will actually receive more protection. Yet, as Lichtman points out, the very reason Wyoming has pushed for delisting is because politicians say bear management is presently "too restrictive." In a stunning confession published in the journal Yellowstone Science after he retired in late 1997, Dick Knight, who oversaw the Yellowstone Interagency Grizzly Bear Study Team for 24 years, voiced strong reservations about delisting. "I can imagine people out there with chain saws and herds of sheep ready to move in when the bear population is delisted, and that scares me. Because I don't know how to protect bear habitat. We just don't know," Knight said. "You can write some laws, but hell, we couldn't protect the Targhee from widespread clearcutting and roadbuilding in grizzly habitat, even under the Endangered Species Act. You get an administrator who wants to get around a law, and he'll do it." Although Servheen insists that political expediency is not a motivation for delisting, several events besides pressure from Senator Thomas and Wyoming Governor Jim Geringer suggest otherwise. According to a memo dispatched over the Fish and Wildlife Service's internal e-mail network, regional agency managers are encouraged to embrace the inevitability of delisting. "Conservation groups try to base their policy decisions on the best available science," says Tim Stevens with the Greater Yellowstone Coalition. "When you look at the delisting question, it's very clear the best available science points away from a delisting conclusion. As such, the conservation community is very nearly unanimously opposed to it." In contrast, Tom France, an attorney with the National Wildlife Federation offers that maybe the grizzly, because of persistent assaults on its habitat and hardened intolerance from humans, is an animal that should be the subject of a new designation for permanently imperiled species created by Congress. "It's something to look at, but we have to live within the bounds of how the ESA operates today, and that is for every animal that gets listed to make every effort we can to delist it," he says. That's a hard pill for most environmentalists in the Rockies to swallow. "When you advocate radical change—and without a doubt, delisting the grizzly is radical—you have to assume a certain burden of proof to show the action you propose will not have disastrous consequences," observes Bob Ekey, the northern Rockies field director for The Wilderness Society. "Right now, the Fish and Wildlife Service has to bear that burden, and their arguments just don't hold up under the weight." Ironically, if delisting proceeds and conditions turn bad for the grizzly, Ekey says that conservationists will bear a burden of proof to show there has been a downturn. "Plus, we would have to overcome the resistance put up by the Fish and Wildlife Service, the state of Wyoming and the IGBC to admitting they made a mistake." Yellowstone's John Varley says the issue is so politically charged he predicts a protracted battle to get to the point where the federal government surrenders authority. "If we ever get to the point where we are delisting, the burden will be on the states to develop an acceptable management plan," he says. "But I don't think it will happen, at least not in my lifetime. This thing is going to be tied up in the courts forever." John Varley might be right. In the end, the long-term stewardship of the Yellowstone grizzly may not be decided by a judge but in the court of public opinion. What the public says about the value of grizzlies holds more weight than a bureaucrat or a politician, or at least that is the way it is supposed to be. Society must judge whether the Yellowstone grizzly, our backyard version of the African lion, the Indian tiger, and Komodo dragon, is worth enough for us to cede it a little more space.

7 The Power to Conserve: The Edwards Dam and its Impact on Endangered Species

IONE HUNT VON HERBING and
ROBERT G. HAND

On July 1, 1999, the 162-year-old Edwards Dam in Maine was explosively breached with a hole 75 feet wide, and water from the dam's reservoir was drawn down, allowing fish access to 17 miles of the Kennebec River not open since the Civil War.

The story that brought about the destruction of the Edwards Dam is complex and has involved 10 years of convoluted debate among private companies and federal and state governments. In addition, it has involved many other segments of society, including fishermen, lawyers, economists, scientists and politicians. The decision made by the Federal Energy Regulatory Commission (FERC) and supported by the State of Maine to remove the dam is a landmark in the annals of the hydropower industry.

Introduction

The Edwards Dam was a small, privately owned hydroelectric dam on the Kennebec River in southern Maine that supplied but a small portion of the state's electricity. On November 22, 1997, a federal agency empowered by local and national environmental groups made the decision to remove the dam but demand that they pay the expense of the removal, as well. Tearing down this dam was unremarkable on its own, since this dam was an extremely marginal, 162-year-old hydropower dam. However, the fact that the decision for dam removal was made by a federal agency against the wishes of its owners is an example of inappropriate use of government power. Furthermore, the forced removal of the dam sets a precedent that will be used as a template by the government for removal of other dams across the country. As a result, the Edwards Dam takes center stage in a national controversy involving private property issues, utilization of the Endangered Species Act, wildlife restoration and energy provision for the next century.

Rivers, Property Rights and Muddied Waters?

For centuries, humans have been harnessing rivers and other waterways to gain economic benefits from the enhanced availability of water and the production of power. Since rivers, aquifers and water in general have been largely socialized in the United States, they suffer from chronic overuse, poor utilization of their resources and a myriad of controls and mismanaged rationing. Unfortunately, the philosophy underlying these regulatory strategies almost always encourages a new set of strategies that are typically more misguided than the original schemes. Economic and political decisions as to the use of water systems are delegated to the government, which, in turn, works closely with selected environmental groups, lobbying interests and chosen members of the U. S. Congress. And to this point, "water socialism" is the most common method of control in the United States as well as other countries around the world.

The most common uses for rivers in the world are generation of hydroelectric power through installation of dams, and tourism/recreational fishing. Environmentalists have long been advocating dam removal, claiming that removal of dams will significantly enhance the riverine ecosystem and thus increase revenue from recreational fishing. Until recently, very few dams have been removed (e.g., the Saint-Etienne-du-Vigan dam in France, which was removed in 1997) and thus provide little data on the restoration of the riverine habitat on which to base future dam removals (Dadswell 1996).

Environmentalists have achieved a major coup with the recently breached Edwards Dam. Of course, little or no evidence exists that removal of the dam will be effective in restoration of the Kennebec riverine ecosystem. Their unfounded claims that removing dams from the Kennebec River and from other rivers will restore the natural habitat has convinced government officials to advocate the removal of the other dams in the nation. Thus dam removal is backed by environmentalists, supported by government officials, and not supported by scientific data, all of whom have taken a gigantic leap of faith that dam removal will bring about bounty derived from tourist dollars and resurgence of fish populations.

And who ultimately benefits? The Edwards Dam Company? Certainly not, since they may pay for its dismantlement and will no longer benefit from the revenues from the power plant. The local communities? No, since in an economic study conducted in 1989 to determine the efficacy of removal of the Edwards Dam for generating tourist revenue, no economic boom was predicted. It did not matter if the dam were removed or not, the predicted revenue from tourist dollars would not be greater than the cost to remove the dam (Boyle et al. 1991). The environmentalists? Since the dam has been removed they may aid the government in forcing removal of privately held dams and laying claim to the use of the rivers. More importantly, however, enhanced political power will increase their overall status as lobbyists for dam removal across the nation and provide them access to future federal funds that would be dedicated to projects involving dam removal.

The History of the Edwards Dam—(1837-1997)

In 1837 the Kennebec River Dam Company built a dam between Augusta and Waterville in southern Maine. The dam stretched across the entire width of the Kennebec (917 feet), rose 20 feet above the surface of the river, and was built below the head of the tide (this is defined as the upstream limit of the estuary where ocean-derived water influences the salinity of the river to greater than five parts per thousand). Its construction raised the level of the water upstream and made the Kennebec River navigable at a time when Maine had no railroad and few roads. However, construction of the dam prevented the migration of anadromous fishes such as Atlantic salmon to spawning sites upriver. Its erection was blamed for a reduction in Atlantic salmon, shortnose and Atlantic sturgeons and other fish populations. At that time, however, sustaining fish populations was considered inconsequential compared to powering large textile mills and providing hundreds of jobs. In 1882, the Edwards Manufacturing Company bought the dam to power a textile mill. In 1913, the company installed electric generators with turbines, which increased downstream mortality for migrating fishes. Sixty years later, in 1973, Bates Manufacturing sold the Edwards Division (mill and dam) to Miller Industries, but in 1980 the textile mill closed. This left the dam without a major buyer for its electricity for 10 years. In 1984, Edwards Manufacturing signed a 15-year contract to sell electricity at a high price to Central Maine Power, a public utility.

As the United States recovered from the energy crisis in the mid 1980s, and the pressure for restoration of natural habitat and wildlife grew in the late 1980s and 1990s, fish restoration programs were begun in the Kennebec River. These programs were sponsored jointly by the State of Maine and by the Kennebec Hydro Developers Group (seven up-river dam owners), which committed money to restore American shad, Atlantic salmon and alewife populations in 1987. In 1988, Edwards installed a fish pump to assist fisheries restoration. One year later, however, the Kennebec Coalition—which included American Rivers, the Atlantic Salmon Federation, the Natural Resources Council of Maine, and the Kennebec Valley Chapter of Trout Unlimited—united to advocate for dam removal.

In 1991, Edwards applied for a 50-year license and authority to increase the electrical output of the dam from 3.5 KW/hr to 4.5 KW/hr. In 1993, the license to operate the dam, issued by the Federal Energy Regulatory Commission (FERC), expired, and FERC issued the first of a series of annual permits. In 1995, Edwards reduced the request for the increase of power output of the dam, and in 1996, FERC issued a preliminary recommendation to relicense the dam, provided a fish passage was installed. However, FERC soon reversed that decision.

Strong public support from local environmental groups such as the Kennebec Coalition persuaded others to join in their fight for the removal of the dam. In addition to members of the Kennebec Coalition, supporters of dam removal included Governor Angus King (a former hydropower developer), Senators Olympia Snowe and Cathy Collins, Representative Tom Allen, U.S. Secretary of the Interior Bruce Babbit, the Maine State Planning Office, Maine Department of Inland Fisheries and Wildlife, the National Marine Fisheries Service and the U.S. Fish and Wildlife Service. In addition, a Final Environmental Impact Statement (FEIS-0097) recommended removal of the Edwards Dam. Thus the fate of Edwards Dam was sealed. After 10 years, advocacy from these various groups was so strong that it crushed the futile attempt of the Edwards Dam Company to stem the tide. Curiously, much of the pressure came from outside the local community from large environmental groups such as American Rivers and the Atlantic Salmon Federation. Clearly these groups significantly influenced the outcome of the decision to tear down the dam. Unfortunately, however, it will be members of the local community who have to bare the brunt of the costs of river maintenance and dam removal.

Mounting Pressure for Dam Removal

Pressure to remove dams began building more than 20 years ago as rivers such as the Kennebec and others across the United States began to be cleaned up under federal and state clean water laws. Until the early 1970s, the Kennebec River was a sewer, polluted with raw sewage from the cities of Augusta and Waterville, as well as industrial wastes from pulp and paper mills, including highly toxic metals such as mercury, arsenic and cadmium. The Kennebec was also clogged with logs cut by logging companies, which transported the logs in the river currents and thus rendered the river barely navigable. Numerous fish kills and the general filth of the river kept fishermen and vacationers away.

In 1974, a ban on log transport went into effect and opened up the river to boat traffic. In addition, dramatic improvements in water quality followed installation of sewage treatment plants along the river and reduced levels of toxic metals. Active fish restocking by the state has turned the cleaner Kennebec into one of the better fishing destinations in Maine. Given the rising focus on the Kennebec as a major fishing and recreational river, environmental and political pressures strongly favored dam removal when the license for the Edwards Dam expired in 1991.

Despite the environmental impacts of dams, an enormous number have been built in the United States. During the past century, Americans have built 75,187 dams with a combined storage capacity of almost one billion acre-feet, which is enough to cover the entire state of Texas with six feet of water. About 5,500 of these are more than 50 feet high. Most dams were built, according to U.S. Army Corps of Engineers records, for recreation (35%), farm ponds (18%), flood control (15%), water supply (12%), irrigation (11%), hydroelectric (2%) and navigation (0.5%). The majority of big dams on western rivers are owned and operated by the federal government and are not subject to FERC licensing. These include some of the largest dams, such as Hoover and Glen Canyon on the Colorado River and Grand Coolee on the Columbia River. More than 2,000 dams around the United States are subject to licensing by FERC, which regulates dams owned by individuals, utilities and local governments. For these dams, removal has become an acute issue, because hundreds of 30- to 50-year licenses are coming up for license renewal by FERC in the next few years. In the state of Maine alone, of 27 generating and storage facilities, 10 are operating under expired licenses and waiting decisions by FERC. Seven of these 10 dams are on the Kennebec River above

Edwards Dam.

How long will it be before the other seven above Edwards Dam will be subject to destruction?

The Edwards Dam Decision

On November 25, 1997, FERC denied the application to relicense Edwards Dam and instead ordered it removed. This action represented the first time that FERC had ordered the removal of an operating hydroelectric dam against the owner's wishes and at the owner's expense. In reaching its decision, FERC conducted an independent analysis of three options: 1) approving and relicensing the dam; 2) approving relicensing only if the dam owners invested nearly $10 million on a fish passage system deemed necessary by the U.S. Fish and Wildlife Service to assist some species of fish to migrate upstream; and 3) retirement and removal of the dam. FERC chose the last option on the grounds that it had the greatest likelihood of improving the habitat and spawning potential for nine species of migratory fish that use the Kennebec River. With removal of the dam, migrating fish would potentially have access to the longest stretch of spawning habitat north of the Hudson River since 1837. However, as we will discuss in due course, there is no empirical evidence supporting their beliefs. The State of Maine believes removal of Edwards Dam could potentially help restore nine to 10 species of fish, including the endangered shortnose sturgeon and two endangered species of mussels, the yellow lamp and tidewater mucket. Again, as we will point out in further discussion, although resurgence of endangered species may have been one of the main reasons for dam removal, it may not be the real one.

The decision by FERC to remove Edwards Dam has prompted environmentalists to claim that the federal government is changing the way it looks at management of river systems. According to one group, American Rivers, dams were once considered as permanent structures on the landscape. With the removal of the Edwards Dam, however, that group believes that dams have a finite life cycle and that removal should come when the value of restoration of the resources outweighs that of the electricity the dam can generate. Congress added weight to this notion in 1986 when it passed legislation requiring FERC, through its hydropower licensing activities, to reach an appropriate balance between power generation and environmental protection. In all cases prior to that of Edwards Dam, FERC had addressed significant environmental impacts through the imposition of license conditions (e.g., requiring the installation of fish passages). However, in the case of Edwards, FERC determined that installing a $10 million fishway would be 1.7 times more costly than retiring and removing the dam. Furthermore, removal of the dam would allow four species of fish that do not use fishways—shortnose sturgeon, Atlantic sturgeon, striped bass and rainbow smelt—to reach 17 miles of historic upstream spawning habitat. Finally, removal of the dam would also increase wetland habitat and provide recreational boating and fishing benefits.

The owners of Edwards Dam have appealed FERC's decision, claiming that federal law does not give FERC the right to order a dam removed or the power to require the owners to pay for its removal. They contend the removal order is unconstitutional and that when private property is taken for public use, the owner must receive just compensation. Therefore, when the government restricts the use of property, its actions constitute a "taking" of that property for which the owner must be compensated under the Fifth Amendment, which provides that "nor shall private property be taken for public use without just compensation." In the Edwards Dam case, however, the owner would be assessed some of the costs ($2.5 to $6 million) to destroy the dam and restore the river to its natural condition. Environmentalists claim that dam owners have profited from a public resource, the nation's rivers, and have an obligation to restore those rivers if the public desires. The National Hydropower Association in Washington, D.C. is supporting the dam owners in their appeal out of concern that FERC's decision will have negative implications for the rest of the hydropower industry.

Another group that is not in favor of dam removal is the anglers or recreational fishermen that will supposedly benefit from the removal of the dam. According to an economic assessment, anglers would prefer installation of the fish ladders to dam removal. Anglers are most interested in the Atlantic salmon and brown trout, both of which can use the ladders. In addition, dams provide for many substitute opportunities for reservoir fishing, and anglers can simply move above the dams to fish in a reservoir environment, as well as have the ability to fish below the dam in a free-flowing environment. More importantly, according to the assessment, in the 10 to 30 years it will take to establish improved sport fisheries on the lower Kennebec River, nonresident angler participation will not increase more than the roughly 300 nonresident anglers who currently fish the nearby Penobscot River for Atlantic salmon each year. In fact, some nonresident anglers may actually switch from the Penobscot River to the lower Kennebec River. If this type of substitution occurs, the resulting nonresident expenditures along the lower Kennebec River can not be considered new money in Maine's economy.

Furthermore, no one knows the role (if any) that small hydropower sources might play in meeting future energy needs. Given that hydropower is perceived as a clean source of electricity, and that Japan and the United States have both set targets for lowering greenhouse gases, the industry position is that this is the time to promote, not cut back on, renewable energy sources such as hydropower. As long as oil remains cheap and there is no energy crisis, dam removal may remain economically practical. However, if oil costs increase in the next decade, the importance placed on smaller dams such as Edwards might increase, and dam removal may no longer be a practical option if the electricity prices are to be kept down. Restoration of riverine ecosystems in the United States, if it involves removal of hydropower dams, must be balanced with responsible decisions about how energy will be generated for urbanized areas when those dams are gone. The question of removing dams on major rivers and their tributaries is part of an intense debate that pits the value of cheap electricity against the often-emotional value of a river as an undisturbed natural resource.

Although the Edwards Dam has been in existence since 1837, its potential to generate electricity has fluctuated over its lifetime. Since 1984 Edwards Manufacturing has provided power to Central Maine Power Company (a privately owned public utility) under a contract that allowed the company and its co-licensee, the city of Augusta, to share a $2.5-million profit by selling power at triple the cost of electricity now available (12 cents per KW/hr versus approximately 3 cents per KW/hr). Central Maine Power will not renew the contract with the Edwards Dam after the contract expires in 1999. The power that the dam generates (3.5 megawatts) represents only 0.1 percent of Maine's total use and can be replaced by other sources.

The Edwards Dam Removal

Costs of removal are estimated from $2.5 million to $6 million depending upon the speed of removal. The higher figure would pay for the work to be done in one season. Initially, FERC asked the owners to pay for the removal. However, Bath Iron Works has stepped in to provide $2.5 million to aid in removal. This is not an altruistic move, but one that will ultimately benefit Bath Iron Works, a private defense contractor that benefits from millions of dollars in tax exemptions each year. The $2.5 million that Bath Iron Works is contributing to dam removal will serve as partial mitigation for the company's own $218 million expansion, which includes building a pier into 15 acres of endangered fish spawning habitat in the lower Kennebec River. Since Bath Iron Works is destroying habitat on the Kennebec River, the contribution of money for dam removal is intended to provide 15 to 17 miles of new spawning habitat for endangered species such as the shortnose sturgeon. Most elements of the various legal documents relating to removing the Edwards Dam have contingencies built into them in the event that the removal of the dam failed to occur. In the case of Bath Iron Works, the $2.5 million it has committed to the process would go instead toward projects prioritized by the state as environmental needs.

The agency responsible for this deal with Bath Iron Works is the U.S. Army Corps of Engineers, which has traditionally been responsible for navigation and flood control. The Corps' responsibilities expanded in the 1980s to encompass environmental restoration under the federal Water Resources Acts (1986, 1988, 1990 and 1992). The agreement with Bath Iron Works is one of several the Corps has made to aid in restoration of American waterways. In this case as in many others, the agreement may appear to have a clear and worthwhile objective, yet the value and likely outcome of such restoration efforts are ultimately unpredictable. It is the faith generated by environmentalists and their effective use of the Endangered Species Act that has resulted in the removal of the Edwards Dam. No evidence exists that suggests that removal of the Edwards Dam will result in a resurgence of endangered species like the Atlantic salmon or shortnose sturgeon. In fact, most state biologists admit that Atlantic salmon will likely never return to spawn in the Kennebec. Clearly, resurgence of endangered fish species is not the driving reason behind the dams removal. However, it's a convenient cause.

The Fish Story

The controversy over relicensing or removing the Edwards Dam has been viewed by many people as one big fish story on a unique river system. However, preservation and enhancement of the 43 species of fish in the estuary and the river may not be the only reason for dam removal. In this case as in other cases such as acid rain and global warming, the cause of the environmentalists was assumed to be a just cause, because we believed that the motives of the environmentalists justified their conclusions. However, no data was ever put forward to prove that removal of the dam would enhance the fish populations and bring back extinct native populations. When the Edwards Dam was erected, the Kennebec River was full of fish, as were most rivers throughout the United States. After erection of the dam, anadromous fish such as Atlantic salmon, rainbow smelt and the shortnose and Atlantic sturgeon could not bypass the dam to continue up the river. Sea-run migrations of all anadromous fish were significantly reduced and, in the case of Atlantic salmon, eliminated. Removal of the Edwards Dam, however, will not necessarily restore the fish communities of the Kennebec River to their former state. The Kennebec River has undergone significant urbanization as two large cities, Augusta and Waterville, and numerous pulp and paper mills were built on its banks. Untreated sewage and industrial wastes have significantly affected the river's fish and bird ecosystems. As a consequence, even after the river was "cleaned up," most of the recreational fishery remains tag-and-release. To this day there are signs posted along the river warning people not to eat fish caught in it. Furthermore, it is likely that even though toxins in the water column have been significantly reduced, they still exist in the sediments. These could cause pollution downstream when water from the impoundment behind the dam is released prior to dam removal. In addition to the effects of pollution, introductions of non-native species, such as brown trout brought in the 1800s from Europe, have significantly changed the composition of the natural fish communities in the river. This unique but unnatural assemblage provides for simultaneous brown trout and striped bass fishing, to the delight of the fishermen, but it hardly approximates natural conditions. In local newspapers, journalists have written convincingly that removal of the dam will bring back native populations of anadromous fishes. However, little mention is made of the fact that the state will continue to stock the river with fish every year and that at least 25 years would be necessary to determine whether the predictions of the environmentalists were correct.

How then will the Edwards Dam removal affect the riverine ecosystem? Will removal significantly increase the numbers of endangered or threatened fish species as mandated by the Endangered Species Act (1973)? Unfortunately, no one really knows. Two factors will determine how fish populations respond to dam removal: 1) whether the fish species can use fish ladders, and 2) the nature of the physical and biological changes that would occur in the 15 to 17 miles of river above the dam after its removal. Some of the predicted physical and biological changes include a decrease in average depth of the river by 18.7 feet, resulting in faster water flow, clearer water and more algal growth, thanks to greater light penetration and colder water temperatures.

Predictions of the effects of dam removal or retention (with the addition of fish passages) on fish populations were published in two major research reports that differ in their fundamental conclusions. One report was produced by Stone and Webster Environmental and Technological Services, which was hired by FERC to access the physical and biological effects of dam removal in comparison to dam retention. This report was used by FERC in a draft environmental impact statement on the Kennebec Basin (FEIS-DEIS-0097). A second report was produced by an independent scientist, Dr. Michael Dadswell, who was hired by the Kennebec Coalition. FERC concluded that for the endangered shortnose sturgeon and the threatened Atlantic sturgeon, there would be either a net negative impact or no impact on the restoration of these species if the dam were removed, since these species are not expected to use the new habitat above the dam for spawning. The state disagreed and concluded that the removal of the dam will result in an increase of both species, because the improved flow conditions and reduced depth of the river would encourage spawning in both these species. Both shortnose and Atlantic sturgeon need fairly high flow conditions (1 to 4 cm/sec) to spawn. Such flows currently do not exist in the impoundment. In addition, neither shortnose nor Atlantic sturgeon commonly uses upstream fish passages, and these populations would not benefit from new fish passages if the Edwards Dam were retained. Atlantic sturgeon in particular grow to very large sizes—six to 10 feet and 100 to 300 pounds—and therefore few lift systems could accommodate them. Shortnose sturgeon were historically known to spawn up to Waterville, and the state predicts that removal of the Edwards Dam will increase habitat available to the sturgeon by 91 percent and thus increase sturgeon populations by 11 percent. However, these estimates depend upon the appropriate physical changes (e.g., increase in current production of beneficial riffle-pool habitat) occurring after the dam is removed. There is no guarantee that these changes in the riverine environment will take place. However, the state predicts that populations of both species would increase after dam removal, and this has accelerated the drive to remove the dam as a way of complying with the Endangered Species Act. The intent of that act is to prevent continuing declines and to restore populations to vital levels. Unfortunately, sturgeon take 10 to 15 years to grow to maturity and reproduce, so the benefits of dam removal for this species will take a long time to be realized.

Although the welfare of sturgeon may have provided much of the initial dam removal effort because of their imperiled status, these fish cannot support the recreational fishing industry on the river. Therefore, restoration of other fishes such as the American shad, rainbow smelt, alewife and striped bass became critical in the justification of dam removal. In general, FERC concluded that there would be little net positive or negative benefit in restoration potential for these species. The Maine Department of Marine Resources strongly disagreed, stating that American shad, rainbow smelt, alewife and striped bass would all be enhanced, because removal of the dam would eliminate upstream and downstream passage inefficiencies (mortalities) through the dam's turbines. Both American shad and alewife can use fish passages, but high mortalities occur in the turbines as juveniles migrate downstream. In addition, with the removal of the dam, shad, rainbow smelt, alewife and striped bass would all be able to utilize upstream spawning sites. However, striped bass would have to compete with brown trout, a non-native species which has thrived in the impoundment in the absence of striped bass for about 100 years. For rainbow smelt, which historically spawned all the way up the river to Waterville, the Maine Department of Marine Resources has predicted the removal of the dam would increase production by 30 to 50 percent annually. All these predictions depend on whether physical and biological conditions will change as predicted in the former impoundment (e.g., increased food abundance, increase in current flows and the development of riffle-pools). Restoration may also be aided by stocking fish in the impoundment after dam removal. American shad and alewives have been stocked behind Edwards Dam for a decade. In 1997, three million shad fry were stocked into the impoundment. Alewife and brown trout are also stocked on an annual basis at a price of millions of dollars to the taxpayer. It is the hope of advocates of dam removal that natural sea-run populations would return to the Kennebec and stocking would no longer be necessary. However, since shad take five years, and alewife three to five years to mature, it would require 15 to 20 years to determine whether removal of the dam has benefited these species.

Finally, removal of the Edwards Dam may not affect Atlantic salmon populations whose numbers are so small that both FERC and MDMR agree that natural sea-run populations are unlikely to return to the Kennebec. Although recent studies suggest that the few resident salmon are genetically unique and may, as a result, end up on the endangered species list, the evidence is not conclusive. Atlantic salmon can use fish passages to move upstream to spawn, but high mortality occurs for the fry as they migrate downstream. Therefore, removal of the Edwards Dam could potentially eliminate these mortalities should a natural sea-run population occur again. There is no active stocking program for Atlantic salmon in the Kennebec, and the Atlantic Salmon Authority does not have the money to initiate one and is unlikely to divert resources from restoration efforts on other Maine rivers.

The Final Days of the Edwards Dam and Future Possibilities

If the best case scenario is realized, all nine to 10 species of fish will be restored, sea-run populations will return and Atlantic salmon will return to spawn in streams. This hoped-for increase in fish populations would trigger construction of fish passages on other dams up-river. Installation of fish passages would be triggered by the shad count taken during a single season at a fish passage facility at the next two dams up-river, the Lockwood and UAH-Hydro Kennebec. If 8,000 shad are counted in one season at the Lockwood Dam, and 15,000 are counted at UAH-Hydro Kennebec Dam, then permanent fish passages would be built on the next dam up-river, the Shamut Dam, no sooner than 2014. Similar triggers in the form of fish passages would be built all the way up the Kennebec, allowing for enhanced access of shad up the river. Shad were chosen because they are an important food fish for striped bass and brown trout, whose populations may rise with increases of shad and other fish such as alewife and smelt.

The predicted numbers of fish that should appear in the Kennebec are very large and exceed many millions. If these increases in fish populations occur, they will likely take at least five years. In the best-case scenario, the recreational fishery will boom in response to increasing fish numbers. The revenue from recreation and tourism will propel communities along the river to new financial heights, and the communities of Augusta and Waterville will thrive. In the worst case, there will be no economic boon, as one report has predicted (Boyle et al. 1991), fish will not utilize the new spawning territory and the wetlands produced will not benefit riparian wildlife. In this case, fish will continue to be stocked by the state at taxpayers' expense to maintain a recreational fishery, and the goals of restoration demanded by the Endangered Species Act will not have been met.

Conclusion

What appears to be on surface levels a rather insignificant and marginal dam removal story turns out to an incredibly complex and perhaps monumental pivotal case.

It is indeed a political, environmental and economic drama with a major cast of players vying for the leading role. However, given the complexity of the Edwards Dam story, it is difficult to discriminate the winners from the losers. Suffice it to say, in this case, private property owners and science are not the winners. Future decisions must be made with respect to private property; a "taking" of private property must be compensated by the government with respect to the revenue lost to the owner. If valuable resources such as our nation's rivers are to be utilized correctly, then it is our responsibility to assure that their use is maximized and that decisions affecting their use are based on sound science.

Update: (from *The Bangor Daily News,* May 26, 1999). A recent result of the breaching of Edwards Dam opened the lower Kennebec and its tributaries to several fish species, including the common carp. The common carp is not considered beneficial to the river, and state wildlife officials say it "endangers other fish by reducing water quality." In response to this threat, which was not brought to the State's attention in the Edwards Dam negotiations, a new dam costing $145,000 may be built on a Kennebec River tributary to keep out the carp and other undesirable fish. This may be the beginning of a new set of problems faced by the Kennebec River and surrounding communities.

Sources

For the information in this chapter, I drew from government reports by the various resource agencies; accounts in reliable journals and newspapers; books on rivers and dams; newsletters of organizations such as American Rivers, European Rivers Network, Trout Unlimited, Reason, and on a few interviews.

Boyle K.J., Teisl M.F., Moring J.R. and Reiling S.D. (1991) Economic benefits accruing to sport fisheries on the lower Kennebec River from the provision of fish passage at Edwards Dam or from the removal of the Edwards Dam. Department of Marine Resources, Augusta, ME.

Bodaly, R.A., T.W. D. Johnson, R. J. P. Fudge and J.W. Clayton. (1984) Collapse of the white-fish (*Coregonus clupeaformis*) fishery in southern Indian Lake, Manitoba, following lake impoundment and river diversion. Can. J. Fish. Aquat. Sci. 41: 692-700.

Bradbury, D. Many gain as activists, shipyard collaborate. Portland Press Herald. July 26, 1998.

Cheever, D. Changing river: history behind the decision. Kennebec Journal Morning Sentinel. July 13, 1998.

Cheever, D. If it's a waterway, it's a U.S. Army Corps of Engineers project. Kennebec Journal Morning Sentinel. July 12, 1998.

Cheever, D. Dam deal to extend fish's run of river. Kennebec Journal Morning Sentinel. July 14, 1998.

Dadswell, M.J. (1996) The removal of Edwards dam, Kennebec, River, Maine: its effect on the restoration of anadromous fishes. Report submitted to the Kennebec Coalition.

DeLong J.V. Dam Fools. Reason magazine. April 1998.

Gerstenzang J. U.S. orders destruction of dam to restore river. Los Angeles Times, November 26, 1997.

Hardin, B. For First Time, Fish Habitat Takes Priority Over a Hydroelectric Dam. The Washington Post, November 26, 1997.

Maine States Planning Office, Natural Resources Policy Division (1993) Kennebec river resource management plan: balancing hydropower generation and other uses.

Maine State Planning Office (1995). Draft Environmental Impact Statement for the Kennebec River Basin (FERC DEIS-0097).

Maine State Planning Office (1997). Final Environmental Impact Statement for the Kennebec River Basin (FERC FEIS-0097).

Palmer, T. (1994) Lifelines. The case for river conservation. Island Press, Washington, D.C. 254pp.

Polson, S. Fish may be winners nationwide in Maine dam dispute. The Christian Science Monitor, July 20, 1998.

Rankin, J. Destroy it and will they come? Kennebec Journal Morning Sentinel. July 14, 1998.

Squires, T.S. (1988). Anadromous fishes of the Kennebec River estuary. Report prepared for the NOAA, NMFS Management Division, State Federal Relations Branch.

8 Management of Columbia River Salmon Under the Endangered Species Act: Environmental Engineering for a Dysfunctional Ecosystem

DANIEL GOODMAN

Treasure from the Ocean

The ocean is estimated to contain something like $50 billion worth of dissolved gold. That is a lot of gold, and a lot of money, but the ocean is a big place. The gold content of the ocean is very dilute: in the parts per trillion range.

The chemist Fritz Haber was awarded a Nobel Prize in 1918 for devising a practical process to extract nitrogen from the air to make ammonia, which is crucial in the manufacture of fertilizers and explosives. This dramatic success at obtaining a valuable commodity from a free component of the environment prompted Haber to turn his attention to the gold in sea water. But air is mostly nitrogen, which was the desired element in Haber's first success, whereas sea water is mostly water and salt with very little of the desired gold. The extreme dilution of the gold in sea water defeated Haber, and no economically practical extraction method has ever been found.

So far in human history, fishery resources have proven to be the real treasure from the ocean. The total biological production of the ocean is immense, but this too must be understood relative to the size of the ocean. Judged per acre, the fertility of the ocean is actually low. The magnitude of the fishery resource is immense only owing to the huge volume of the ocean. Because the oceans' fishery resources are "dilute," the cost of obtaining these commodities is actually high. Large capital investments in ships, and high operating expenses in fuel and manpower, are necessary for quantity harvests in most commercial ocean fisheries.

The Fish that Laid the Golden Egg

Salmon are a remarkable exception to the rule that valuable ocean fish are widely scattered and inherently expensive to harvest. Salmon breed in fresh-water rivers, but migrate out to sea, usually as minnow-sized fish a year or less old; adults return from the ocean in a mass migration, years later, as fish generally weighing five to 50 pounds, to repeat the cycle. The salmon accomplish a biological equivalent of Haber's dream, feeding on the dilute resources of a huge ocean, and then providentially concentrating the resulting commodity by collecting themselves in predictable locations at predictable times, as they return to fresh water, where they can be harvested easily at very little expense.

The magnitude of this fishery resource can be enormous. To this day, the annual salmon run in Bristol Bay, for example, is several tens of millions of fish.

The wild salmon resource is as close to a free lunch as Nature will offer us. And it is a good lunch, too. The adult salmon do not feed much when they re-enter fresh water, and their upstream migration to the breeding grounds can be long and physically demanding. To succeed in their adult migration, the fish must be muscular and carry large energy stores in the form of body fats and oils. This makes for very high-grade table fare.

Paradise Lost

The Columbia River was once one of the world's great salmon rivers. It supported the predominant salmon fishery in the lower 48 United States. At the peak of the commercial Columbia River salmon fisheries, in the years around World War I, annual production of the canneries was about 25 million pounds. There was even a plan for a cannery as far upstream as Red Fish Lake, in Idaho, almost a thousand miles from the river mouth. But before the cannery was actually built, the Red Fish Lake salmon fishery declined below a level that could make such a facility profitable.

The Red Fish Lake sockeye salmon was the first salmon stock listed under the Endangered Species Act. This stock today exists almost entirely as a captive population, in which most adult individuals are kept in hatcheries and complete their entire life cycle in a combination of artificial freshwater and saltwater facilities.

The first petition for federal "listing" of a Columbia Basin salmon stock under the Endangered Species Act was filed in 1979. On the heels of this petition, the Northwest Power Act of 1980 created a new entity, the Northwest Power Planning Council, with representation from the four states in the U.S. portion of the Columbia Basin. Initial hopes were that the Council would provide a forum for salmon management without the need for invoking the Endangered Species Act. The pending petition for listing was withdrawn when the Northwest Power Planning Council was formed, but it was re-submitted later, as the salmon declines continued.

The first official declaration of extinction of a Columbia Basin salmon stock was that of the Snake River coho salmon in 1988. The first official listing of a Columbia Basin salmon stock was that of the Snake River sockeye salmon, listed as endangered in 1991. Since then, more Columbia Basin stocks have been listed, some as endangered, some as threatened, and more are under review for listing.

Commercial harvest of Columbia Basin salmon is now very small, and, ironically, much of the harvest pressure is from economically inefficient ocean fisheries. The population sizes of most Columbia Basin stocks are generally too small to sustain much harvest. Direct intentional harvest of the stocks listed as "endangered" is prohibited automatically under the Endangered Species Act. Direct harvest of the stocks listed as "threatened" is subject to control of the National Marine Fisheries Service, the agency responsible for administering the Endangered Species Act as applied to ocean fish. And direct harvest of stocks that are not listed is still subject to control if those harvests coincidentally take any listed stocks.

Federally funded activities intended to restore Columbia Basin salmon now have an annual price tag of several hundred million dollars. Cumulative expenditures have now reached several billion dollars. Many millions of dollars have recently been invested in a paper exercise of analyzing the potential ecological and economic consequences of a proposal to breach some of the dams at huge hydropower installations in the Columbia system in an effort to restore the salmon runs. Flow regulation restrictions, imposed following court intervention under the Endangered Species Act, affect electricity generation, irrigation projects and barge traffic. By some calculations, the dollar value of the electricity generation lost because of flow regulation for the salmon is in excess of $100 million per year.

Returning adult salmon can be collected to breed in hatcheries. There, concrete or plastic tanks with pumped water are substituted for natural spawning habitat for adults, natural incubation habitat for the eggs, and natural rearing habitat for the young. In the hatcheries, prepared food is provided to the fish, and the small fish are protected against predation losses, which in nature are quite high.

The elimination of predation mortality allows a hatchery breeding to produce more outmigrating young fish per adult breeder than would a natural breeding. The multiplier is often on the order of tenfold. Against this multiplier must be counted the capital cost of the hatchery infrastructure, the energy costs of pumping and filtering water, and costs of the feed and labor. Since the preponderance of the adult salmon's mass results from growth in the ocean, subsidizing the freshwater portion of the life cycle might still result in a profitable leveraging of total output. Forty years ago, the salmon outmigration from the Columbia River was almost 100 percent fish of wild origin. At present the outmigration is thought to consist predominantly of hatchery fish. Many of the hatchery stocks are declining along with the wild stocks.

More than half of the salmon now sold for consumption in U.S. markets are "farmed" fish raised in net pens along the coasts of Chile, Norway, British Columbia and Washington state. The salmon farming operations must feed their fish an expensive high-protein diet for the entirety of the life cycle.

The degree of federal control of Columbia Basin salmon management seems to be growing, albeit slowly. A recent federal court decision has ruled that a plan put forward by Oregon to manage salmon recovery efforts under state control does not satisfy requirements of the Endangered Species Act. Another recent federal court decision has ruled that Indian treaty rights applying to Pacific Northwest salmon are not exempt from authority of the Endangered Species Act.

As of the date of this writing, the Columbia Basin salmon are, for the most part, continuing to decline, and the listings are proceeding apace.

What's Wrong with this Picture?

Superficially, the case of the Columbia Basin salmon is grist for the mill of the classic conservative critique of the Endangered Species Act. With the right spin, the story is one of heavy-handed federal intervention, enormous expenditures, and programs which failed to meet their objectives. But this isn't the whole story, and it isn't even the most important or most interesting part of the story.

In order really to understand the case of Columbia Basin salmon management in relation to the federal Endangered Species Act, we need to consider a list of fairly pointed questions. And the answers to some of these questions may be a little surprising. We need to ask: Why has the Endangered Species Act been invoked in the case of Columbia Basin salmon? How much of the Columbia Basin salmon management effort is driven by the federal Endangered Species Act as distinct from other federal, state and tribal sources of authority? How much of the money spent on these programs originates with Endangered Species Act mandates? To what extent is the level of effectiveness and efficiency achieved in this management program a reflection of the functioning of the Endangered Species Act, as distinct from other social forces? And finally, is the case of Columbia Basin salmon reasonably representative of the way the Endangered Species Act operates? This chapter will examine the story from the perspective of these questions.

The first hint that this story may prove to be somewhat unusual is the obvious mismatch between the nature of the resource at risk and the overt objectives of the management tools that are being brought to bear. Salmon is such a valuable commodity in the market that even inefficient high-input salmon farming is economical. Wild salmon are preeminently a valuable commodity that nature provides essentially for free, as long as the environment and harvest are managed properly. Managing such a renewable resource under terms of legislation that is intended to prevent extinction of the last remnants of a population is surely to miss the point.

In this light, it is clear that something went very wrong in the management of Columbia Basin salmon long before the Endangered Species Act was even written. And the costly and unsuccessful federal programs intended to rebuild the Columbia Basin salmon runs got underway before the Endangered Species Act was applied to Columbia Basin salmon. An understanding of this history of management failure reveals that almost none of the blame for the situation to date rests with the Endangered Species Act. If anything, the Endangered Species Act may offer the last hope of resolving some problems of fragmented jurisdiction that have played a large role in past institutional failures to manage Columbia Basin salmon, and the Endangered Species Act offers perhaps the last hope for an institutional framework that could rationally weigh economic costs against the objective of preventing local extinctions of salmon stocks.

It is believed that the present annual Columbia salmon runs are smaller by something on the order of 10 million adult fish, compared to the pristine status. If we simply went out and bought salmon at $50 per fish, we could make up this difference and stay more or less within the total budget of the present restoration effort. But buying fish from somewhere else doesn't satisfy the intention of the Endangered Species Act, and it doesn't address the public concerns for conservation of the Columbia ecosystem. We don't really know if we can re-create a good salmon ecosystem at a unit cost per adult salmon carrying capacity of $50 per fish.

If the present total restoration budget were put into hatcheries, the numbers of fingerlings produced annually might be somewhere between half a billion and a billion. But, at the present apparent rates of ocean survival, even such an enormous hatchery output would not generate enough returning adults to make up the supposed deficit in the adult runs. And, of course, the artificiality of a hatchery approach is not ecologically satisfying. The acceptability of a hatchery strategy under the Endangered Species Act is a complicated issue.

The very applicability of the Endangered Species Act to Columbia Basin salmon stocks is a matter of interpretation. The astute reader will have noticed that this chapter has consistently referred to the depleted Columbia Basin salmon populations as "stocks," not species. The relation between stocks and the population units that qualify for protection of the Endangered Species Act warrants a closer look.

The Biological Reality of Salmon Stocks

There are many species of salmon. In the Columbia Basin, there are four species (sockeye, chinook, steelhead and chum) of which stocks have been listed, and there is one additional species (coho) of which stocks have been declared extinct. These five species are by no means restricted to the Columbia; all are widely distributed along the north Pacific rim.

Salmon populations of a given species are subdivided into "stocks," based largely on geography. Salmon adults have astonishing navigation and homing abilities which they use to direct their upstream migration so that they return to spawn in the same area where they were born. Thus, each tributary stream or mainstream gravel bar that serves as a salmon spawning area defines a genealogically distinguishable population. Almost all the salmon spawning in a particular area are fish that hatched there and are themselves descendants of fish that hatched and later spawned in that same area.

There is a small amount of "straying," which allows for colonization of new spawning habitats and recolonization of old spawning areas that may have lost their original salmon population. But the rates of exchange of individuals between spawning areas are very slow compared to potential normal annual rates of salmon population growth and decline. So, from the standpoint of management for harvest, where there is a desire to adjust the harvest rate to maximize production without depleting the population, it makes sense to treat each local population as a distinct management unit, called a stock.

The considerable genetic isolation of each local population allows for genetic differences between the local populations within a salmon species. With modern scientific techniques, such as DNA sequencing, the genetic differences between local populations of salmon can actually be measured. Some of the genetic difference between local populations controls differences in life history traits that are important to the success of each respective stock.

Time and place are critical for a fish that may use many hundred miles of river, from river mouth to tributary headwaters, and that may use thousands of miles of ocean, during its life cycle, in a northern environment that is strongly seasonal. In addition to differing with respect to spawning location, salmon stocks of the same species can differ with respect to spawning time, incubation period of the eggs, emergence time of the fry, locations where the small fish reside and grow prior to their outmigration, seasonal timing of the outmigration, age and size at outmigration, number of years at sea, locations favored in the ocean, adult size at return, and seasonal timing of the return migration.

Each combination of these traits embodied in a successful life history pattern constitutes a "solution" to the problems the fish must face in finding favorable and productive habitat during each stage of its life cycle, in sequence, avoiding crowding, avoiding competition, avoiding predators and avoiding hostile conditions of temperature, flow or turbidity that may occur at different seasons in different locations. For any given stock, all the pieces of the life history puzzle have to fit together in a way that works as a whole. For example, a seasonal run timing that is effective for a fish that spawns in a mountain headwater and overwinters as a young fish in fresh water might be disastrous for a fish that spawns in the river mainstream a hundred miles from the estuary and migrates out to sea before its first winter.

Unlike the homing fidelity to spawning location, which is almost entirely governed by a kind of "instant learning" recognition of the site where the fish hatches, many of the other life history traits which differ between stocks are subject to a considerable degree of genetic adjustment. It is known that life history traits in fish evolve relatively rapidly, on a time scale of decades, and are under strong pressure from natural selection. So, not only does the homing of the salmon give the respective stocks a demographic reality that is important to harvest management, there is also a genetic reality underlying the life history differences. These genetic differences make the respective stocks non-substitutable in the short term, though successful life history patterns can re-evolve independently in the long term.

Very large numbers of salmon stocks are recognized for practical purposes of harvest management. By some accounts, for example, there are about 3,000 stocks of the various species of salmon in the Columbia and its tributaries.

Harvests of different stocks can be managed to some extent separately, because of differences in respective run timing, and because harvests can be geographically targeted. So for harvest purposes, the stock is the natural management unit.

Management Units Under the Endangered Species Act

For plants and invertebrate animals, decisions under the Endangered Species Act pertain to the entire species. In order to declare a population of such a species "endangered" or "threatened," and thereby bring it under the protection of the Endangered Species Act, the determination must be that the entire biological species is in danger of extinction. Since a species is a fairly well defined biological unit, the management unit for plants and invertebrates under the Endangered Species Act is natural, and generally unambiguous.

The wording of the law is less straightforward for vertebrates. The Endangered Species Act offers the option of declaring a "distinct population segment" of a vertebrate species to be in danger of extinction, and then providing for this population the full range of protection. This allows the flexibility to list a local population, such as the population of grizzly bears centered in Yellowstone Park, that may indeed be in danger of local extermination, and that may be of great public interest, even though elsewhere, other populations of this same species may be healthy enough. But the language of the law does not really define where the line should be drawn in exercising this flexibility, for the phrase "distinct population segment" has no special scientific meaning and does not necessarily correspond to an unambiguously recognizable natural unit.

Because of the known multiplicity of stocks for each salmon species, salmon present an opportunity for extreme micromanagement of subpopulations under the Endangered Species Act, if stocks are interpreted as qualifying for the status of "distinct population segment." Given the large number of declining stocks, just the administrative process of making the listing decisions could turn into a growth industry for the responsible agencies. While the fanfare of listings might appear "protective," the consequence could actually be the opposite if the preoccupation with assembly-line listings distracts from the jeopardy decisions and recovery plans that must make up the substance of a management program that really protects the listed populations. There may also be some risk that pushing the implementation of this "distinct population segment" option to an extreme might diminish the credibility and support for the Endangered Species Act.

In the actual event, the National Marine Fisheries Service has pursued a middle ground. The agency has developed a concept of "evolutionarily significant unit" as their interpretation of a biological basis for defining a "distinct population segment." In application, this definition rests more on genetic than on demographic criteria. The agency has declared a large number of such evolutionarily significant units for some species of salmon in the Columbia Basin, but the number is not as large as the number of stocks that might be identified. And the potential for the number of listing decisions to overwhelm the administrative process has been controlled somewhat, in practice, by the sensible expedient of making some listing decisions for aggregates of evolutionarily significant units.

But the fact remains that the population units of salmon being managed under the Endangered Species Act in the Columbia Basin each represent a very small fraction of the total populations of the respective biological species. And these units are defined under a set of criteria that were invented for this purpose.

The suitability of salmon hatcheries as a management tool for endangered salmon falls into a strange gray area, created by the tension between the stock concept for conventional fisheries management of salmon, and the evolutionarily significant-unit definition of the basic population unit that is managed under the Endangered Species Act. Since the salmon's homing behavior automatically returns the adult fish to their location of origin, hatchery raised fish return to their hatchery. So each hatchery operation constitutes its own stock for each species that it raises. Thus the question naturally arises what status these "hatchery stocks" have relative to the Endangered Species Act.

The annual hatchery production of 100 to 200 million young salmon now constitutes the bulk of the annual outmigration from the Columbia Basin. The roughly 100 salmon hatcheries now operating in the Columbia Basin could make up a large fraction of the still extant stocks, if they were so counted, and might also represent a large number of evolutionarily significant units, if they were so designated. But this count could cut both ways.

Demographically, hatchery stocks seem to qualify as stocks, without much question. The picture is less clear from a genetic standpoint. Hatchery stocks are often assembled out of mixtures of bloodlines from other hatcheries and from various wild stocks as well. In the first generations of hatchery breeding, a hatchery stock will undergo some amount of "domestication" as traits that confer good performance in the hatchery are selected for during the hatchery phase of the life cycle, and bad behavior, such as jumping out of the tanks, is selected out. At the same time, during the ocean and migration phases of the life cycle of these hatchery stocks, there will be selection on life history traits in the direction of forming a total life cycle that "works" by adjusting the ocean phase to be compatible with the age, size, condition, behavior and season of the outmigration after the young fish are released from the hatchery.

So, on the one hand, a hatchery stock is in part a creation of human fish cultivation practices, and might not be thought to qualify for Endangered Species Act listing any more than a breed of show dogs. Further, since a successful hatchery stock has evolved a combination of life history traits that work well for a stock that does breed and rear in the hatchery and begins its outmigration at the age, season and size when the hatchery fish are released, such a stock's life history traits may prove very disadvantageous to any strays from this hatchery which attempt to breed in nature, where because of differences in growth rate and temperature they will outmigrate at some other age, size and season. For the same reasons, these strays could represent a genetic threat to any wild fish with which they might interbreed, as the resulting new patchwork of life history patterns may not suit a fish either for hatchery life or for life in the wild.

But on the other hand, the numerical multiplier effect, achieved in hatchery rearing by superabundance of food and by elimination of predation on the early life history stages, could appear to be an attractive option for giving a numerical boost to a population that has reached perilously low numbers. And when no further options are left for a wild population, preserving the last remnants of that population for the entirety of their life cycle in artificial facilities seems as logical a last resort for salmon as it has for a number of bird and mammal species that now exist only in captivity, and are perpetuated only through captive breeding.

The National Marine Fisheries Service, in making decisions about salmon population units that qualify for protection under the Endangered Species Act, generally has not extended protection to hatchery stocks, has not accepted hatchery production as a legitimate means to augment the population size of listed stocks, and has acted to attempt to limit the straying of hatchery fish into listed populations. But the same agency has so far taken one listed salmon stock into captive breeding when that stock was about to disappear. As more salmon stocks reach that brink there will be more decisions about taking them into captive breeding.

There is an underlying logic to this set of decisions by the agency, but it also requires some fancy footwork. If this logic is pursued to its apparent conclusion, the implications for the eventual recovery program are sobering. If each evolutionarily significant unit of each endangered Columbia Basin salmon stock must eventually be taken into captive breeding as the stocks continue to decline, the large number of such captive breeding operations will be extremely costly—and unlike conventional production hatchery operations, this cost will not be offset by a real or supposed contribution to valuable sport or commercial harvest, for the numbers will be far too small, and the fish never leave the artificial facilities.

The smaller the population subunits qualifying for Endangered Species Act protection, the more these listed stocks will be geographically intermixed among the few remaining healthy wild salmon stocks and the several productive hatchery stocks. This geographic proximity exacerbates the inevitable conflicts between managing the healthy salmon population units for human use and protecting the listed weak stocks. These conflicts are at their sharpest when harvests targeting healthy stocks coincidentally increase the fishing pressure on weak stocks, and when strays from productive hatcheries mingle with wild weak stocks on their spawning grounds.

It will be interesting to see whether the present evolutionarily significant unit policy, as an approach to implementing the "distinct population segment" provision of the Endangered Species Act for Columbia Basin salmon, will stand the test of time. In the few years that the Endangered Species Act has been applied to Columbia Basin salmon, things have not run smoothly. The massive hatchery program in the Columbia Basin is controversial. Jeopardy decisions in connection with harvest and with management of the federal hydropower system in the Columbia Basin have been bitterly contested, and courts have intervened on several important occasions. No recovery plan for Columbia Basin salmon has yet to go beyond the "draft" stage.

Follow the Money

The Endangered Species Act is in some respects draconian, for the law is quite definite about prohibitions on activities that would be detrimental to species listed as endangered. But the Act does not mandate budgets for recovery measures, monitoring or scientific investigations. Budgets for most endangered species programs are paltry. Under a 1988 amendment, the responsible agencies are required to report all reasonably identifiable costs associated with Endangered Species Act recovery efforts. As of 1995, when the last such set of audits were compiled, the total annual federal spending for recovery efforts of all listed species, including salmon, was smaller than the total annual federal spending for Columbia Basin salmon. Where has the huge Columbia Basin salmon budget come from? And what directs those portions of the budget that are not counted as Endangered Species Act implementation?

Columbia Basin salmon first encountered the big money of big government programs with the Rivers and Harbors Acts of 1925 and 1927. These planned for ten mainstream dams in the Columbia system, to be built by the U.S. Army Corps of Engineers, for stated purposes of electricity generation, flood control and navigation. The first dam, Rock Island, was completed in 1933; by 1957 six big dams had been completed on the Columbia; by 1975, when the last big dam was completed, the total was 11 on the Columbia River and seven on the Snake River, which itself was a major salmon producing tributary that in turn was fed by important tributaries such as the Grande Ronde River, the Imnaha River, the Salmon River and the Clearwater River.

It was obvious from the outset that dams would pose obstacles to upstream migration of adult salmon, so fish ladders were constructed at all the dams below Chief Joseph Dam on the Columbia. It was believed that Chief Joseph Dam (and before it, Grand Coulee Dam) would be too high for a fish ladder to be effective. And the high Hells Canyon Dam on the Snake, though provided with a fish ladder, nevertheless proved impassable to upstream migration. Thus, simple blockage removed a substantial fraction of the Columbia Basin from natural salmon production by the middle of this century. By this time, new declines in some important salmon stocks were very evident.

Less obvious, but known to some scientists at the time, were other adverse effects of the dams. Most notably, the turbines of the hydroelectric facilities were exacting a mortality on the young fish as they passed each dam during their downstream migration. Further, the replacement of many miles of river with many miles of reservoir simply eliminated large amounts of important salmon habitat. The idea that there was some need to "compensate" for the effects of the dams on the Columbia Basin salmon first gained political currency with the Mitchell Act that initially provided approximately $20 million in federal funding for hatcheries in the period 1947-1957, and which continues at a higher level of funding to this day.

As the dam building continued, and the salmon decline continued, it was natural to blame the dams, with primary focus on the federal Bonneville Power Administration and the US Army Corps of Engineers. The nominal revenues from electricity generation by the Bonneville Power Administration fall somewhere between $2 and $3 billion annually. Thus there was an obvious deep pocket to target in a federal program which in any case does not do its bookkeeping like a business. And so, the lion's share of the costs for salmon restoration in the Columbia Basin has been borne, and continues to be borne, by the Bonneville Power Administration. Some of the restoration activities are written by congress into the mandate for the Corps of Engineers, some for the Fish and Wildlife Service, some are carried out by the National Marine Fisheries Service, and some are carried out in programs managed by Bonneville Power Administration itself. But one way or the other, almost all the bills ultimately are sent to Bonneville. At present, the annual bill is roughly 15 percent of the nominal electricity revenues.

Columbia Basin salmon at one time were significant to the local economy. Salmon were once the mainstay of the Indian tribes of the region, and rights to salmon harvest were written into the Treaty of 1855, which established for most of those tribes the basic legal status under which they continue to govern themselves and relate to the federal government. And salmon naturally are a kind of environmental emblem for the Pacific Northwest. Given this economic, legal and symbolic prominence of salmon, it was inevitable that considerable political pressure would develop to respond to the salmon decline. Given the ease of isolating the federal hydrosystem as a villain in the story, and given the size of the electricity revenues account, tapping that account was a politically painless way to pay for a politically necessary large and visible restoration program.

This military-environmental-industrial complex, its relation to the federal government, and the mechanism for bankrolling it, was fully evolved before any of the Columbia Basin salmon stocks were listed under the Endangered Species Act. Now, the same funding mechanism is paying for Endangered Species Act implementation. But the National Marine Fisheries Service, which is responsible for Endangered Species Act implementation for the salmon, does not have direct control over the bulk of the salmon restoration money from Bonneville, and this fact accounts in part for the very modest level of focus apparent in the overall program.

So this is how, and why, Columbia Basin salmon have come to constitute an unrepresentive, high-budget outlier in the distribution of endangered species programs.

What Went Wrong?

Columbia Basin salmon stocks have been in a state of decline for over a century. Many measures of environmental deterioration in the salmon ecosystem of the Columbia Basin show trends of increasing damage over the same time.

During the nineteenth century, and through the early years of the twentieth, the primary cause for salmon decline unquestionably was overharvest. But soon other factors complicated the picture. Irrigation withdrawals reduced tributary stream flows necessary for spawning and rearing, raised stream temperatures, stranded fish on fields, and returned silty and contaminated water to the rivers. Logging caused siltation, increased runoff at the expense of groundwater recharge, and removed cover; and the removal of cover and the reduction of recharge raised stream temperatures. Mining operations destroyed spawning and rearing habitat in stream channels. Dams converted river habitat to lake-like habitat, impeded upstream migration of adults, caused mortality of outmigrating young fish in turbine passage, and caused dissolved gas supersaturation; deliberate water management drastically altered the seasonal pattern of flow, affecting salmon outmigrations and return migrations; the new patterns of water level fluctuations stranded eggs and young of mainstream spawning populations. Hatcheries flooded the system with fish that often were derived from different geographic locations, fish that generally were domesticated stocks adapted to hatchery conditions and not to reproduction in the wild, and that were released to migrate at a size and age different from the life history pattern of the wild fish. Some studies indicate markedly lower ocean survival rates for hatchery fish compared to wild fish, and higher mortality due to predation while migrating. Also, hatchery stocks often return as adults at a younger age, and a smaller size, and carrying fewer eggs per female, compared to the corresponding wild stocks.

Since the cumulative history of environmental damage accompanies a history of population decline, it is tempting to say that this particular list of factors "caused" the decline. Human nature being what it is, the temptation for various constituencies to single out one factor or another as "the" cause of the decline has been all but irresistible. But such finger pointing fails to quantify the role of each factor in contributing to the decline of the salmon; it fails to account for interactions between the effects of the various factors; and it neglects the possible role of other environmental factors operating in the ocean and estuaries.

Nature is never really constant, even without human modification of the environment. Large scale shifts in ocean conditions are part of the normal "background" variation in the world, and these can have far-reaching ecological effects. In the past two decades ocean survival rates for some Columbia Basin stocks have been unusually low, and over more or less the same period there has been a detectable shift in patterns of ocean currents, sea surface temperatures, and biological productivity in the North Pacific.

It is not known how much of this depressed ocean survival is genuinely attributable to "natural" variation in the ocean. If the dominant cause is natural variation, the ocean conditions could swing back to a more favorable state quite independent of our interventions. Human-caused factors besides the dams, that could possibly affect ocean survival, have also changed for the worse during this same time interval. And outside the Columbia Basin, not all stocks in the Pacific Northwest have exhibited declines across the board, so there is more to the story than simply poor ocean conditions.

The Iron Law of Replacement of Generations

For a population to sustain its numbers, each individual in the population must, on the average, during its lifetime, produce one offspring which itself survives to reproduction. If this relationship is maintained, each generation on average replaces itself. If an individual produces more than one surviving offspring on average, the population will increase. If an individual produces less than one surviving offspring on average, the population will decline. If the decline persists, the population will go extinct.

We may analyze the factors which contribute to the replacement of generations with a graphical device, shown in Figure 1 (next page), where the vertical axis is a logarithmic scale. First, we plot the number of female eggs per adult female as a white bar reaching up from the value one to the number of eggs. Then we plot the rates of survival of various mortality factors in the life history as black bars, stretching down from the value one to the respective survival rate of each life history episode. Then, in Figure 2, we take all the black bars, representing survival of mortality factors, and stack them one atop the other alongside the white bar representing the reproductive rate. Finally, we observe whether the stack of black bars is higher or lower than the white bar.

For fairly elementary mathematical reasons, this sequence of graphing operations constitutes a precise quantitative assessment of the combined effects of reproduction and mortality in the population. If the stack of black bars exceeds the white bar in height, the population must decline, as each individual on average does not replace itself in its lifetime. If the stack of black bars is lower than the white bar, the population must grow, as each individual more than replaces itself.

For the declining salmon stocks, the stack of black bars is higher than the white bar. But it is the total height of the stack of black mortality bars in relation to the white reproduction bar that matters. No one of the bars is necessarily overriding. We see, therefore, that it makes no sense to single out any one mortality factor as "the" cause of the salmon decline. And even the cumulative effect of all the mortality factors is not "the" cause, for any cumulative total mortality (short of 100 percent) could still be sustainable if the per capita reproduction were high enough.

Thus, for example, for a declining stock, if there is any harvest at all, that harvest is, prima facie, an "overharvest." But this does not guarantee that reducing the harvest, or even eliminating the harvest, will necessarily reverse the decline.

The "real" cause of the Columbia Basin salmon decline is that the cumulative effect of all the sources of mortality exceeds the reproduction in the declining stocks, and has done so fairly consistently, and by a substantial margin, for several decades.

Figure 8.1 Components of population replacement rate per generation

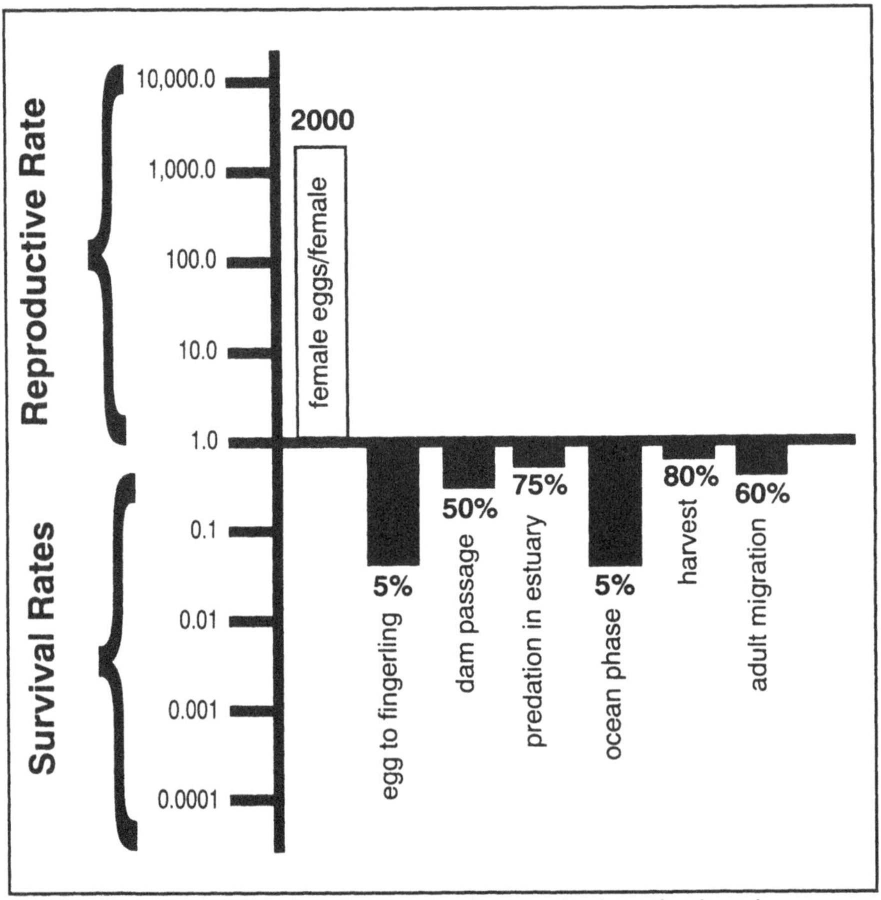

Lengths of bars, on a logarithmic scale, show the vital rates that determine the replacement rate of a population in each generation. The white bar shows the reproductive rate of a female salmon that has survived to reach the spawning grounds. The black bars show the survival rates of each stage of the salmon life cycle: survival from egg to a fingerling ready to start the migration from its freshwater rearing area, survival of dam passage and other hazards during the outmigration through the river mainstream, survival of predation on the small fish as they make the transition to salt water in the estuary, survival of the several years of growth to mature size in the ocean, survival of harvest as the adults gather for the start of their return migration, and survival of the upstream migration through the river to return to the spawning grounds. The critical lengths of the black bars are the distances (up or down) from the value 1 to the respective reproductive rate or survival rate. The values in percents at the tips of the black bars list the survival rates. And 100 percent minus the listed value would be the corresponding mortality rate. Thus the five percent survival rate shown for the egg to fingerling phase corresponds to a 95 percent mortality in passing through this stage of the life cycle. The specific numbers in this graph are plausible for a "generic" Columbia River wild salmon population in recent decades.

Figure 8.2 Replacement rate

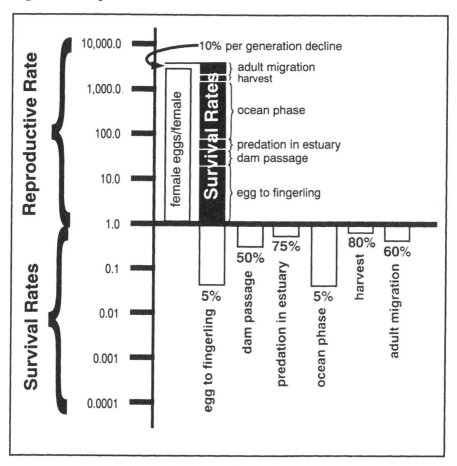

When the black survival bars from Figure 1 are stacked alongside the white reproductive rate bar, starting from the reference value 1 on the logarithmic scale, the combined height determines the replacement rate of generations. If the stack of black bars is taller than the white bar, then the generations fail to replace themselves fully, and the population must decline. If the stack of black bars is shorter than the white bar, then each generation more than replaces itself and the population increases. In the case illustrated, this population declines by 10 percent per generation. (The mathematical principle behind this graphical device is the same used in the mechanical slipstick slide rules that were the mainstay of engineering calculation in the days before the invention of electronic calculators and computers.)

A salmon recovery program need not be built on improving survival during just one particular stage of the life cycle, or reducing just one source of mortality. Recovery can be brought about with any combination of interventions that raise the white reproduction bar and/or lower the stack of black mortality bars enough that the white bar is then higher than the stack of black bars. An intervention program that increases reproduction somewhat and/or reduces some sources of mortality somewhat, but not enough that the white bar is then higher than the stack of black bars, will not accomplish recovery. It will merely slow the continuing population decline.

Engineering Solutions

The salmon problem in the Columbia Basin has been the subject of many well-meaning and well-funded attempts at solution. Judging from the fact of the continued decline of the stocks, it is difficult to find a basis for concluding that the combined efforts, so far, at solving the problem have "worked," though some of the individual efforts may well have had the intended effect of somewhat increasing reproduction or somewhat decreasing some component of mortality.

At a simple, common sense level, it is easy to sympathize with the motivation for the various investments in attempts at salmon restoration, however "un-ecological" they may seem. If the problem is not enough salmon, why not invest in hatcheries to raise more salmon to the age of outmigration? If downstream passage through inhospitable reservoirs is a problem, why not transport juvenile fish downstream in barges? If turbine mortality is a problem, why not put in a system of screens and conveyor belts to route fish around the turbines? If insufficient flows are a problem, why not mandate minimal flow? If gas supersaturation is a problem, why not modify the spillway structure? If predation at the bypass outfall is a problem, why not extend the outfall pipe to a location less attractive to predators, string up piano wire to discourage birds, and put a bounty on squaw fish? If irrigation diversions are a problem, why not screen them? If temperatures and flows are outside of the range for successful adult spawning migration, why not collect adults at the fish ladders below the problem section and truck the fish the rest of the way upstream?

The above questions invite the easy answer that these efforts should be undertaken. And indeed these efforts have been undertaken on a scale that would satisfy an environmental technocrat's wildest dreams. So many millions of young fish are released from Columbia Basin hatcheries each year that now the outmigration is made up almost entirely of hatchery fish. So many millions of young fish are barged or trucked around the dams on the lower Snake River and the lower Columbia that roughly half of the total outmigration is now transported by the U.S. Army Corps of Engineers. Almost 20 million annually of the outmigrating young fish have implanted in their snouts little pieces of wire marked with a code in notches, so that the wire tags, detectable by a magnetic device, when recovered from a dead fish identify the time and place of that fish's origin. Around one million of the outmigrating young fish have implanted in their body cavity a tiny transmitter which is energized each time the fish passes an "interrogation" coil, identifying the individual live fish with a unique signal code as it passes through the appropriately equipped passageway in a dam.

But at another level, these questions of "why not..." are not mere rhetorical flourishes. The salmon have continued to decline while these efforts were implemented, so the answer to an individual "why not..." might well be "because it is ineffective, (or maybe even counter productive)," or perhaps the answer could be "because it is too expensive relative to the effect achieved."

But such an answer will have to be very authoritative to carry weight in an atmosphere where many constituencies are ready to go to court to promote their interests, and where the network of causal interactions is so complex that many hypothetical causal scenarios are plausible. For example, it is believed in some quarters that some combination of poor avoidance behavior by hatchery fish, disorienting effects of barge and truck transportation, and concentration of young fish by the dam bypass facilities have increased vulnerability of the outmigrating fish to predation. Near the mouth of the Columbia River, some artificial islands, created in recent decades out of dredge spoils, have become home to the largest colony on this continent of Caspian terns, a seagull-like bird, which were hardly known to be present in this location 20 years ago. By some estimates this bird colony now imposes a mortality on the salmon comparable in magnitude to the turbine mortality of several of the mainstream dams combined. It comes as no surprise that lawsuits have been filed in an attempt to force a management decision to reduce the tern population; it might give the reader pause, however, to learn that some national bird advocacy groups oppose elimination of this tern colony and wish to have a say in how the bird population is to be managed.

Risks of Failure and Risks of Success

The attempted solutions for restoration of the Columbia Basin salmon largely reflect an engineering approach in which a factor is identified as contributing to the salmon decline, and then some intervention, generally artificial, and often involving large structures or capital equipment, is initiated in an effort to counteract or ameliorate that factor. A striking general feature of these types of attempted solutions is that they often are accompanied by side effects that are detrimental to the salmon.

Further, if such interventions are planned, implemented and evaluated one factor at a time, serious incompatibilities between interventions can arise when uncoordinated interventions fail to complement, or perhaps even negate one another. Considering the entire suite of one-factor engineering solutions, it is possible that the attainment of the immediate objectives of some may be to the detriment of others, not merely because of competition for programatic resources, but because an outcome that is a solution with respect to one objective may be a problem with respect to another. A program made up of such a mixture of uncoordinated efforts faces both risks of failure and risks of success.

There are many examples of such a potential for counterproductive side effects in the salmon restoration program. Hatcheries can indeed produce large numbers of young salmon, under favorable circumstances, but hatchery rearing selects for traits that are probably disadvantageous when hatchery strays reproduce in the wild or interbreed with wild fish. Barging young fish past the dams and reservoirs does reduce mortality of downstream passage for some stocks, but barging only favors the particular life history types and stocks that are taken in the collectors at the chosen times, and it creates a dependency on maintaining this artificial intervention on this particular schedule. Turbine bypass structures do allow young fish to avoid the mortality associated with turbine passage, but the bypass system is designed to pass the maximum number of fish with a minimum amount of water, so it concentrates the young fish at the bypass outfall, attracting predators. Routing water over the spillways rather than through the turbines at the dams reduces turbine mortality, but spill over these tall dams creates gas supersaturation that at high enough levels is lethal to fish. There are special modifications that can be made to spillway structures to reduce gas entrainment, but these structures increase mechanical injury to spilled fish. And the list goes on.

So, being convinced that a particular action qualitatively has some desired effect on one particular factor is not enough to justify its adoption. The effect on some identified factor, considered in isolation, may be rather different from the net result for the salmon.

An intervention is liable to affect the salmon through more than one mechanism. A comprehensive evaluation of an intervention needs to consider whether the positive effects on the salmon are greater than the negative effects. This is a lot to ask from an evaluation, for it requires quantification of both the positive and negative effects. And it requires that both be quantified with enough precision to have confidence in the estimate of the numerical difference between the two.

Further, there are interactions among the various direct effects of these attempts at solution. The mechanism of interaction can be social and economic. For example, if hatchery production is successful at increasing run size, this will encourage demands for increased harvest, which will increase the incidental fishing mortality on weak wild stocks that cannot sustain it. Or the mechanism can be ecological. For example, ecological crowding can create a survival bottleneck at one stage of the life cycle as a result of enhanced survival earlier in the life cycle.

Because of this complicated interplay, a high level of quantitative understanding would be needed to design a recovery program that was both effective and efficient. Effects of proposed or ongoing interventions need to be quantified in order to determine how much of that intervention would be required to achieve the desired level of effect. If a population is declining 10 percent per year, an intervention that, say, reduces mortality enough to change the rate of decline to six percent a year is a positive effect, but it does not achieve recovery. Knowing this, we would then want to investigate whether an increased investment in that same intervention could raise the positive effect to the point that population decline was reversed. This is important for planning purposes, since we might find that the level of investment required for that particular intervention far exceeds the recovery budget, or we might find that no amount of investment in that particular intervention was capable of achieving the desired quantified level of response. Either case would indicate that a successful recovery program must adopt some other strategy, perhaps employing some amount of investment in the intervention in question in combination with other interventions, or perhaps not employing that particular intervention at all.

Thus, the determination that a system of interventions should have a net positive benefit on the salmon cannot be carried out by evaluating one factor at a time. Designing an effective recovery program requires a quantitative analysis of many trade-offs between good and bad consequences of many interventions; and it requires a quantitative coordination of many interventions that otherwise might work at cross purposes; and it requires a gauging of the level of each intervention so that the combined effect will be sufficient to achieve the desired goal of recovery.

Rational Management and the Endangered Species Act

Restoration of Columbia Basin salmon will not be achieved just by "fixing" a problem associated with one environmental factor or technological modification. The environmental changes in the Columbia have been so pervasive, and have occurred on such a wide scale, that what was once a "salmon ecosystem" now is some other kind of ecosystem. This new ecosystem may be productive enough for walleye pike, smallmouth bass or squaw fish, but it is not, under its own dynamics, going to produce much salmon. And the salmon it does produce will be from a few lucky stocks whose life histories happen to be attuned to the new set of conditions.

There are a few apparent "spontaneous" successes that have arisen among those wild and hatchery stocks that do seem capable of coping with the new reality of the Columbia ecosystem. It is believed, for example, that among the many Columbia Basin stocks, the wild sockeye salmon from the Okanogan River, wild fall chinook salmon from the Hanford Reach of the mainstream of the Columbia, and wild steelhead from the John Day River are still robust populations. The spring chinook stock from the Lookingglass hatchery returns so many adults straying onto the natural spawning grounds in the Grande Ronde River that it has been classified as a problem in a "biological opinion" by the National Marine Fisheries Service. But these successful Columbia Basin stocks are the exception rather than the rule.

And the particular reasons for these few, scattered successes have not been determined. It is not known how these sorts of successes might be achieved at other locations in the Columbia and on a larger scale. And it is not known whether these sorts of successes are possible for the listed stocks of greatest concern.

No doubt there are lots of possible interventions—such as the many components of the multi-hundred million dollar per year set of efforts that is now underway—that could incrementally improve some aspects of the Columbia

Basin for salmon. But such a collection of disjoint activities is not necessarily assured of success—as indeed the present program seems not to be succeeding. The ecosystem in question encompasses over a thousand miles of rivers, and many thousands of square miles of watershed. Because the salmon depend on many different kinds of habitats in many locations, in sequence, during their life cycle, the whole ecosystem has to function correctly for successful salmon production. This is a very long chain with many weak links, and any one broken link breaks the chain.

What would it take to succeed—to meet the present avowed goal of "doubling the salmon runs" in general and to achieve "recovery" of the listed stocks? How compatible are these goals? Is either goal achievable at a socially acceptable cost? Short of turning back the clock in an implausible "de-development," the specifications of an actual blueprint for success are unknown. And the fact that the necessary blueprint is unknown is itself a commentary on a program that has spent many tens of millions of dollars on monitoring, data management, analysis and modeling, and many millions more on administrative and participatory "processes."

There is little centralized control of the salmon restoration effort, and the priorities that are served are not necessarily those of recovery of the stocks listed under the Endangered Species Act. Many of the important quantitative questions about salmon management that have gone unanswered have also effectively gone unasked.

Despite the huge numbers of marked, tagged and radioed fish, there has been poor design, lack of coordination and outright omission of important categories of fish from the fish tracking projects. These programmatic flaws have undermined the effectiveness of the monitoring for purposes of addressing many of the critical management questions. As a consequence, key variables that need to be known with some quantitative precision, and that could be known with this precision if the right monitoring designs had been implemented, are not now known with that precision. For instance, not enough is known about the reproductive rates and mortality rates at various life stages of the remaining wild stocks in the Columbia Basin; not enough is known about the incidental mortality rates of the wild fish in various fisheries; not enough is known about the effects of different routes of upstream and downstream dam passage at different dams on survival to reproductive age; not enough is known about the ecological effects of reservoir flow releases on survival, about the effects of crowding by hatchery fish on wild populations, about the effects of interbreeding between hatchery fish and wild fish, and about the effectiveness of various kinds of habitat improvement efforts.

Just enough is known about these various factors affecting Columbia Basin salmon to raise, alternately, dire suspicions or rosy expectations. Not enough is known with enough quantitative precision to compare the trade-offs, to identify which interventions really work under which circumstances, to define what mix of interventions will be most efficient at achieving the goal of recovery, or to determine the actual minimal cost of achieving the goal of recovery under the Endangered Species Act.

The Endangered Species Act vests considerable authority in the agencies responsible for implementation, but this power is largely negative—the power of Section 4 prohibitions. On paper, the National Marine Fisheries Service has the authority to wield great power by declaring that federal actions, such as issuing fishery quotas, operating the hydrosystem, operating hatcheries, or permitting logging, constitute a "take" or pose "jeopardy" to the listed salmon. In practice, such declarations would almost certainly be contested vigorously in court by affected parties. And the plaintiffs' first line of argument could readily be based on scientific uncertainty of the grounds for the determination.

The last line of defense against Endangered Species Act rulings that appear to cause undue social or economic hardship is appeal to the "endangered species committee," commonly referred to as the "god squad." The endangered species committee, on paper, has the power to declare the costs excessive and to let the take or jeopardy proceed, or even to let the species go extinct. In practice, no endangered species committee has ever made such a determination—a reflection, perhaps, of the political unpalatability of acknowledging responsibility for a visible extinction.

Plenty of extinctions have occurred while the Endangered Species Act was in force, but these were all cases that hardly anyone cared about, and the extinctions took place quietly. In order for a recovery program to reach a cost threshold where there is any reason to invoke the endangered species committee as a safety valve, it is almost certain that there had to be enough previous public opinion pressure or special interest involvement that a subsequent endangered species committee decision against the population at risk is politically unthinkable.

On the side of positive recovery actions, rather than prohibitions, on behalf of an endangered species, the Endangered Species Act does not provide much of a power base. The National Marine Fisheries Service does not have a very large budget of its own to devote to Columbia Basin salmon, and it does not have the direct power to simply commandeer the huge Bonneville salmon budget and redirect it toward endangered species priorities. It is amusing to imagine a kind of endangered salmon poker game, in which threats by the National Marine Fisheries Service to shut down economic activities that nominally fall under their jurisdiction are issued in order to negotiate more influence over the Bonneville salmon budget. But these threats would also have to be gauged to stop short of provoking too many lawsuits or a call for intercession by the endangered species committee. In fact, present changes in the balance of power in the complex institutional network managing Columbia Basin salmon restoration are occurring very slowly.

Postscript: Columbia Basin Salmon and the Endangered Species Act

This chapter has provided an account of the odd circumstances surrounding the Endangered Species Act recovery effort for Columbia Basin salmon. Hopefully the story is scientifically interesting—most investigations of complex ecological systems are.

Because the stakes are so high, the story is also important. The stakes are high from the perspectives of biology, economics, and policy. Biologically, some salmon extinctions have already taken place in this ecosystem, and more are imminent. Economically, the investments in the recovery attempt are enormous, and seem likely to grow. And from a policy perspective, the Columbia Basin may serve as a proving ground for several subtle ideas, most notable among these being the concept of "evolutionarily significant unit" as a basic population unit to be protected under the Endangered Species Act.

Notwithstanding the interest and importance of the story, in these terms, the story does not provide a general window into the usual workings of the Endangered Species Act. The forces behind many of the odd circumstances surrounding the Endangered Species Act recovery effort for Columbia Basin salmon have to do mostly with money—huge amounts of money, that could potentially be mobilized for salmon management and salmon restoration. The Endangered Species Act does not mandate such budgets. Indeed the Columbia Basin salmon budget did not originate under Endangered Species Act actions; and authority of the Endangered Species Act does not control the way the preponderance of the salmon budget has been spent, so far. Very simply, the money, and political interest, was there before the Endangered Species

Act applied; and the money, and the brute fact of continuing salmon decline, has governed much of the way the story has unfolded. In this respect, the Columbia Basin salmon story has more in common with the institutional dynamics of a very small number of other, unusual, big-budget environmental programs, such as Superfund, and much less in common with the large number of usual Endangered Species Act recovery programs which actually operate on a shoestring and draw little national attention.

Part III

Reform

9 A Public Health Model for Species Preservation

FREDERIC A. MORRIS

When people approach problems of public policy, they often bring with them a distinctive conceptual framework. Such a framework, whether called a model, a paradigm or a vision, provides coherence by establishing a basic set of working assumptions that defines for the individual how the world works.[1] Because these assumptions are usually implicit, they are not ordinarily held open to examination. Instead, they provide an unacknowledged basis for the issues that are debated.[2] In devising policy to preserve species, many people seem to employ what might be labeled a medical model, in which endangered species are like individuals with a life-threatening illness or injury that requires emergency medical treatment. For example, Edward O. Wilson compares conservation biologists to "doctors in an emergency ward," who "look for quick diagnoses and procedures that can prolong the life of species until more leisurely remedial work is possible."[3]

The medical model undoubtedly captures much of the reality underlying species preservation. But as students of public policy have persuasively argued, exclusive reliance on a single model can obscure important elements of a problem. Use of a complementary framework can often illuminate them.[4] In this case, a logical alternative to the medical model is a model based on public health, in which species are like human populations that enjoy increased life expectancy through preventive measures that prevent untimely death.

Trends in human mortality suggest that the public health perspective at least deserves a look. From the beginning of the nineteenth century to the middle of the twentieth century, average life expectancies in Western nations rose from roughly 25 to 75 years, but much of this gain occurred before the main advances in modern medicine. The decisive factors seem to have been a combination of measures which prevented the major infectious diseases, such as improved nutrition sanitation and personal hygiene; direct efforts to reduce the spread of disease; and immunization. Even in recent years prevention seems

161

at least as important as treatment in extending life expectancy. For example, only one-third of the drop in general mortality in the developed world between the 1950s and the 1970s is attributable to causes of death considered to be treatable.[5] If prevention works for humans, might it not also work for species?

Human Mortality and Species Mortality

Viewing species preservation from either a medical perspective or a public health perspective begins with a common premise: namely, that the lives of species are in important respects analogous to lives of humans. The similarities are obvious but interesting.

First, like humans, all species are mortal. Extinction is as inevitable and irreversible as death. Of five to 50 billion species that have existed in the history of life on earth, probably no more than 10 to 40 million currently exist. Thus only about one tenth of one percent of all species which have ever lived are still alive.[6] By way of comparison, as of 1995 about five percent of all humans who have ever lived were estimated to be living (5.7 billion living of 105 billion ever born).[7]

Second, like humans, species have definable life expectancies. "No species of complex life has existed for more than a small fraction of the history of life."[8] The fossil record indicates an average species life span on the order of one to four million years.[9] In an average year the background rate of extinction is on the order of 10 per year.

Third, like that of humans, the life expectancy of species varies over time, space and circumstance. Species have been subject to several rare but extremely deadly mass extinctions. The largest scale versions of these appear about once every 100 million years and kill off on the order of 65 percent of the then-living species.[10] Humans may be causing a mass extinction today, at least in certain locations. Wilson estimates that in tropical rain forests, humans have increased the extinction rate 1,000 to 10,000 times over the pre-human background rate and argues that "we are in the midst of one of the great extinction spasms of geological history."[11]

In summary, species mortality is in important respects like human mortality. We can no more eliminate extinction than we can eliminate death. However, just as we seek to reduce the number of premature deaths, we can attempt to reduce the incidence of premature extinction. In the case of humans, life expectancy has been dramatically extended over the past two centuries through a combination of public health measures to prevent illness and medical interventions to treat illness that cannot be prevented. In the case of species, the emphasis has been decidedly on the side of treatment.

The Medical Model of Species Preservation

The medical model for saving human lives provides emergency medical treatment to individuals with life-threatening illness or injury. As embodied in the Endangered Species Act (ESA),[12] the medical model for preserving species operates in a remarkably analogous fashion.

The statutory scheme begins with the duty of the Secretary of the Interior (through the U.S. Fish and Wildlife Service and the National Marine Fisheries Service) to identify species that are endangered (in danger of extinction throughout all or a significant portion of their range) or threatened (likely to become an endangered species in the foreseeable future).[13] Only such listed species qualify for protection. Thus the ESA is concerned exclusively with saving species that are in danger of dying or soon likely to be so.[14] Once a species is listed, the Secretary is required to prescribe a course of treatment in the form of a recovery plan.[15] Every species, defined to include any subspecies of fish, wildlife or plants and any distinct population of fish or wildlife that interbreeds[16] is an individual patient, each with its own recovery plan.

While undergoing treatment, species are protected from further injury through the prohibition on illegal take.[17] As defined in the statute, "take" means to harass, harm, pursue, hunt, shoot, wound, kill, trap, capture, collect, or to attempt any of the foregoing.[18] By regulation, "take" is defined also to include death or injury from significant habitat modification.[19] Under specified circumstances, the Secretary can issue a permit allowing "incidental take" where the applicant agrees to measures that minimize and mitigate the impacts through an approved Habitat Conservation Plan.[20] Federal agencies have the additional duties of carrying out programs for the conservation of listed species and ensuring that their actions are not likely to jeopardize the continued existence of listed species or destroy or adversely modify their habitat.[21]

If the course of treatment proves effective, the Secretary may downgrade a species condition from endangered to threatened ("downlisting") or remove it from the lists entirely ("delisting").[22] In the latter case, after thus discharging the patient from treatment, the Secretary is required to monitor the delisted species status for at least five years.[23] If during this monitoring period the Secretary discovers a significant risk to the well-being of the recovered species, he must promptly issue an emergency regulation to address the risk. Once the monitoring period ends, the species exits the system and as a healthy species is no longer the concern of the ESA.

Accomplishments and Limitations

Within its frame of reference, the ESA seems to have had some success in restoring the health or slowing the declined of imperiled species. As of January 31, 1999, 1195 U.S. species were listed as endangered or threatened, of which 518 have approved recovery plans.[24] According to the Fish and Wildlife Service, "nearly half of all species listed for a decade or more are now either stable or improving in status" and only seven such species "have been found to be extinct."[25] Within the next several years, the Fish and Wildlife Service plans to downlist or delist 20 to 25 species, including the peregrine falcon, the bald eagle and the gray wolf.[26]

At the same time, however, the medical model as implemented through the ESA has inherent limitations.

First, like a physician treating an individual patient, the ESA protects individual species, defined to include any subspecies of fish, wildlife or plants and any distinct population of fish or wildlife that interbreeds.[27] Focusing on species one at a time ignores the place of the species in the larger ecosystem, the relationships among species, and the habitat that supports them. In justification, conservationists have tended to assume that areas rich in one group of species, such as birds or mammals, will also be rich in others, such as plants and insects, and thus the efforts to preserve the habitat of the more readily surveyed species in an area will tend to protect many other species as well. In practice, the distribution of species may not overlap in this fashion.[28] Moreover, the habitat needs of species that do occupy the same ecosystem may differ. Actions that help conserve one species may undermine another.[29] Increasingly, conservation biologists have moved their focus from individual species to ecosystems.[30] As Stuart Pimm has put it, "No species exists in isolation, so no species can recover until all the other species to which it is dynamically linked (directly and indirectly) have also recovered."[31] But the ESA has not caught up.

Second, like an emergency room that accepts all comers, the ESA in principle renders all threatened and endangered species (except insect pests) equally deserving of treatment. Once listed, each species is entitled to all statutory protection without discrimination (except when a federal action is exempted by the "God Squad" from the requirement not to jeopardize a listed species).[32] From an environmental valuation perspective, it would seem clear in principle that not all species are created equal; each affords a distinct bundle of value.

Consider the framework for valuing resources which natural resource economists have created. It defines value based on the various forms of benefits that resources (including species) confer.[33] Sources of value derive from the consumptive uses of species, such as harvesting salmon for food or the western yew for medicine; non-consumptive uses of species, such as bird watching or catch-and-release fishing; the knowledge that others can use a species, such as tribal fishing for salmon; retention of the option to use species in the future, even if those uses are at present unknown, such as heretofore undiscovered medicinal or agricultural uses; knowledge that the species will be available for future generations, and thus can be enjoyed by them; knowledge that the species exists, independent of any present or future use, known or unknown; and the services provided by a species in supporting other species, including humans: butterflies that pollinate wildflowers, trees that provide food and shelter for songbirds, beetles that recycle wastes into nutrients.[34] Such ecosystem services may seem mundane, but are enormously important.[35] If all insects and other land-dwelling arthropods were to become extinct, humanity would likely follow in a few months.[36]

Given such diverse sources of value, it would be surprising if all species were valued equally. Empirical research is consistent with this intuition. Lay people tend to prefer large, familiar animals such as panthers, bald eagles or grizzly bears to spiders, snails or insects.[37] Conservation biologists also distinguish among species, in this case by virtue of the ecosystem services that they provide. As Wilson has put it, "there are little players and big players, and the biggest players of all are the keystone species," those whose removal from an ecosystem "causes a substantial part of the community to change drastically."[38] However, the keystone species are not necessarily big in either size or charisma, and may well include tiny invertebrates, algae and microorganisms.[39]

In practice, federal expenditures may tend to reflect the lay preference for large, familiar animals.[40] But the ESA establishes no statutory basis for allocating protection resources based on species value, however determined.

Nor does it provide any but the most limited basis for taking into account the cost of preservation efforts, public or private. In allocating medical care to humans, such even-handed treatment may be ethically required in principle though rare in practice.[41] In preserving species, the obvious inefficiencies in such an approach are much more difficult to justify.

Third, just as the medical system can treat only patients that seek care, the ESA protects only known species. A recent United Nations study estimates that worldwide approximately 1.75 million species are known to science and that on the order of 14 million species may actually exist.[42] In the United States, scientists have identified 100,000 or more native species, which again is likely to represent only a fraction of the actual total.[43] Protecting only species that have been identified ensures that many species will go unprotected. The sheer number of species is so vast that biologists can identify only a small fraction of those which are endangered or threatened. As a result, a great number of species inevitably become extinct before they are discovered, much less protected.[44]

Assuming a budget constraint for species preservation, those species that are identified are overprotected at the expense of those species that are not identified. From a psychological standpoint, this emphasis is understandable; in the realm of human health and safety, we readily expend almost any available resource in order to save the life of an identified individual in peril. In contrast to statistical lives, as Thomas Schelling has observed, "If we know the person, we care."[45] Aldo Leopold made the almost identical observation about the loss of a species: "We grieve only for what we know. The erasure of Silphium from western Dane County is no cause for grief if one knows it only as a name in a botany book."[46] As a guide for allocating species protection resources, this understandable emphasis seems misplaced.

Fourth and most fundamentally, the ESA protects only those which are endangered or threatened. It is remedial rather than preventive. Only listed species qualify for protection. The ESA is intended only to bring unhealthy species back from the brink of extinction, not to protect healthy species.[47] Experience in extending human mortality strongly suggests that an exclusive emphasis on treatment of the ill or injured is to forego significant opportunities in averting premature extinctions. Consider the following highlights from John Cairns's fascinating account of the history of human mortality.[48]

According to Cairns, during the first three million years or so of human existence, patterns of mortality changed very little. Except in times of pestilence or famine, average life expectancy has been on the order of 25 years.

Then at about the end of the eighteenth century, life expectancy began to climb upward, reaching 75 years or more in advanced Western nations by the mid-twentieth century. The causes of this increase are still not well understood, but a variety of factors appears to have been at work. Beginning in the eighteenth century, several of the basic conditions of life began to change. Innovations in agriculture and trade with the new world led to a more varied diet and presumably better nutrition. Improved building design eliminated the black rat and with it, Bubonic plague. As the replacement of wool with cotton clothing made clothes washing practical, washing of the person became more worthwhile. Except for immunization against smallpox, direct steps to contain the main cause of death—infectious disease—did not begin until the nineteenth century.

Establishing the basic truth that germs caused most mortality of the time and taking steps to prevent infection was a long and difficult process that was as much political as scientific. Each disease was ultimately conquered through combination of general improvement in living conditions, specific measures to prevent the spread of the disease, such as immunization, and treatment, in that sequence.

Declines in mortality for each disease have generally preceded the development of effective treatment. Tuberculosis is a case in point. The death rate from tuberculosis in England declined from nearly 400 per 100,000 in 1850 to zero by 1970, with a similar decline in the United States. Yet immunization was never widely adopted in either country and no really effective treatment became available until the 1950s. "Cross-sectional" data is similarly suggestive. "If we ask what factors are associated with high life expectancy in the different nations of the world, it turns out not to be the numbers of doctors or hospital beds for every 10,000 in the population, but things like the provision of a clean water supply and the level of literacy."[49]

A Public Health Model for Species Preservation

Medicine deals with individuals through treatment of disease and injury. Public health deals with population through prevention of disease and injury. Both have been powerful factors in extending human life spans in the past two centuries. A public health model for species preservation would complement current medical models by seeking to improve species health in the aggregate and before species are endangered or threatened with extinction. What might such a model look like in practice?

First, the model would recognize the types of human activity that are believed to endanger previously healthy species: "habitat destruction or degradation, the introduction of invasive non-native species, pollution, and over-harvesting of wild species."[50] Of these, the latter three can be addressed by conventional environmental and fish and wildlife regulation. Addressing the first and likely most important factor underpins the fundamental approach of the public health model: preserving species health by protecting the habitats and ecosystems on which healthy species depend.

Second, the model would be appropriately humble about the extent to which one can manage ecosystems for the preservation of particular species. Recent assessments have criticized many habitat conservation plans prepared under the ESA as lacking the scientific theory and empirical data necessary to identify steps that would protect the endangered species of concern.[51] This criticism seems fair enough, but applies with equal force to recovery plans developed by the Fish and Wildlife Service and other government agencies. Our understanding of how to "treat" endangered species to prevent their extinction is at a stage of development comparable to that of medicine before the major discoveries of the twentieth century.

Third, therefore, the public health model would focus on the preservation of healthy habitats and ecosystems generally rather than targeting specific species for individualized care. And just as many of the early public health measures were enabling and voluntary rather then coercive, so too are many promising steps to protect ecosystems. They emphasize steps that encourage land management that supports healthy ecosystems.

Consolidation of public land holdings

For example, in a recent transaction, Plum Creek Timber exchanged more than 62,000 acres of its land in west-central Washington for 16,500 acres of national forest land. Like other similar deals, the exchange eliminates the checkerboard pattern of land ownership created by nineteenth century land grants to the railroads. In this case, the land obtained from Plum Creek includes old growth and other woodlands adjacent to the pristine Alpine Lakes Wilderness.[52]

Establishment of conservation easements

For example, the New England Forestry Foundation, a private non-profit group, recently bought the development rights to over 750,000 acres of Maine woods as a conservation easement from the Pingree family. Limited logging and recreational use will continue on the land, which includes more than 2,000 miles of river and stream shoreline, more than 85 lakes and ponds, and nesting areas for bald eagles and peregrine falcons.[53]

Placement of land in conservation trusts

For example, the Nature Conservancy recently purchased outright 185,000 acres of remote Maine wilderness from International Paper Company. The two tracts involved include about 40 miles along the Upper St. John River and provide habitat for deer, bears, osprey, great herons and a variety of rare plants including the Furbish lousewort, a wild snap dragon that is unique to the area.[54]

Hybrid strategies

For example, the Conservation Fund recently bought almost 300,000 acres of forests, river frontage, lakes and wetlands in New York's Adirondack region, Vermont, and New Hampshire from Champion International Company. Acting as intermediary, the Conservation Fund will, at closing, transfer title of various tracts to a combination of state governments and private investors. The three states will own the most fragile and unspoiled areas, while private investors will obtain the remainder subject to easements guaranteeing public access for recreation and allowing environmentally sensitive logging.[55]

Conclusion

"Endangered means there's still time!" So reads the motto of the (quite informative) endangered species home page of the U.S. Fish and Wildlife Service. However admirable this impulse to make lemonade with the available lemons, delaying protection until a species becomes endangered invites inefficiency. In human terms, this approach is the equivalent of foregoing public health measures and preventive medical care, deferring treatment until the patient becomes critically ill and thus requires intensive care or exotic life support systems, at predictably huge cost. Or to use another analogy, the practice is like triage in reverse, in which care is lavished on those least likely to survive. In bringing human life expectancy to its current levels in developed countries, prevention rather than treatment has played the decisive role.[56] It would be surprising if species preservation could not benefit by balancing Wilson's emergency room with the ecological equivalents of public health measures and preventive care.

Notes

1   See, for example, Thomas Sowell, A Conflict of Visions (New York: William Morrow, 1987); Graham T. Allison, Essence of Decision (Boston: Little, Brown, 1971); and John D. Steinbruner, The Cybernetic Theory of Decision (Princeton, NJ: Princeton University Press, 1974).

2   Robert F. Coulam, Illusions of Choice (Princeton, NJ: Princeton University Press, 1977), 11.

3   Edward O. Wilson, The Diversity of Life (Cambridge, MA: Harvard University Press, 1992), 228.

4   See especially Allison, Essence of Decision.

5   John Cairns, Matters of Life and Death (Princeton, NJ: Princeton University Press, 1997), Chapter 1, "A History of Mortality."

6   David M. Raup, Extinction: Bad Genes or Bad Luck? (New York: W.W. Norton, 1991), 3.

7   "How Many People Have Ever Lived on Earth," Population Reference Bureau, http://www.prb.org/prb/news/answers/everlive.htm, from Population Today (February 1995).

8   Raup, Extinction, 181.

9   Raup, Extinction, 108 (background rate of one extinction per four million years); Wilson, Diversity of Life, 280 (background rate of one extinction per one million years)

10 Raup, Extinction, 84-85.

11 Wilson, Diversity of Life, 280.

12 16 U.S.C. 1531-1544.

13 16 U.S.C. 1533.

14 See, for example, the statutory definition of conservation, 16 U.S.C. 1532 (3) (methods and procedures which are necessary to bring any endangered species or threatened species to the point at which the measures provided pursuant to the ESA are no longer necessary).

15 16 U.S.C. 1533 (f).

16 16 U.S.C. 1532 (16).

17 16 U.S.C. 1538.

18 16 U.S.C. 1532.

19 50 C.F.R. 17.3; Babbitt v. Sweet Home Chapter of Communities for a Great Oregon, 15 S. Ct. 2407 (1995) (upholding rule defining harm to include habitat modification).

20 16 U.S.C. 1539 (a).

21 16 U.S.C. 1536.

22   16 U.S.C. 1533 (c).

23   16 U.S.C. 1533 (g).

24   U.S. Fish and Wildlife Service, Box Score, Endangered Species, http://www.fws.gov/r9endspp/boxscore.html.

25   U.S. Fish and Wildlife Service, News Release, "Nation Marks 25 Years of Endangered Species Protection," December 23, 1998, http://www.fws.gov/r9extaff/25th.html.

26   U.S. Fish and Wildlife Service, News Release, "Babbitt Announces New Policy and Plans to 'Delist' Endangered Species," May 6, 1998, http://www.fws.gov/r9extaff/delstvnt.html.

27   16 U.S.C. 1532 (16).

28   William K. Stevens, "Study Undercuts Beliefs on Preserving Species," The New York Times (September 28, 1993).

29   See Lorin L. Hicks, "Plum Creek's Cascades Habitat Conservation Plan: A Corporate Approach to Ecosystem Management, Endangered Species Update (July/August 1997).

30   Wilson, Diversity of Life, 283.

31   Stuart L. Pimm, The Balance of Nature? (Chicago: University of Chicago Press, 1991), 371 (emphasis in original).

32   16 U.S.C. 1536.

33   See, for example, A. Myrick Freeman III, The Measurement of Environmental and Resource Values: Theory and Methods (Washington, D.C.: Resources for the Future, 1993).

34   Bruce A. Stein and Stephanie R. Flack, "Conservation Priorities: The State of U.S. Plants and Animals," Environment (May 1997): 6, 39.

35   Edward O. Wilson, The Diversity of Life (Cambridge, MA: Harvard University Press, 1992), 308.

36   Ibid., 133.

37   Don L. Coursey, "The Revealed Demand for a Public Good: Evidence From Endangered and Threatened Species," New York University Environmental Law Journal (forthcoming).

38   Wilson, Diversity of Life, 164.

39   Ibid., 309.

40   Coursey, "Revealed Demand for a Public Good."

41   See Guido Calabresi and Philip Bobbit, Tragic Choices (New York: W.W. Norton, 1978).

42   V.H. Heywood, ed., Global Biodiversity Assessment (Cambridge, U.K.: Cambridge University Press, 1995), cited in Stein and Flack, "Conservation Priorities," 8.

43   T. Eisner, J. Lubchenco, E.O. Wilson, D.S. Wilcove, and M.J. Bean, "Building a Scientifically Sound Policy for Protecting Endangered Species," Science (September 1, 1995): 1231-32, cited in Stein and Flack, "Conservation Priorities," 8.

44   Edward O. Wilson, "Is Humanity Suicidal?," The New York Times Magazine (May 30, 1993).

45   Thomas C. Schelling, Choice and Consequence (Cambridge, MA: Harvard University Press, 1984), 115.

46   Aldo Leopold, A Sand County Almanac (New York: Oxford University Press, 1989), 48.

47   See, for example, the statutory definition of conservation, 16 U.S.C. 1532 (3) (methods and procedures which are necessary to bring any endangered species or threatened species to the point at which the measures provided pursuant to the ESA are no longer necessary).

48   Cairns, Matters of Life and Death

49   Ibid., 36.

50   Stein and Flack, "Conservation Priorities," 10.

51   "Many Habitat Conservation Plans Found to Lack Key Data," The New York Times, December 23, 1997.

52 Editorial, "Transfer Plum Creek Lands with Eyes Open," The Seattle Times, April 20, 1998; "Congress' Land Swap Will Be First of Many, Conservationists Fear," The Seattle Times, November 1, 1998.
53 "Deal Protects Maine Woods from Development," The New York Times, March 4, 1999.
54 "Nature Conservancy Buys Maine Forest Tract," The New York Times, December 16, 1998.
55 "$76 Million Deal to Save Woods and Wetlands," The New York Times, December 10, 1998.
56 Cairns, Matters of Life and Death.

10 Balancing Business Interests and Endangered Species Protection

ANDREW J. HOFFMAN,
MAX H. BAZERMAN and
STEVEN L. YAFFEE

If you ask most Americans what they know about the Endangered Species Act (ESA), they will likely respond, "the spotted owl." This Pacific Northwest controversy epitomizes the conflict between jobs and the environment that the ESA has come to symbolize. To protect the spotted owl, large tracts of federal lands were withheld from logging, the supply of raw timber decreased, mill capacity was eliminated, logging jobs were lost, and prices increased. As this example illustrates, endangered species protection can alter local, regional and national economies. It also shows the kind of win-lose negotiations that typify ESA debates. Each side in the debate sees beating the other as the way to achieve its goals. Environmentalists want a better environment and are willing to sacrifice economic development toward that end. Development interests want economic growth and consider it unacceptable to forfeit jobs or economic prosperity for species protection.

As species protection is weakened, we move toward satisfying development interests at the expense of environmental interests. As species protection is strengthened, we move toward satisfying environmental interests at the expense of development interests. Undoubtedly, such a tug-of-war debate will always persist, but we argue that there are opportunities to expand the scope of debate, finding solutions that will improve the potential outcome simultaneously for both environmental and development interests.

In the managerial negotiations literature, scholars used to argue over whether to follow a win-lose philosophy or a win-win philosophy.[1] But more recent formulations argue that either is costly. Rather, rational negotiators now think about how to first create a larger pie and then claim a significant portion

of that pie, subject to concerns for fairness and the ongoing negotiation relationship.[2] But environmentalists and developers are still trapped in win-lose
debates. While political debates have fueled the dichotomy between environmentalists and development interests, we see the need for a balanced perspective to manage the two sets of concerns simultaneously.

In this article, we begin with an overview of the ESA and its surrounding controversies. We then argue that, when viewed from a broad economic
perspective, the benefits derived from nature can, under certain circumstances,
create mutual gain solutions for both economic and environmental interests.
It becomes clear that it is not the objectives of the Endangered Species Act
that cause economic dilemmas but its implementation. To that end, we offer
practical ways to improve ESA implementation.

The ESA and Controversy

In species protection debates, public opinion is often formed by anecdotes
rather than by the substance or objectives of legislation. The attention that the
ESA garners centers on costs to individual landowners and ignores the aggregate economy. For example, Ben Cone, a forester in North Carolina, shifted
from a 60-year tradition of sustainable forest management to clear-cutting
when he feared finding the endangered red-cockaded woodpecker on his property.[3] Clearly, this is not the solution that the ESA intended. But this kind of
image captures national attention and comes to symbolize ESA outcomes. In
reality, it was not the act's implementation that caused Cone's actions but
rather his misperceptions, which precipitated a hasty reaction. Only after the
story became a touchstone for ESA critics was it revealed that endangered
species considerations affected only 15 percent of Cone's land. He was free to
continue thinning trees on the remaining land. Furthermore, the Fish and Wildlife Service (FWS) repeatedly offered Cone habitat conservation proposals,
insulating him from future ESA reponsibilities, but he refused to cooperate,
fearing further economic loss.[4] Cone's fear of the complete devaluation of his
assets led him toward a radical protective strategy.

To understand such controversies, we must first understand the ESA. In
1973, the ESA was created to protect endangered or threatened species and
restore them to a secure status in the wild.[5] It is administered by the FWS
(Department of Interior) for land-based species and the National Marine Fisheries Service (NMFS, Department of Commerce) for marine species. Each

agency maintains a list of plants and animals considered worthy of protection under the act. Species listed as "endangered" are at risk of extinction throughout all or a significant portion of their range. Those "threatened" are likely to become endangered in the foreseeable future. Once a species is listed, the act forbids its import, export or interstate or foreign sale. Further, it becomes illegal to kill, harass, possess or remove the protected species from the wild ("taking" a species). The agencies draft recovery plans to ensure the species' long-term survival. Most important is Section 7 of the ESA, which requires all federal agencies to review their own actions and those they fund or permit to ensure that they do not jeopardize any listed species or destroy or modify critical habitat. Section 7 is administered through an interagency consultation process, in which the FWS or NMFS gives biological opinions to development and permitting agencies on proposed action.

Of the 781 domestic species for which the FWS was responsible as of May 1993, the majority lived on private land (see Figure 1).[6] Although no court has ever found that operation of the ESA has taken private property in violation of the Fifth Amendment, the costs associated with endangered species protection are real, at times resulting in significant economic impacts at the local and regional level.[7] Economic effects are due to: (1) delays from providing permits and petitioning, (2) alterations to development plans to accommodate endangered species protection, and (3) in the most extreme cases, job loss due to endangered species restrictions. The last category is the most visible, but all three incur economic costs to private developers.

The FWS is attempting to minimize these impacts by offering private landowners a flexible compliance option. To balance the objectives of species protection and economic development, Section 10 of the ESA allows private landowners to formulate habitat con-

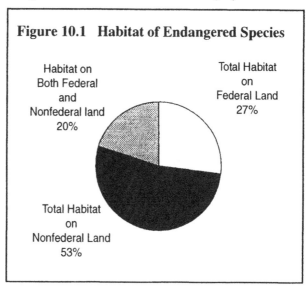

Figure 10.1 Habitat of Endangered Species

Habitat on Both Federal and Nonfederal land 20%

Total Habitat on Federal Land 27%

Total Habitat on Nonfederal Land 53%

servation plans (HCPs). Once the FWS approves an HCP, it gives landowners permits to "incidentally take" listed species during development, provided that the landowner takes certain steps to conserve that species. There are approximately 150 currently approved HCPs and more than 200 in development.[8]

Viewing the ESA from an Economic Perspective

Overstated Costs and Understated Benefits

To accurately assess the economic impact of the ESA, we must step back from individual cases and consider the broad economic context. In the aggregate, the picture is often quite different. Stephen Meyer, director of the Environmental Politics and Policy Center at Massachusetts Institute of Technology, studied the impact of endangered species listings on state economies and the agricultural sector. He found that, first, "endangered species listings have not depressed state economic development activity as measured by growth in construction employment and gross state product" and, second, the assertion that the Endangered Species Act has harmed the American farmer, hobbled agricultural production, and decimated the forest industry is baseless.[9] And the number of projects hindered by ESA implementation between 1987 and

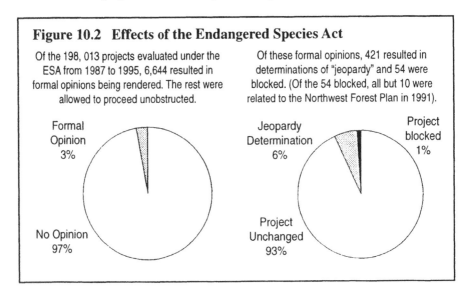

Figure 10.2 Effects of the Endangered Species Act

Of the 198, 013 projects evaluated under the ESA from 1987 to 1995, 6,644 resulted in formal opinions being rendered. The rest were allowed to proceed unobstructed.

Of these formal opinions, 421 resulted in determinations of "jeopardy" and 54 were blocked. (Of the 54 blocked, all but 10 were related to the Northwest Forest Plan in 1991).

Formal Opinion 3%

No Opinion 97%

Jeopardy Determination 6%

Project blocked 1%

Project Unchanged 93%

1995 is very small (see Figure 2).[10]

Even in the spotted owl case, the story has been one not of economic recession but rather of economic transition. While some logging companies were hurt by restrictions on timber supply from federal lands, windfall profits accrued to others that relied on timber from private lands and smaller, more efficient timber mills. As a result, in the ensuing debate, some had an interest in resisting and trying to delay this market transformation, while others quietly capitalized on the opportunity it created. Some in the forestry industry deftly placed blame for their economic circumstances on the ESA, while others successfully adapted to its goals by formulating HCPs (for example, Weyerhaeuser and Plum Creek) or implementing sustainable forestry techniques (for example, Collins Pine Co.).

The state of Oregon continues to be one of the U.S.'s largest producers of timber products. But, instead of relying on 300-year-old trees from public lands, the industry there is relying on wood from privately held, sustainable tree farms. Despite a cutback in timber use, most timber-dependent counties report rising property values, increasing timber wages and an overall increase in jobs. This is due to newer, leaner operations that have replaced the aging mills and workforce retraining for the region's growing high-tech industry.[11] Tom Powers, a University of Montana economist, recently reported that from 1988 to 1994, jobs in the region grew by 18 percent, contrary to dire predictions.[12]

Developers do not exist within a social, economic or environmental vacuum, free from the effects of their actions. An accurate appraisal of the costs of endangered species protection should also consider the external effects of individual development decisions. For example, consider a timber sale by the Bureau of Land Management. BLM in southern Oregon would allow increased logging, which the NMFS has determined would adversely affect the nearby Umpqua River, the centerpiece of a $36 million sports-fishing industry and the habitat for the threatened Umpqua cutthroat trout. Portions of the river are part of the Wild and Scenic River system, which supports rafting, sight-seeing, and, most economically important, fishing.[13] Traditional land-use decision-making has often been ineffective in forcing developers to consider the external costs of individual actions. Ironically, the decision-making processes of the ESA have provided interactions in which one economic interest can influence the actions of another.

Other tangible economic benefits are associated with endangered species protection. Some are direct, while others are more generalized benefits of ecosystem protection for which endangered species are useful indicators. Here we highlight five areas that illustrate the broader economic potential of endangered species protection: pharmaceutical products, advanced materials, food production, flood control and drinking water filtration, and recreation.

• Pharmaceutical Products. Some pharmaceutical companies view nature as the best available R&D operation. Plants and animals vary both genetically and chemically, and the subtle distinctions between species found in different regions can provide the needed component of a new medicine or industrial product. After millions of years of evolution, adaptation and diversification, organisms have fine-tuned antibiologicals and other compounds that are effective for their existence and could help ours. Nature has already done the testing; labs can replicate it only at high cost and still not match the number of generations of product variability that evolution has provided. Hence it is more cost-effective to look for new products with benefits to humans in nature than in the artificial, costly lab environment. Digitalis, derived from the purple foxglove, saves the lives of three million heart disease sufferers in the United States per year.[14] The ancient horseshoe crab has a blood-clotting system that produces proteins for detecting gram negative sepsis, a potentially life-threatening bacteria affecting more than 10,000 people annually.[15] Taxol, a promising treatment for ovarian and breast cancer (which kills approximately 40,000 women per year), comes from the bark of the Pacific yew tree, found primarily in endangered ecosystems of the Pacific Northwest.[16] The rosy periwinkle, a native of a seriously endangered habitat in Madagascar, provides a critical component in the treatment of childhood leukemia and Hodgkins disease.[17] The nearly extinct Houston toad produces alkaloids that may prevent heart attacks and an anesthetic more powerful than morphine.[18] The National Cancer Institute is now studying four plant compounds that protect against the replication of the HIV-1 and HIV-2 viruses. One is derived from the leaves and twigs of a tree in the Malaysian rain forest, and the other comes from a tropical vine in the rain forest of Cameroon.[19]

Between 25 percent and 40 percent of all prescriptions in the United States are based on substances derived from natural sources. Fewer than 10 percent of these compounds can be synthesized economically. The World Health Organization estimates that 80 percent of global health problems are treated by plant-based medicines. However, only about five percent of the world's known plant species have ever been investigated for pharmaceutical properties.[20] Those with no apparent utility today may reveal their hidden potential tomorrow. Beyond the simple respect for diverse life forms, prudence and responsible management would dictate the protection of species for which we can find no current direct use.

So valuable are the potential medicinal benefits that pharmaceutical companies are investing in biological diversity protection. For example, in 1991, a Costa Rican biological diversity organization called Instituto National de Biodiversidad (INBio) agreed to catalogue all plants and animals in Costa Rica. In exchange for the right to screen the results of this "chemical prospecting," Merck pays INBio $1 million up front and royalties on any drug developments; 10 percent of the initial fee and 50 percent of the royalties are used for conservation and biological diversity protection through an arrangement with the Costa Rican government.[21]

In another example, Shaman Pharmaceuticals of San Francisco, California, sends medical anthropologists to work with indigenous peoples of Central and South America, Africa and Southeast Asia to identify plants used for medicinal purposes. In an industry where speed to market can mean success or failure through the control of crucial patent rights, Shaman foresees that this targeting will help it bring drugs to market in seven to eight years, compared with the industry average of ten to 12 years. With the blessing of the Food and Drug Administration, the company is running two drugs through clinical trials, one that fights respiratory syncytial virus and another that shows promise against drug-resistant herpes.[22]

Advanced Materials

Materials made from plants and plant by-products could challenge the foundations of the petrochemical and composites industries. For example, biopolymers, which are stronger and more lightweight and biodegradable than synthetics, are derived from microbial systems, extracted from higher organisms such as plants, or synthesized chemically from basic biological building blocks. A wide range of emerging applications includes medical materials, packaging, cosmetics, food additives, clothing fabrics, water treatment chemicals, industrial plastics, absorbents, biosensors and even data storage elements.[23] As applications and production techniques expand, so too will the search for new sources of biological raw materials. As in the case of pharmaceuticals, most of the available plant feedstocks have yet to be investigated.

Food Production

Genetic diversity is critical to the strength and continued production of plant and animal stocks. Crop production and fish supply need diversity to maintain strains that resist new diseases, predators and natural disruptions. This diversity is best maintained naturally. For example, a National Research Council report states that salmon hatcheries, once thought to be key to survival, are pushing many naturally spawning salmon species to extinction by inadequately maintaining the unique biological traits of hundreds of salmon varieties that eventually could become endangered.[24] Scientific researchers have confirmed that increasing the number of species improves an ecosystem's productivity.[25]

Monocultures drive the gene pool toward increasing homogeneity through inbreeding. The economic side effects are tangible. In 1978, 15 percent of the U.S. corn production was destroyed by Southern leaf blight, with losses estimated at $1 billion. Seed producers were able to limit the damage by introducing new strains of corn that were less vulnerable to the blight. One, the endangered Mexican wild corn, is immune to a serious agricultural viral corn disease. Furthermore, through cross-fertilization, new types of strains can be created as well. For example, crossing corn with an endangered grass from Mexico produced a corn strain with increased resistance to Northern leaf blight.[26]

Flood Control and Drinking Water Filtration

Habitat destruction can contribute to increased flooding and increasing demands on drinking water purification. Much flooding in the Mississippi River has been attributed to the elimination of vital wetlands, the straightening of river courses, and the construction of extensive levees. In response to the 1993 floods that killed 50, left 70,000 homeless, and caused farm and property losses in excess of $10 billion, researchers and the government are beginning to realize that reserving bottom land for wetland conservation is more cost-effective in controlling floods. Thus far, federal expenditures of nearly $250 million have been allocated to buy more than 8,000 bottom-land homes from Midwesterners willing to move.[27] At the same time, the government has chosen not to reinforce or rebuild levees in some less populated areas to allow wetlands to re-form. Across the country, the U.S. Army Corps of Engineers is returning altered and straightened rivers to their original, meandering courses.

Wetlands act as purification and detoxification systems for aquatic environments. As such, endangered species can signal when ecosystems are in crisis, much like the canary in the coal mine. For example, the threatened Ozark cavefish is an indicator of water quality in the region; efforts to protect the cavefish also provide a valuable monitoring system for protecting the water supply.[28]

Recreation

Economic and social demographics are altering land-use demands. The needs and desires of an increasingly urban and environmentally concerned population are supplanting the traditional interests of logging, mining and grazing. The 1990 census showed that the West (the location of nearly all BLM and much of Forest Service land) has become nearly as urban as the Northeast, with more than 83 percent of its residents living in cities. In Idaho, where 60.6 percent of the land is federally owned, the state commerce department estimated that tourism returned $1.4 billion to the state's economy in 1989—slightly more than the $1 billion generated by the state's livestock and mining industries combined.[29]

Currently, 50 million anglers drive a $69.4 billion-a-year economy and are responsible for millions of jobs in the United States.[30] Nationwide, their numbers have increased 11 percent from 1985 to 1991. The number of hunters has similarly increased three percent, with a corresponding increase in expenditures of seven percent to $12 billion.[31] Texas draws more hunters than any other state, generating $1 billion in annual income. Of this, 39 percent accrues to private landowners; the rest goes to restaurants, motels, and equipment suppliers.[32] And the number of "nonconsumptive" participants (hikers, birders, and so on) increased by 10 percent from 1985 to 1991. Overall, Department of Commerce data reveal that more than 108 million Americans (nearly two of every five) participated in a wildlife-related activity in 1991.[33] Leading the list, birding has become one of North America's fastest-growing hobbies, with enthusiasts spending $18 billion a year on travel and equipment.[34]

Some corporations and landowners have capitalized on this trend. For example, International Paper has implemented a fee-based recreation program in its commercial forests in Texas, Louisiana and Arkansas. The program charges hunters for access and leases small tracts of land on which families can park their motor homes and enjoy the woods. After three years, the company's revenues from the program have tripled, growing to 25 percent of its total profits from the area. Deseret Land and Livestock in south Texas pursued a similar strategy when its cattle ranch fell on hard times. By charging fees, the company now makes 60 percent of its income from hunters and nature lovers.[35]

In each case, the focus of the land value shifted from extraction to natural beauty and a balanced ecosystem. This shift, and the reality that 73 percent of sportsmen consider themselves to be conservationists, has led the country's environmental and conservation groups, such as the Sierra Club and the National Audubon Society, to form coalitions with hunting and sporting groups.[36] Constituting a powerful economic and political interest block, many sportsmen now oppose the efforts of logging, mining and oil interests to release federal lands to state control for fear that they will be sold and lost to sporting interests.[37]

Cities and states are also tying economic prosperity to ecosystem protection. Sauk Prairie, Wisconsin, became a steward of the American bald eagle. By attracting tourists with events like Bald Eagle Days, the town reaps $1 million annually into its economy. Louisiana has identified the link between restoration of alligator populations for viewing and carefully controlled hunting and the state's economy.[38] In New Jersey, The Nature Conservancy acquired 3,257 acres of primeval river, pine and oak forest, and abandoned salt mines near the state's southern edge in 1994. It plans to create a wildlife sanctuary that the local community expects will attract bird-watchers and hikers. The Rio Grande Valley Birding Festival in Harlingen, Texas, attracted approximately 1,500 people in 1995, representing 41 states and providing an estimated $1.6 million for the five-day event; 465 species of birds were sighted, including 34 species not found elsewhere in the United States.[39]

Nonmarket Value

Not all the value of endangered species is tangible. For example, economists have priced the annual (nonmarket) benefits of spotted-owl protection in excess of $1 billion, which represents the popularity of endangered species protection among the U.S. public.[40] In a recent survey, 42 percent of Americans believed that the Endangered Species Act does not go far enough, and 33 percent said it strikes about the right balance, whereas only 22 percent said it goes too far.[41] In the same survey, 63 percent opposed any reduction in protecting endangered species; 59 percent opposed the expansion of logging, mining, and ranching on public land; and 67 percent were against opening the Arctic National Wildlife Refuge to gas and oil exploration.[42]

Natural Capital and Economic Transitions

We are not arguing that economics should be the sole criterion for determining the merit of endangered species protection. Clearly, the economic costs of protection are often overstated, and the direct and indirect economic benefits are often understated. Indeed, when viewed more broadly, environmental protection is an important component of economic systems, both in providing natural capital and in inducing economic transitions that promote efficiency and productivity over the long term.

The Role of Natural Capital

In building the natural resource base of democracy in the United States, Thomas Jefferson noted, "The greatest service which can be rendered any country is to add a useful plant to its culture, especially a bread grain."[43] Now, just as in Jefferson's time, we need to invest in natural capital to maintain a sustainable economy for the long term.

It is inconsistent to argue that we are morally obligated to ensure that future generations are not burdened with massive debt and then not ensure a sound resource base and a stable living environment. Responsible economic foresight necessitates present day ecosystem management. As plants and animals become scarce, the costs of protecting them rise exponentially.

It is better to invest small amounts of resources and proactively avoid such catastrophes as the spotted-owl and salmon controversies. While the spotted owl case was a costly effort to protect an endangered species, it was also a mistake that could have been avoided, had the agencies and interest groups dealt with the underlying issues early and proactively.[44]

• *Economic Transitions.* Including natural capital in the conception of a healthy economy introduces the notion of environmental protection as necessary to economic management. Endangered species signal the need to make environmental, technical and economic corrections and indicate stresses to the natural system that often lead to problems in local economies and human health. For example, declining eagle populations in the 1960s signaled an ecosystem overburdened by DDT spraying. The overlapping declines of spotted owls, murrelets and Pacific salmon species point to declining water quality, affecting both fisheries and overall forest health.

Economic transitions are underway at all times. As consumer demands change, technologies advance and regulatory priorities evolve, certain industries face demise, while others rise to fill their place. For example, the typewriter industry was virtually eliminated by the computer, the compact disc replaced the phonograph album, and the dissolution of the Bell system wrought structural changes in the telecommunications industry. With changing federal forest management due to spotted-owl protection, price fluctuations have made steel studs an economically viable alternative to framing lumber in new-home construction and have stimulated a new, more sustainable market in engineered wood products.

The protection of endangered species promotes economic transitions designed to protect the natural resource base. By moving away from a purely extractive view of natural resources, it shifts us toward stewardship. Rather than using resource scarcity as a last-minute signal to stimulate rapid economic transitions, we should rely on distressed species as an early warning that gives more time for a balanced response. For example, the diminishing supply of large timber from old-growth forests signals that this resource will eventually be exhausted and that an economic transition may occur.

Negotiation Biases and Joint Gains

Any assessment of the economic implications of endangered species protection must include the long-term interests of diverse stakeholders to communicate economic transitions and develop alternative strategies consensually. Unfortunately, this is not occurring in policy development discourse. Most people have the common, unfortunate perspective that "what is good for the other side is bad for us" in terms of the economy and the environment. But, to the extent that environmental and economic interests weigh issues differently, we can find new opportunities by shifting our mind-sets.[45]

According to a 1995 poll, 69 percent of Americans believe that environmental protection and economic development can work together.[46] Some companies are following the trend. Carrier Corporation, a division of United Technologies, invested $500,000 to eliminate the toxic solvents for cleaning copper and aluminum parts in the manufacture of air conditioners. After one year, it had recouped $1.2 million in reduced manufacturing costs.[47] DuPont announced a $500 million capital improvement plan at three North and South Carolina chemical plants, which will reduce air emissions by 60 percent and increase production by 20 percent.[48]

A shift in mind-set is critical if the ESA is to enhance economic competitiveness rather than diminish it. It is a useful, but imperfect solution to an implicit dispute. As Howard Raiffa explains: "We must recognize that a lot of disputes are settled by hard-nosed, positional bargaining. Settled, yes. But efficiently settled? Often not...They quibble about sharing the pie and often fail to realize that perhaps the pie can be jointly enlarged...There may be another carefully crafted settlement that both [parties] might prefer to the settlement they actually achieved."[49] Moving beyond preconceptions is possible. For example:

• Riverfront Plaza, an outlet mall along the banks of the Kansas River in Lawrence, Kansas, was originally slated for construction in a bald eagle nesting area. Through a negotiated settlement, the city established permanently protected easement areas on both sides of the river to defend some of the best remaining habitat, planted replacement trees, and closed the outside walkway of the mall when most eagles are present. Subsequently, architects designed one-way windows for viewing the eagles, which attracted customers to the mall.
• In Cleveland, Ohio, the 1993 Independence Day fireworks threatened to harm a pair of nesting falcons. Various groups resolved potential conflicts through negotiations and produced an alternative fireworks plan. As a result, the newly hatched falcons became a spotlight attraction, benefiting the Tower City Center shopping mall and other downtown businesses.[50]
• A California developer proposed building a retail mall on the wetland habitat of the Sebastopol meadowfoam, a protected plant. After consultation with the Army Corps of Engineers and the FWS, the developer agreed to establish a new Sebastopol meadowfoam colony offsite and acquire and protect additional habitat with an existing natural population of the species.[51]

Under Sections 7 and 10 of the ESA, federal agencies can negotiate the provisions of their projects to ensure that they do not jeopardize endangered species and can expand this process to private landowners. HCPs are a way for companies to develop plans that serve the interests of the endangered species and the proposal. Many private landowners have used these plans to work with other stakeholders in finding optimal solutions.

Implementation of the ESA

An enhanced Endangered Species Act that will integrate economic and environmental interests must have three objectives: first, it must work within the market system to create individual incentives for protecting biological diversity; second, it must foster an inclusive regulatory program that incorporates the interests and needs of all affected parties; and third, it must evolve beyond the single-minded focus on individual species and consider the whole ecosystem. Relevant parties in the debate must acknowledge that the environment and the economy are intertwined.

To improve the implementation of the ESA, we propose: (1) the promotion of economic incentives, (2) a reduction in the uncertainty facing affected groups, (3) the allocation of adequate resources, (4) more stakeholder involvement in the ESA decision-making process, and (5) a move toward ecosystem based management.

Promote Economic Incentives

Other environmental programs, such as the Clean Air Act, utilize market incentives to achieve their goals. To make the ESA consistent with this, we should incorporate policies to harness the power of the marketplace so landowners and corporations find it in their interest to protect biological diversity based on properly adjusted prices. The policies include tax incentives (estate, property and income), special trust funds, transfer of critical habitat from private to public control and user fees on federal lands.

• Tax Code Reform. Currently, both estate and property taxes are calculated based on land's highest and best-use value, which usually involves development. The taxes are an incentive for landowners to (1) develop the land, (2) harvest the land's resources to pay the taxes, or (3) sell off parcels of land to pay the taxes, thereby breaking up biologically valuable properties. Estate tax reform would allow heirs to defer or avoid applicable estate taxes on inherited land in return for managing their land in ways that benefit endangered species. The agreement could be revocable, and the estate taxes would become due when heirs have stopped managing the land as agreed on. For example, a bill before the 104th U.S. Congress proposed easing inheritance taxes to give landowners incentives to create and maintain wildlife habitats.[52] Estate tax reform could also allow the estate (or heirs) to make tax-deductible gifts of land or an interest in land to a qualified organization.

Property tax reform could create credits for the cost of land management programs that benefit endangered species on private lands. In a move that has gained the support of both property rights advocates and environmentalists, the Texas legislature recently approved Proposition 11, a law that allows owners of agricultural land to convert it to wildlife management uses without losing valuable property tax exemptions.[53] Or an income tax deduction could allow for the costs of land improvement to enhance its value as an endangered species habitat.

Tax law could also establish a program of tradable permits in endangered species protection.[54] Based on a system for measuring the conservation value of land, increases or decreases could be measured in standardized units, for which the landowner would receive a credit. Any landowner wishing to decrease the conservation value of his or her land would do so by offsetting this decrease with credits gained by arranging an equivalent increase elsewhere or by purchasing those credits from another landowner.

• ESA Special Trust Funds. Two impediments to reestablishing endangered species are (1) building adequate local support and (2) providing enough funding for management of a particular species. Authorizing a species-specific trust fund with nonfederal cost-sharing requirements could relieve these impediments. Individual and corporate donors could contribute to the protection of particular species, as Exxon Corporation has worked with the National Fish and Wildlife Foundation to establish the international "Save the Tiger" fund. This technique engages private-sector and local interests in recovery of endangered species while also stimulating the local economy associated with species recovery.

An innovation grants program could promote and reward ecosystem-level partnership efforts. All nonprofit organizations and government agencies would be eligible for ecosystem management grants on a matching basis. Such a program would motivate competitive forces and provide flexible funding arrangements.

• Government Land Exchanges. In the few situations in which all or most of the development of a property is precluded because of the needs of an endangered species, a program could be devised to trade federal lands with low biological diversity value for private land with high biological diversity value, thereby shifting some ESA costs back to the government and reducing the burden on private landowners. A recently proposed swap involved $380 million in federally owned oil and gas fields and timberland in exchange for thousands of acres of old growth in the Headwaters Forest in California, currently owned by Maxxam Inc. Through such trades, the Department of the Interior can use its surplus land portfolio, including oil and gas subsurface leases, as assets in exchange for private-sector lands. By targeting economically valuable federal lands that lack biological diversity, the department can sell them to the highest bidder and use the money to benefit endangered species. Such a program should be for implementation, not as compensatory entitlement for private landowners.

A test of this concept is underway in the Umpqua River Basin, which extends from the crest of the Cascade Mountains to the Pacific Ocean. With funding from the National Fish and Wildlife Foundation, the timber industry and others, an interdisciplinary team of resource experts is analyzing fish and wildlife habitats to identify areas critical to the basin's long-term health. The team will then determine the feasibility of land exchanges between private owners and the government landowners in the area (such as the Bureau of Land Management, the Forest Service and the state and local counties) to protect vital areas.

User Fees for Natural Resources

Increased user fees for federal lands could be charged for hunting, fishing, hiking and camping. The Forest Service, by charging market value for national forest recreation, could collect as much as $6.6 billion per year. Extending this to lands that the other federal agencies manage could bring the total to $11 billion.[55] These fees could offset the tax burden for operating expenses and link users and land managers to ensure that managers provide the resources that users most want.

• The Pitfalls of "Takings" Legislation. Current proposals call for "takings" legislation to offset the loss of private land value. (Unlike the term's connotation as harmful to endangered species, "takings" refers to government control of private land.) We are concerned that providing a subsidy for takings would promote opportunism and excessive costs to state and federal treasuries. The complications are threefold. First, takings compensation is based on anticipated, not necessarily real, loss of value. Developers' estimates of what they can make on the land are not adequate measures for just compensation. Second, there are tremendous opportunities for speculation. If a parcel of land is a known habitat for an endangered species, a developer could obtain the property with the intention of extorting rewards at the expense of the federal or state government. Third, takings can often assign property rights to the wrong individual. If clear-cutting is the stated right of the logging industry, should loggers be compensated for not creating runoff that damages the downstream salmon fishery? If a developer chooses to fill in a wetland, should it be compensated for not destroying fish-breeding grounds, natural water-filtering capacity, or the ability of the river to absorb rising floodwaters?

Each complication affects sport fishermen and downstream municipal water plants and communities. Which party should be assigned the property right of a balanced ecosystem? How can the social costs of habitat destruction be included in development economic formulas? Takings legislation resolves neither issue, while market incentives offer an efficient solution to both.

Reduce Uncertainty Facing Affected Groups

The most problematic aspect of ESA controversies is the uncertainty that they generate for the landowner. The timber industry in the Northwest might have been relatively satisfied with less national forest land on which to log commercially if it had been guaranteed availability in perpetuity. Sawmills with millions of dollars in capital on the line cannot make wise investment decisions without knowing the long-term viability of their raw materials supply. Thus far, most encounters between the developer and the ESA have resulted in negotiated solutions. But the time that these solutions take and the uncertainty about whether the final agreement will be satisfactory and permanent is problematic. Current congressional indecision on the ESA increases uncertainty about the HCPs of such companies as Weyerhaeuser, Georgia-Pacific, the Scofield Corporation, and Simpson Timber. To cut funding would undermine their efforts, creating costly uncertainty, delaying corporate expenditures already allocated, and ultimately increasing overall costs.

At the same time, we know that information on species' needs, development impacts, and the most cost-effective protection methods will change over time. Landowner agreements such as HCPs could include provisions for ongoing monitoring, preferably with all parties' active involvement. We could establish such agreements for a fixed time period to provide investment certainty for the midterm (five to ten years) but not preclude efficient, effective solutions in the long term. Protection provisions included in an agreement should be conservative enough to allow for adaptive change. If monitoring indicates that a species can tolerate more disturbance, the landowner could expand development. If new information suggests that protection needs to be altered significantly and imposes increased costs, the public should share or largely underwrite the burden of that change.

Another way to reduce landowners' uncertainty is to streamline ESA review procedures where possible. We should review deadlines in place to make more timely decisions. We might consider small-scale blanket exemptions to specific provisions of the ESA (such as for small landowners) to facilitate decision-making and ease the burden on such landowners.

But the primary ways of ensuring more certainty are to (1) generate more information about species needs and ecosystems, (2) encourage collaborative problem-solving by all participants considering all available information, and (3) provide adequate resources for local, regional and federal implementation. These critical points correct market inefficiencies and involve the business community in species protection.

Allocate Adequate Resources for Implementation

Developing ecosystem management requires adequate funding and resources for generating the scientific and economic information essential to wise investment decisions. And, in resolving ESA disputes, high-quality information is needed to resolve conflicts. Developers must understand the regulatory consequences of various features of their land.

The National Biological Service now operates the GIS-Gap analysis program in 43 states. Gap analysis represents state-of-the-art inventory and landscape mapping to identify areas needing protection. The public will be able to learn about identified areas through interactive geographic information systems (although it might be necessary to withhold the identity of some parcels to discourage opportunistic collecting of endangered species).[56]

Several analysts have suggested that inadequate resources have led to delays and problems in the ESA's history.[57] In fiscal 1994, Congress appropriated $67.5 million for the FWS's endangered species program, of which only 20 percent was for consulting. On an absolute basis, this was only 0.5 percent of the total federal outlay on natural·resources and 1.5 percent of the budget for the Environmental Protection Agency. On a relative basis, this amount is out of proportion with the increased activities that the service is undertaking. Formal project opinions grew by 280 percent, and species listings increased by 37 percent (see Figure 3). By most accounts, "The endangered species program is severely short of money and overwhelmed by a backlog of hundreds of imperiled species—and by almost as many lawsuits demanding action to save them."[58]

It is economically irresponsible to create an endangered species protection program and then starve it of needed resources. An impoverished program is likely to lead to delays, uncertainties and impasses, which create uncertainty for business, which, in turn, cause more delays and cost overruns. Complete, credible data, coupled with more stakeholder interaction, require personnel who are trained and skilled in negotiation, communications and development processes.

Involve Stakeholders in Decision Making

Generated information must incorporate the perspectives of multiple stakeholders. Currently, recovery planning teams are composed almost exclusively of scientists. Science-based assessment of alternative conservation strategies is critical, but it is also important for affected interests to participate in recovery planning. Advisory boards of affected and interested groups can identify ways to minimize local impact and future impasses. Development proponents should understand the ramifications on natural systems and propose actions that are both scientifically and financially sound. Unless all parties find solutions that consider as much information as possible, impasses will remain.

The current process for granting federal protection to species requires no formal involvement of affected groups beyond an opportunity for public comment in the rule-making process. On one level, it seems appropriate to limit consideration of a species' status to scientific input and assessment. At the same time, it would be more efficient to consider the ramifications of federal listing earlier, allowing affected groups to act before listing is needed.

Through HCPs, public and private parties can interact and devise plans that are sensitive to local economies while protecting endangered species.[59] By learning from recently completed HCPs, we can improve the planning process and reconsider the level of public involvement and review, post-HCP monitoring, and legal standards to ensure that HCPs are effective ecologically

Figure 10.3   U.S. Fish and Wildlife Service Project Load

Species Listed

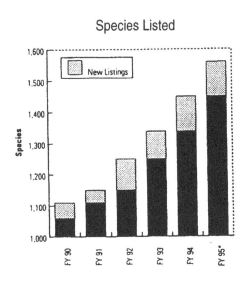

Development Projects Evaluated

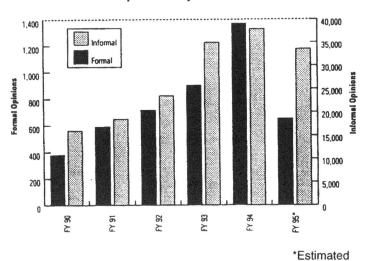

*Estimated

Source: Information provided by the National Fish and Wildlife
Foundation, B. Cairns, deputy director.

and economically.

Ultimately, an overarching federal mandate can help ensure that interested parties negotiate. Multiparty negotiation can function in an incentive structure that encourages parties to bargain in good faith and seek creative solutions. In the many negotiations already conducted under the ESA, it is clear that the absolute mandate to protect species helped motivate various public and private interests to simultaneously protect environmental and economic concerns.[60] Without incentives, integrated solutions are unlikely.

In many ways, this approach parallels that of other market-based mechanisms to pollution control, in which government standards set binding objectives but affected interests determine how to reach those standards. Having clear performance measures and flexibility will yield the most efficient, effective strategies for achieving economic and environmental objectives simultaneously.

Move Toward Ecosystem-Based Management

A new type of resource management, called ecosystem management, incorporates many themes: science-based decision-making, stakeholder involvement, articulation of social values, and long-term planning. Ecosystem management attempts to shift from a single-minded focus on individual species to a broad-based focus on regional resource management. Endangered species management is useful as an indicator of ecosystems in crisis, but the ultimate objective is a stable ecosystem. From an economic standpoint, healthy ecosystems are needed more than most individual species. But ecosystems are composed of assemblages of species and natural processes, overlaid by human communities. Hence it is necessary to protect species as components of ecosystems and as proxies for ecosystem integrity.

Early research on ecosystem-based approaches to resource management suggests that they may be appropriate for the future.[61] They are regional in scale, emphasize collaborative decision making by a full range of public and private interests, and seek to balance economic and environmental concerns. Their ability to focus public and private resources on shared problems and work through conflicts that have often led to impasse can yield substantial efficiencies for all parties.

One way to move toward an ecosystem-based approach might be to delegate aspects of ESA implementation to state and local officials.[62] Many states already have sensitive-species programs underway that might result in program efficiencies and more sensitive, local decision making. But other parties, including nongovernmental organizations, can play a role in consortia to protect valuable ecosystems. These consortia must have the capacity, motivation and authority to implement endangered species programs. Since enforcement requires the policing powers of a government unit, government must be one partner in a regional consortium.

Encouraging multi-state and other regional decision-making would also help facilitate ecosystem-level action. For example, the current ESA state-grants program could promote the regional consortia's ecosystem-level action with a provision to delegate program authority. Such a program could also introduce competition between states and consortia to promote innovation. Any program that delegates federal powers must be subject to strict performance criteria and ongoing monitoring. Providing ways for citizens to sue guarantees that such innovative approaches are monitored for effective implementation.

Ecosystem-based approaches to species management, underway in many places, are likely to represent the future of natural resource management in the United States. A recent University of Michigan study examined 105 situations in which individuals from both the private and public sectors used and lauded ecosystem-based approaches.[63] For example, the Georgia Conservancy has proposed a statewide watershed protection project centered on clusters of community-based groups in 15 major watersheds in Georgia, while the Conservation Fund has formed a voluntary land protection program along Georgia's Ebenezer Creek. In Maine, three large paper companies, Baskahegan, Champion International and Georgia Pacific, have banded together to form the Salmon Habitat and River Enhancement Project (SHARE) to protect the habitat of the Atlantic salmon. And landowners in southwest Florida are joining to voluntarily protect more than 3 million acres that make up the habitat for the endangered Florida panther. This project is anticipated to accomplish its goal at taxpayer savings of $1 billion. These kinds of locally based, public-private partnerships will move resource management debates from a reactive, crisis mode to a more proactive, deliberative community approach.

Conclusion

When first written, the ESA was intended as a policy of last resort, in which species deserving intensive care received protection. But our understanding of resource management, policy implementation and the interrelationship between the economy and the environment have evolved considerably. Now the ESA is part of a framework of laws, institutions and national capabilities that collectively promote sustainable societies, both economically and environmentally. Ultimately, the goal of endangered species protection represents the goal of the entire framework. Rather than pursuing environmental goals based on the fluctuations of "best available technology" or most practicable economic calculations, endangered species protection has the goal of maintaining valuable, productive ecosystems. By developing management plans that are guided by the objective of balancing local, regional and state economies with the health of the ecosystem on which they are based, the ESA seeks the end-point of all environmental objectives: economic and environmental sustainability.

Species protection is not only for ourselves but for future generations. As stewards, we can enhance the benefits of our actions, minimize the costs, limit the hidden externalities, maintain our natural capital, and avoid the precipitative effects of boom-and-bust economic transitions only if we promote improvements in the ESA process. One way to be more proactive is to move toward ecosystem-scale management that includes human populations while still providing a safety net for the most endangered organisms. By including the human population, the ESA process must become more inclusive and negotiations more creative. By taking a broad look at all aspects of this process economic, environmental and political—cooperative ecosystem management is the best way to foster joint gains in environmental protection and economic growth over the long term.

Acknowledgments

Reprinted with kind permission from "Balancing Business Interests and Endangered Species Protection" by Andrew Hoffman et al, Sloan Management Review, Fall 1997, pp. 59-72 by permission of publisher. Copyright 1997 by Sloan Management Review Association. All rights reserved.

The authors would like to gratefully acknowledge the financial support of the Henry and Munson Foundations and the National Fish and Wildlife Foundation. Special thanks also go to Francisco Benzoni, Grant Gund, Don Moore, and Jon Wilk for providing research support and to Amos Eno,

Barbara Cairns, and the anonymous reviewers from the U.S. Fish and Wildlife Service and Sloan Management Review who provided valuable feedback
and comments.

Notes

1   H. Cohen, *You Can Negotiate Anything* (Secaucus, New Jersey: Lyle Stuart, 1980); andR.
    Fischer and W. Ury, *Getting to Yes* (New York: Penguin Books, 1981).
2   H. Raffa, *The Art and Science of Negotiation* (Cambridge: Harvard University Press,
    1982);D. Lax and J. Sebenius, *The Manager as Negotiator* (New York: Free Press, 1986);
    and
    M. Bazerman and M. Neale, *Negotiating Rationally* (New York: Free Press, 1992).
3   J. Baden, "The Adverse Consequences of the ESA," *The Seattle Times*, 25 October 1995.
4   T. Bethell, "Species Logic," *The American Spectator*, volume 28, August 1995, pp. 20-22.
5   7 U.S.C. 136; 16 U.S.C. 460 et seq. (1973); as amended by P.L. 94325 (1976); P.L. 94-359
    (1976); P.L. 95-212 (1977); P.L. 95-632 (1978); PL 96-159 (1979); P.L. 97-304 (1982);
    P.L. 98-327 (1984); and P.L. 100-478 (1988).
6   U.S. General Accounting Office, *Endangered Species Act: Infirmation on Species Protec-
    tion on Nonfederal Lands* (Washington, D.C.: U.S. GAO, 1994) CRED-95-16.
7   Ibid.
8   U.S. Fish and Wildlife Service, *Facts about the Endangered Species Act* (Washington,
    D.C.: U.S. Department of the Interior, 1995).
9   S. Meyer, *Endangered Species Listings and State Economic Performance* (Cambridge,
    Massachusetts: MIT Project on Environmental Politics and Policy, working paper no. 4,
    1995); and
    S. Meyer, *The Economic Impact of the Endangered Species Act on the Agricultural Sector*
    (Cambridge, Massachusetts: MIT Project on Environmental Politics and Policy, working
    paper no. 5, 1995).
10 Data provided by B. Cairns, deputy director, National Fish and Wildlife Foundation, Wash-
    ington, D.C.
11 T. Egan, "Oregon, Foiling Forecasters, Thrives as It Protects Owls, *New York Times*, 11
    October 1994, p. 1.
12 "Economics and the Environment," *Greenline*, number 30, 4 January 1996, p. 1.
13 T. Egan, "Recriminations as Northwest Loggers Return," *New York Times*, 5 December
    1995, pp. 1, A13.
14 N. Myers, *The Sinking Ark* (Elmsford, New York- Pergamon Press, 1979), p. 71.
15 National Wildlife Federation, *Nature's Pharmacy: Human Life Depends on the Rich Di-
    versity of Life* (Washington, D.C.: National Wildlife Federation, 1994).
16 G. Kolata, "The Aura of a Miracle Fades from a Cancer Drug," *New York Times*, 7 No-
    vember 1993, p. Al.
17 N. Myers, *A Wealth of Wild Species* (Boulder, Colorado: Westview Press, 1983), p. 90.
18 B. Wagner, "Nature's Tropical Medical Chest," *U.S. News & World Report*, 1 November
    1993, p. 77; and
    E. Permisi, "Pharming Frogs," *Science News*, volume 142, 18 July 1992, pp. 40-42.
19 M. Grever, *Drug Discovery and Development from Natural Sources: The National Can-
    cer Institute Experience* (Washington, D.C.: U.S. House of Representatives, Committee
    on Merchant Marine and Fisheries, Subcommittee on Environment and Natural Resources,

9 November 1993).

20 Endangered Species Coalition, *The Endangered Species Act Protects U.S.* (Washington, D.C.: The Endangered Species Coalition, 1995).

21 T. Eisner, "Chemical Prospecting: A Global Imperative," *Proceedings of the American Philosophical Society*, volume 138, September 1994, pp. 385-392.

22 Information provided by S. Hall, Strategic Environmental Associates, Underwood, Washington; see also:
    "A Rare Species," *The Economist*, volume 334, 28 January 1995, p. 76.

23 D. Byrom, *Bionzaterials: Novel Materials from Biological Sources* (New York: Stockton Press, 1991).

24 G. Borg, "Salmon-Saving Program May Do Harm," *Chicago Tribune*, 9 November 1995, p. 16.

25 C. Yoon, "Ecosystem's Productivity Rises with Diversity of Its Species," *New York Times*, 5 March 1996, p. B8.

26 Endangered Species Coalition (1995).

27 B. Ayres, "Lessons from '93 Flood Help Soggy Midwest Now, *New York Times*, 24 May 1995, p. 14.

28 Endangered Species Coalition (1995).

29 "Cry for Preservation, Recreation Changing Public Policy," *Congressional Quarterly*, 3 August 199 1, pp. 2145-2151.

30 R. Boyle, "President Clinton Signs Order for Fishing Area Restoration," *Outdoor Life*, volume 196, 1995, p. 10.

31 U.S. Department of Commerce, *National Survey of Fishing, Hunting and Wildlife-Associated Recreation* (Washington, D.C.: U.S. Government Printing Office, 1991).

32 S. Pendleton, "Birds Get a Break in Texas with Land Conversion Law," *Christian Science Monitor*, 15 November 1995, p. 8.

33 U.S. Department of Commerce (1991).

34 Pendleton (1995).

33 J. Hood, "How Green Was My Balance Sheet," *Policy Review*, volume 74, Fall 1995, p. 80.

36 Times Mirror, *The Environmental Two Step*, Times Mirror Survey, 1995.

37 R. Lacayo, "This Land Is Whose Land?," *Time*, 23 October 1995, p. 68.

38 "Tourists Pour In," *Greenline*, number 6, 28 November 1995, p. 1.

39 Information provided by N. Miflar, Harlingen, Texas.

40 D. Hagen, J. Vincent, and P. Welle, "Benefits of Preserving Old Growth Forests and the Spotted Owl," *Contemporary Policy Issues*, volume 10, April 1992, pp. 13-26.

41 Times Mirror (1995).

42 Lacayo (1995).

43 U.S. Department of the Interior, *Why Save Endangered Species?* (Washington, D.C.: U.S. Department of the Interior, 1993).

44 S. Yaffee, *The Wisdom of the Spotted Owl: Policy Lessons for a New Century* (Washington, D.C.: Island Press, 1994).

45 M. Porter and C. van der Linde, "Green and Competitive: Ending the Stalemate," *Harvard Business Review*, volume 73, SeptemberOctober 1995, pp. 120-134.

46 Times Mirror (1995).

47 "Industrial Switch: Some Firms Reduce Pollution with Clean Manufacturing," *Wall Street Journal*. 4 December 1990, p. Al.

48 "DuPont to Spend Big to Cut Plant Pollution," *Engineering News Record*, 5 August 1991, p. 22.

49 H. Raiffa, "Post-Settlement Settlements," *Negotiation Journal*, volume 1, January 1985,

pp. 9-12.

50 Sierra Club Legal Defense Fund, "The Endangered Species Act Works - Success Stories" (Washington, D.C.: Sierra Club Legal Defense Fund, 1995).

51 U.S. General Accounting Office (1994).

52 H. Dellios, "Nature vs. Human Nature: Incentives May Be the Solution," *Chicago Tribune*, 26 June 1995, p. 1.

53 House Bill No. 1298 from the 72nd Legislature, Regular Session, 1991; see:Pendleton (1995).

54 H. Fischer and W. Hudson, eds., *Building Economic Incentives into the Endangered Species Act* (Washington, D.C.: Defenders of Wildlife, 1994).

55 R. O'Toole, "Incentives and Biodiversity" (Smithsonian Earth Day Conference on Biodiversity, speech, 22 April 1995.

56 National Biological Service, *National GAP Analysis Status Report: 1994 and 1995 Fiscal Years* (Washington, D.C.: National Biological Service, 1995).

57 National Research Council, *Science and the Endangered Species Act* (Washington, D.C.: National Academy Press, 1995), p. 84; and
F. Campbell, "The Appropriations History," in K.A. Kohm, ed., *Balancing on the Brink of Extinction: The Endangered Species Act and Lessons for the Future* (Washington, D.C.: Island Press, 1991), pp. 134-146.

58 J. Cushman, "Moratorium on Protecting Species Is Ended," *New York Times*, 21 May 1996, p. Al.

59 T. Beadey, *Habitat Conservation Planning. Endangered Species and Urban Growth* (Austin, Texas: University of Texas Press, 1994).

60 S. Yaffee and J. Wondolleck, *Negotiating Survival: An Assessment of the Potential Use of Alternate Dispute Resolution Techniques for Resolving Conflicts between Endangered Species and Development* (Ann Arbor, Michigan: University of Michigan, research report to the Administrative Conference of the United States, 1994).

61 S. Yaffee, A. Phillips, I. Frentz, P. Hardy, S. Maleki, and B. Thorpe, *Ecosystem Management in the United States: An Assessment of Current Experience* (Washington, D.C.: Island Press, 1996).

62 R. Kiefer, "Beyond the Boundary Line: Constructing a Law of Ecosystem Management," *University of Colorado Law Review,* volume 65, Spring 1994, p. 293.

63 Yaffee et al. (1996).

11 Fixing the Endangered Species Act

RANDAL O'TOOLE

The Endangered Species Act is a wonderfully idealistic piece of legislation that was apparently written by people who had absolutely no idea about how society works. The law's goals are so noble and uplifting that few could disagree with them. Yet the law's means for achieving those goals are doomed to failure.

The fundamental cause of species decline in the United States is that wildlife are a commons. Under British common law, wildlife inhabiting a piece of land were owned by the owner of that land. Landowners thus had an incentive to protect habitat for wildlife they considered desirable, and wildlife lovers had a tool to protect habitat for wildlife by buying land or paying landowners to protect habitat.

But early Americans considered wildlife ownership by landowners to be inegaletarian, and they changed British common law to hold that wildlife were owned by all the people in common. This was good for the people who didn't own land but not so good for the wildlife. If anyone owned wildlife, then anyone could, and did, shoot it. Owners of wildlife habitat were less likely to protect that habitat if they could not benefit from it. Common ownership also diminished the tools available to wildlife lovers.

A second major cause of species decline is a large variety of government subsidies that create incentives to destroy wildlife or wildlife habitat. These subsidies range from below-cost sales of resources from public lands to protective tariffs that prop up the Florida sugar industry to the detriment of Everglades-loving species.

Rather than deal with these fundamental problems, the authors of the Endangered Species Act chose to treat diminishing species as a moral issue. They embodied their ideals in a program that takes punitive measures against public land managers or private land owners whose land happens to be habitat for a threatened or endangered species. To avoid such punitive measures, the

199

landowners and managers sometimes rush to destroy the habitat for diminishing species of wildlife before someone declares that species to be threatened or endangered, demonstrating that poorly written laws often accomplish exactly the opposite of what their authors intended.

In short, the Endangered Species Act took a system of bad incentives and made them worse. People are beginning to understand the perverse incentives that have been created by the act, and such policies or proposals as "safe harbor" and "no surprises" are attempts to correct those incentives. But none of these corrections deal with the fundamental problems of species decline.

If we are to do more than tinker at the edges of a law that doesn't work, we must write a new law that addresses the fundamental causes of species decline. That new law must actively discourage federal subsidies to activities that harm listed species. One way to do this would be through a process similar to the base closures commission: An active committee that identifies harmful subsidies and eliminates them.

The new law must also reform public land management to give managers incentives to protect species rather than to resist protection efforts. Currently, Congress gives agencies such as the Forest Service and Bureau of Land Management budgetary rewards for commodity production that often conflicts with species protection, but offer no similar rewards for protecting biological diversity.

Finally, the new law must give private landowners incentives to protect diminishing species rather than, as the current law does, incentives to "shoot, shovel and shut up." One way to do this is to provide compensation for landowners to protect habitat. An equally important, but little discussed, idea is to create private property rights in species or individual animals. Depending on the species involved, such property rights can go far to protect rare species.

The Prairie Dog and the Ferret

Insight into what is wrong with the act, and how to fix it, can be gained by examining two species: the black-footed ferret and the Utah prairie dog. One hundred years ago, millions of black-footed ferrets thrived in the prairies of the Great Plains and the intermountain West. By the end of 1985, only ten were left. The ferret, which is a member of the weasel family, is a classic example of a species endangered by human activities.

Unlike species whose ecological relationships are complex and whose declines are puzzling, the black-footed ferret's needs and the reasons for its disappearance are simple. The ferret lives almost exclusively on prairie dogs. It eats prairie dogs, it feeds prairie dogs to its young, and it makes its home in prairie dog burrows. So, for the ferret, the survival equation is simple: Prairie dogs equal life; no prairie dogs equals extinction.

In the last decades of the nineteenth century, western ranchers heavily overgrazed the plains and mountain range. This actually improved prairie dog habitat.[1] Prairie dogs cannot colonize in the dense grasses of ungrazed ranges, but with overgrazing prairie dog colonies grew to cover 700 million acres. Although no one was counting at the time, biologists now estimate that black-footed ferret numbers increased to as many as six million.

Growing prairie dog populations were a symptom of overgrazing. But a 1902 federal research report tragically confused cause and effect and blamed the effects of overgrazing on the prairie dogs.[2] This put ranchers on the war-path against prairie dogs.[3]

By themselves, a few ranchers thinly scattered across the West probably could not have done much about prairie dogs. Two Texas ranchers once attacked a prairie dog colony with rifles. For two solid weeks they shot prairie dogs, spending thousands of bullets to kill as many as they could. At the end of that time they couldn't see that they had even made a dent in prairie dog populations.

Strychnine is more effective than bullets, and plowing more effective still at eliminating prairie dog colonies. Using poison and plows, ranchers managed to reduce prairie dogs to about 20 percent of their historic range by 1916. Relying on their own resources, that might have been as much as they could or would do—especially since (as recent research reveals) the benefits to livestock of killing prairie dogs fall short of costs even on the most productive grasslands.

But ranchers had a friend to help them in their crusade against prairie dogs: a friend named Uncle Sam. As long as Uncle Sam would pay, it wouldn't matter whether the benefits exceeded the costs. Many of the overgrazed lands were federal, so that's where many of the prairie dogs were found. Since ranchers had to pay the government to use those lands after 1905, they convinced Congress that the government had an obligation to help them wipe out prairie dogs—on both public and private land.

The agency in charge of controlling prairie dogs was the U.S. Biological Survey. As its name suggests, its original mission was fairly benign: mapping plant communities and counting wildlife populations. But an important law of government is that an agency with a mission that has no constituency will soon find a constituency who will give it a new mission. Ranchers were the constituency, and the new mission was to rid the range of predators and prairie dogs.

Congress gave the Survey this new mission in 1916. The Biological Survey attacked this mission with a vengeance, not to mention every poison, trap and other animal control device science could come up with. In just four short years, it had eradicated prairie dogs from 47 million acres, or almost half of their remaining range.[4] By 1960, with the active help of the Forest Service, Bureau of Land Management, Bureau of Indian Affairs, and even the Park Service, the agency had eliminated prairie dogs from all but about two percent of their historic range.[5]

An important law of ecology is that, when you go after a prey species, the predators disappear first. With prairie dogs making up 95 percent of its diet, the ferret is an obligate associate of prairie dog colonies. This makes the ferret an indicator species for prairie dog habitat in the same way that the spotted owl is an indicator for old-growth habitat.

Biologists say that well over 100 species, including pronghorn and (at one time) bison, find food and shelter in areas colonized by prairie dogs.[6] Many of these species, including the mountain plover, the ferruginous hawk and the swift fox, depend on prairie dog colonies as a critical part of their habitat. Several of these species are declining and may be threatened by prairie dog eradication programs.

Although their range is limited, prairie dogs are prolific and plenty still survive. But by 1940, remaining prairie dog colonies were so small and so far apart that the far less numerous and less prolific ferrets were too few to form a viable gene pool. Ferrets suffered from inbreeding and were highly susceptible to diseases such as plague and distemper.[7]

Available information suggests that the ferret was endangered, as the term is currently defined, well before 1940. In 1973, when the Endangered Species Act was passed, fewer than 100 ferrets were known to be alive and biologists called the ferret "the rarest mammal in North America."[8] Of course, it was immediately listed as endangered.

Up to this point, the ferret's problems seem to be just another case of greedy and selfish people conflicting with the natural world. In fact, virtually all of the ferret's difficulties stem from government failure, not market failure.

- Government mismanagement of the range led to the overgrazing that caused prairie dog populations to initially explode.
- Poor government research concluded that prairie dogs were the cause, not an effect, of overgrazing.
- After 1916, government subsidies destroyed 98 percent of western prairie dog colonies that had survived up to that year.

If the problem really was just one of individual greed, then passage of the Endangered Species Act should have signaled a turn-around point for the ferret. Biologists knew that the ferret was endangered and they knew why.

Other than listing the ferret, what did the Fish & Wildlife Service do to protect the species after the act was passed? Nothing. In fact, it did less than nothing. Even though biologists knew that prairie dog eradication programs were responsible for the ferret's decline, the federal government continued to poison prairie dogs.[9]

Under Section 7 of the act, federal agencies should have stopped killing prairie dogs as soon as the ferret was listed. Under Section 9 of the act, private landowners who poisoned prairie dogs could have been charged with "taking" any ferrets that depended on those prairie dogs for food. A recovery plan could have promoted the spread of prairie dogs, and in turn ferrets, across millions of acres of federal land.

That's not what happened. By 1973, the Biological Survey had been incorporated into the Fish & Wildlife Service—the very same agency entrusted with saving the black-footed ferret. For another 13 years, the Fish & Wildlife Service gave lip service to saving the ferret even as it went out and poisoned prairie dog colonies. Ranchers didn't have to risk being charged with taking ferrets when they poisoned prairie dogs—they merely had to ask the agency in charge of protecting ferrets to do it for them.

In 1986, Congress—worried that the Fish & Wildlife Service was not eager enough at its job of killing coyotes and prairie dogs—transferred the Service's animal damage control program to the Department of Agriculture. Under that program, as well as the Forest Service, Bureau of Land Management and other federal agencies, prairie dog poisoning continues to this day.

With one exception. In 1976, the government's prairie dog eradication programs were so successful that one species of prairie dog, the Utah prairie dog, was near extinction. So the Fish & Wildlife Service listed the species as endangered and stopped poisoning it. Within a few years, the prairie dogs had fully recovered. Although the species is now listed as threatened, that is mainly as a reminder to the agency not to poison it.

Meanwhile, the Fish & Wildlife Service finally wrote a recovery plan for the black-footed ferret in 1978. The plan called for capturing ferrets and breeding them in captivity. Of nine ferrets captured, four immediately died from a vaccine meant to protect them against distemper. The other five had two litters between them, but by 1979 all of them—parents and kits—had died as well.

By this time, the last known wild population was also gone. The Fish & Wildlife Service spent three years looking for ferrets, to no avail. As far as anyone knew, the species was extinct.

Then, in 1981, a new population of ferrets was found near Meeteetse, Wyoming, a ranch community about 30 miles south of Cody. A dog belonging to Lucille Hogg, owner of a local cafe, brought to its owner a dead animal that Hogg didn't recognize. She showed it to a state wildlife manager, who recognizes it as a black-footed ferret.

Immediately, biologists began combing the area, using a variety of search methods. They soon identified 61 ferrets living on 7,400 acres of prairie dog habitat.[10]

Fish & Wildlife Service officials ingratiated themselves to the local populace by threatening to charge Lucille Hogg for letting her dog "take" an endangered species. As a result, ranchers clammed up. The New York Zoological Society offered a $10,000 reward for confirmed ferret sightings, but state biologists said that no amount of money would have broken local silence about other possible ferrets. To this day, local biologists believe that more ferrets could have been found if ranchers had cooperated.

Otherwise, the Fish & Wildlife Service didn't have the budget to do much about the ferrets, so it was happy to let the Wyoming State Game & Fish Department take the lead. The state at least had a better relationship with ranchers, but it decided to do little other than monitor the local prairie dog and ferret populations.

At first, things went well, and the 61 ferrets multiplied to 129 by 1984. Some biologists urged the state to capture a few ferrets for breeding and as backup to the wild population. The state declined to do so until 1985, when biologists discovered that sylvatic plague is decimating the Meeteetse prairie dog population. Worse, they soon learned that canine distemper was wiping out the ferrets.

In July, 1985, biologists found no new litters and only 58 live ferrets. By October, the ferret population had fallen to 16. Biologists captured six of them, and only four of the remaining ten survived the winter in the wild. In 1986, biologists captured those four along with their two new litters, for a total population of eighteen in captivity and, as far as anyone knew, none in the wild.[11]

Since then, Wyoming and, later, six zoos have managed to breed hundreds of ferrets in captivity.[12] The Fish & Wildlife Service decided to reestablish a wild population by releasing captive-bred ferrets in at least ten different locations. But so successful has the prairie dog eradication program been that only three locations were found.

Since 1991, hundreds of ferrets have been released into the wild. The cost per released animal averages around $40,000. But more than 90 percent of the ferrets, unused to life in the wild, end up getting gobbled by coyotes or dying of other causes, so the cost per surviving ferret is more than $500,000.[13] In an ironic touch, the Fish & Wildlife Service has asked the USDA animal damage control program to kill all of the local coyotes before more ferrets are released.

How to Save Them All

Most Americans agree with the Endangered Species Act's goal of trying to save as many endangered species as possible. We don't need to quibble about whether this means species, subspecies or populations—we want to save them all. Stories such as that of the black-footed ferret show that the real question is not whether to save species, but how? Answering this question is a four-step process:

1. We first need to clearly understand the basic problem—that is, why are species ever endangered?
2. Next we must look at how well efforts to save endangered species have worked to date.
3. If they haven't worked, we need to understand why not.
4. Finally, we must look at other fields to see what tools we can apply that may be more successful.

My analysis, which is detailed in the following pages, can be summarized in a few paragraphs.

The Basic Cause is Institutional

It is tempting to view endangered species as an ethical or moral problem: Endangered species are good, anyone who does anything to hurt them is bad. But this view is both deceptive and polarizing.

It is much more productive to view the issue as an institutional problem: Outcomes such as extinction or recovery are a product of institutional design. Given the same people, some institutional structures are more likely to lead to extinctions while others are more likely to recover rare species.

The basic institutional problem with endangered species is that U.S. law treats wildlife as a commons. Thus, no one is allowed to capture any of the benefits from saving species.

The Current Act is Not Working

Our goal, then, is to design institutions that will avoid extinctions and promote recovery of threatened and endangered species. Does the current Endangered Species Act accomplish this goal?

While quantitative analysis is difficult, the short answer appears to be "no": There is little evidence that the act is actually saving species. Of the 1,000 or so species listed as threatened or endangered, no more than two—the Utah prairie dog and the Aleutian Canada goose—have recovered because of actions taken under the act.

The act does impose huge costs on private landowners and public land users. These costs are self-defeating for four reasons.

1. The law has stopped few of the numerous federal subsidies that pose the real danger to many, if not most, listed species. Federal funds are still used to poison prairie dogs a full 25 years after the ferret was listed as endangered.
2. Even where federal agencies are supposedly trying to protect endangered species, they often put up obstacles to recovery.
   The Forest Service, for example, has actively resisted proposals to release captively bred ferrets on national forest lands because managers fear the presence of the ferrets would limit their other activities.
3. The act has given some private landowners incentives to harm habitat and has certainly produced a serious backlash against endangered

species preservation. Some forest landowners have cut their trees to preclude restrictions that might happen if their forests were habitat for marbled murrelet or spotted owl; some ranchers may poison prairie dogs just to avoid having ferrets near their land.
4. Most fundamentally, the law has not addressed any of the institutional problems that lead to species decline in the first place. Whether listed as endangered or not, the law still treats wildlife as a commons.

At best, the law does nothing about existing institutional structures that give people the wrong incentives. At worst, the law itself creates incentives to destroy wildlife habitat. Recent amendments to the law have modified some of the perverse incentives in the 1973 act, but neither the original law, amendments, nor the major proposals being considered by Congress do anything about the perverse incentives that predated that act.

We Must Fix the Act with Incentives

If our goal is to save endangered species, and we consider the problem to be institutional rather than moral, then the approach we should take must emphasize incentives rather than command. The best system of incentives ever devised is the free market, because markets respond quickly to need, learn quickly from failure, and fairly assess trade-offs and costs.

Many endangered species aren't easily amenable to markets; if they were, they might not be endangered. But some species could be included in the market, yet are not because of government regulation. Other species may not be marketable, but have proxies that are. Market-like incentives could even be created to save many species that are totally unmarketable.

Understanding Species Decline

There are several ways of looking at species decline. The popular view blames disappearing species on habitat loss and overhunting. But the question still remains, Why is there habitat loss and overhunting? Are species disappearing because of greed and poorly evolved ethics? Or are there institutional problems leading to species decline?

The Ethical View

It is tempting to regard endangered species as a clear case of good and evil. Extirpating a species is morally wrong. Since the species, and anyone trying to protect them, are by definition "good," then anyone who stands in the way of species protection must be "evil."

Eventually, say some proponents of the ethical view, everyone will have such a refined sense of ethics that few would willingly contribute to an extinction, just as today few people would willingly kill or enslave another person. To guard against those few who would harm species, however, we must have strong laws protecting species, just as we have strong laws against murder or slavery.

We don't reward people for not murdering others; instead, we punish them if they do kill someone. By the same token, endangered species laws should punish people for harming rare species or their habitat. In fact, anyone who would consider harming a rare species deserves punishment, so we should feel no compunction in making such people pay a large share of the costs of protecting wildlife.

The ethical view has several weaknesses. First, although everyone may agree that murder is wrong, we have far less agreement about other issues, including abortion, drug use and endangered species.

A second problem is that not everyone has identical views of "good" and "evil." For some, "good" equates to freedom, including freedom for private property owners to use their property as they see fit, so long as they don't harm other people. From this point of view, endangered species advocates are "evil" if they want to regulate private property use.

Some believe that this is a backwards view, held only by people whose ethics haven't "evolved" to the point where they include wildlife in their definitions of life that shouldn't be harmed. At one time, people only behaved ethically towards their own families or tribes. Later, they expanded their ethical views to include all men within their own race. Eventually, all races and genders were included. The natural next step, then, is to include wildlife.

Yet there is little evidence that human ethics actually "progress" or that they will eventually embrace wildlife. Instead, ethics spread through a process of natural selection in response to changes in wealth and technology. As Stephen Jay Gould says with respect to another form of natural selection, "Natural selection is, first of all, a theory about adaptation to changing local environments, not a statement about 'improvement' or 'progress' in any global sense." Changes in technology and human institutions, not internal ethics, led to a broadening of ethical views from tribe to race to all humanity.

If these questions are to be decided by majority rules, rather than a consensus over ethics, then the majority must be willing to compel the minority to act contrary to the minority's own ethical standards. Should a raped woman . be forced to have a baby? Should a farmer or forest land owner be forced to pay most of the costs of protecting a species that is suddenly found on his or her property? Most ethicists would consider such compulsion unethical.

Even if the majority is willing to use compulsive force, society may not have or be willing to use the resources needed to gain full compliance. Prohibition showed that the social costs of enforcement of alcohol laws can be far greater than the benefits. The same is almost certainly true for the current war on drugs.

I reject the ethical view not because it is wrong, but because it does not work. It may be ethical to save endangered species. But it is neither ethical nor feasible to force people to save species against their will—or rather, against powerful incentives to destroy species habitat. In fact, attempts at compulsion often lead to more habitat destruction.

The Institutional View

An alternate view of endangered species, which to a large degree is mutually exclusive with the ethical view, is an institutional one. The institutional view holds that most outcomes are more a product of institutional design than of human ethics. Given the same people, some institutional structures will produce one outcome, while others could produce very nearly the opposite outcome.

Compare, for example, Germany in 1930 versus Germany in 1960. The same country; the same people (more or less); totally different institutional structures—leading to totally different outcomes.

Or compare bison in the nineteenth century versus cattle. The bison were an open-access resource, free for the taking. Anyone who left a few to ensure sustainable herds merely saw those few shot by someone else. So no one had an incentive to manage bison sustainably. Cattle are a closed-access resource and could be legally consumed only by their owners. The owners therefore had an incentive to maintain their herds. The result: North America has plenty of cattle but few bison outside of parks or other reservations.

Zimbabwe and Zambia are both home to the African elephant, but the two take very different approaches to elephant conservation. Zimbabwe treats elephants as the property of the villages near which they roam. Villages sell hunting rights to the elephants and share in the hunting fees as well as the meat.

In contrast, elephant hunting in Zambia is illegal. With a less well-developed system of property rights, Zambian villages consider elephants a cost since elephants may trample their gardens and eat their crops. Villagers do get a personal gain by guiding poachers—if they are willing to take the risk of getting caught. Elephant conservationists in Zambia have a simple policy: They shoot poachers on sight and leave their bodies for the wild animals.

Status of elephant herds in Zimbabwe: large and growing. Status of elephant herds in Zambia: tiny and shrinking. People in Zimbabwe are no more ethical than those in Zambia, but the different institutions they face lead to different outcomes.

The institutional view has two important advantages over the ethical view. First, it works: Once the proper institutional structures and incentives are in place, resources are sustainably produced in abundance. Second, this view holds out the hope of resolving environmental issues without polarization because it encourages us to view people as partners rather than enemies.

Species Decline in the U.S.

Species decline and extinction became apparent in the U.S. during the nineteenth century. At the time, common law generally applied the "rule of capture" to wildlife, meaning that wild plants and animals are owned by no one unless captured or killed. This meant wildlife were an open-access resource, and—like a bottle of soda pop with two straws—everyone's incentive was to get the wildlife before someone else did.[14]

The U.S. policy significantly differed from its British precedent. "Throughout much of British history," says bird watcher and property rights advocate R. J. Smith, "the right to harvest wildlife belonged to owners of the land." The U.S. changed this policy on the grounds that it was "undemocratic": Wildlife, Americans believed, should be available for anyone even if they could not afford to own their own land.[15]

The result of the U.S. policy, says wildlife legal expert Thomas Lund, was that "American wildlife populations fell as if afflicted by a plague." "The affliction upon wildlife must be attributed" not to habitat decline, continues Lund, but to "those democratic policies that were injected into wildlife law."[16]

The tension between democratic or egalitarian principles and a property rights system that would encourage sustainable wildlife management pervades much of American wildlife history. In Britain, the red grouse has thrived because landowners sold hunting rights and thus had an incentive to enhance grouse habitat and maintain grouse numbers. In the U.S., the prairie chicken, which could have benefited from a similar system, was nearly driven to extinction by hunters.

Early American sport hunters blamed the decline of prairie chicken and other species on "market hunters," meaning commercial hunters. As a result, commercial hunting is almost completely banned in nearly every state. But hunting for commercial markets is common in Britain; the real problem is the lack of incentives for American landowners to protect habitat.

Even migrating animals have been successfully managed through a system of property rights. The English gave landowners rights to any geese that lived part of the year on their land; Icelanders treated eider, famous for their eiderdown, the same way. Canada, Scotland, England and other countries have historically granted exclusive fishing rights to individuals or groups of people. In all cases, the owners have an incentive to manage sustainably rather than to overhunt or overfish.

Clashes between the British and American systems continued as North America was settled—to the detriment of wildlife when the Americans won. The story of the near extinction of beaver due to nineteenth-century fur trappers is well known. What is not so well known is that many trappers, including the Montagnais Indians of Quebec and British trappers throughout western North America, managed beaver on a sustainable basis. This worked only so long as the trappers could defend their exclusive rights to trap in certain watersheds.

Hudson Bay Company trappers managed beaver for decades in the territories that became western Canada and the northwestern U.S. When American trappers insisted on trapping in the same areas, however, Hudson Bay trappers adopted a policy of "trapping out" the beaver so as to drive the Americans away. After the Americans took over the Oregon territory that had been occupied by Hudson Bay trappers, only a decline in the market for beaver furs saved the species from local if not total extinction.

In the late nineteenth and early twentieth centuries, sport hunters and anglers led by Teddy Roosevelt convinced states to ban market hunting and manage game sustainably for recreational hunting. Efforts to ban commercial fishing were unsuccessful, but sport anglers were able to legally curtail many of the most efficient fishing tools, such as fishwheels and certain types of nets.

As the twentieth century progressed, state wildlife agencies found it lucrative to promote game fish and wildlife. This sometimes meant destroying species thought harmful to game, including wolves and "trash fish" such as bull trout. At other times it meant introducing exotic species that were in demand by sports hunters and anglers, such as mountain goats in Washington's Olympics and brook trout in many Western streams.

While the states successfully managed and restored many game species, they often refused to take the full responsibility for those species that "ownership" would imply. The traditional rule of capture held that no one owned the wildlife. The states did not want to change that because if they owned the wildlife, then they would be responsible whenever the wildlife damaged someone's crop or other property.

If you shoot a deer out of season, the state can prosecute you. Does this mean that the state owns the deer? No, because if the deer trespasses on your property and eats your garden, the state is not liable for the damage. Thus, the states have the rights but not the responsibility (though, to their credit, some states do have compensation programs).

If the ownership of wildlife is unclear, the ownership of habitat is even more murky. If my sheep cross into your pasture and eat your grass, you are entitled to compensation. If I pay you to pasture my sheep for several years in a row, and then you decide to pave the pasture, I am not entitled to any compensation just because I can no longer use your pasture.

Suppose cattle and sheep owners convinced Congress to pass a law saying that landowners who let other people's livestock graze in their fields would be required to compensate the livestock owners if ever they decided to use the fields for something else. Though intended to promote livestock grazing, such a law would have the opposite effect, since landowners would deny grazing requests to avoid obligations for future grazing.

Yet rights are different if it is not sheep that are eating your crops but some form of wildlife. For some kinds of wildlife, such as coyotes, the government will actually help you kill it or drive it away. But for other kinds, such as deer or elk, you can only do something about it with the government's permission. For still other kinds, such as many insects, you are on your own.

The rules for fish habitat are even murkier. Legally, many streams are owned by the states. But water is also governed by the rule of capture, meaning I can take it out if I have a water right—even if I leave none for the fish. In fact, if I leave some for the fish, anyone else may take it, and I could lose my water rights. I can also pollute the water by eroding the soil.

States also often preempt the incentives that would encourage private landowners to promote game habitat. Most states discourage private landowners from charging user fees for hunting, and some ban such fees entirely. Even more states forbid landowners from charging for fishing in a stream on their property.

In 1973, Oregon passed a land use planning law that, among other things, protected wetlands. After an Oregon rancher named Dayton Hyde spent much time and money turning one of his pastures into an artificial wetland for waterfowl, Oregon officials told him that, under the new law, neither he nor anyone he sold the property to would ever be allowed to use that pasture for anything else. Hyde loves wildlife and wants to encourage other ranchers to improve wildlife habitat—but few will listen if protecting wildlife means losing the rights to use their property for something else.

So while federal subsidies to agriculture, water power, timber, mining and other activities provide plenty of incentives to destroy wildlife habitat, state wildlife management programs offered few to no incentives to protect that habitat. Yes, biodiversity is a public good, but many species—especially game fish and wildlife—could be treated as private goods except that the government stood in the way.

In insisting that wildlife were commonly owned, American law gave private landowners few incentives to protect habitat. The federal government doesn't help when it subsidizes so many activities that are harmful to wildlife. State governments don't help when they preempt potential markets for hunting and fishing on private land. Nor do other states help when they refuse to compensate landowners for crop damage by game.

While these misincentives are the prime causes of species decline, the Endangered Species Act didn't fix any of them. Instead, if anything, it added to them.

Why the Endangered Species Act Does Not Work

The Endangered Species Act makes the saving of all species, unless exempted by the "god squad," the absolute top priority of the U.S. government. Certainly the extinction of any species is a tragedy. But there are no absolutes in this world. Certain species may be beyond all hope of recovery. Others might be recoverable, but the costs of recovery are far greater than any imaginable benefits. Some—smallpox is an extreme case—we might not want to recover.

The law also imposes most of the costs of saving many species on a few private landowners. Less than half of all listed species are found on federal land, and two-thirds find most of their habitat on private land. The act imposes most of the costs of recovering species on the landowners, yet the benefits are shared by everyone. Even if we could overlook the unfairness of this law, the fact is that it does not work.

Unfortunately, it is difficult to quantitatively measure whether the law is succeeding or failing. One simple way might be to compare the number of species that have gone extinct since the law was passed against the number that have been recovered.[17]

Between 1973 and 1996, eight species in the U.S. proper have gone extinct, including one mammal, three birds, and four fish. Three more Puerto Rican species have gone extinct, including one bird and two amphibians. Another six species that had been listed were later determined to have gone extinct before 1973.

During the same time period, 15 species were removed from the endangered species list and declared "recovered," while ten others were reclassified from "endangered" to "threatened" status. The Fish & Wildlife Service is quick to take credit for many of these delistings or upgrades, but few were due to the Endangered Species Act.

For example, the agency recently upgraded the bald eagle from "endangered" to "threatened." At the time, Fish & Wildlife Service director Mollie Beatty was quoted as saying, "Without the act in place, we might have lost our national symbol." In fact, a ban on DDT that the Environmental Protection Agency put into place before the Endangered Species Act was passed had more to do with eagle recovery.

- Nine "recovered" species were removed from the list when new populations were found; the species were never actually in danger.

- Several others recovered on their own, with no help from humans. Prominent among these were several birds found in U.S. territories in the Pacific Ocean; their populations had been decimated by World War II, but recovered naturally.

- Like the bald eagle, the brown pelican and peregrine falcon improved primarily because of the ban on DDT, which went into effect a year before Congress passed the Endangered Species Act.

- Four species of endangered trout were reclassified as "threatened" not because the species were better off but to allow some fishing of the trout and therefore to maintain the support of the angling community.

- Similarly, the gray wolf in Minnesota was changed from "endangered" to "threatened" to allow local residents to kill them to protect themselves—with the expectation that fewer animals would be killed legally than if killing were illegal.

- The American alligator recovered after it was protected from hunting under the act. But the states in which it is found insist that is was their work, not the Endangered Species Act, that led to the alligator's recovery. At the time of its listing in 1973, its populations were already increasing or stable due to state efforts in most of its range. Of all reclassified or delisted species, only two have clearly improved as a result of the act. Both were once endangered; they are now listed as "threatened" but for practical purposes are probably fully recovered.

- The Aleutian Canada goose, which nests on Alaskan islands, was threatened by a fox that had been introduced for its furs by Alaska settlers. The Fish & Wildlife Service's animal damage control program controlled the foxes, which led the goose population to quickly recover.

- As noted, the Utah prairie dog recovered after the Fish & Wildlife Service halted federal poisoning campaigns. So the scorecard seems to be: eight species extinct, two recovered. But that doesn't prove that the act is failing because we don't know what would have happened if the act had not been passed. Conceivably, without the law, the California condor, black-footed ferret and several other species would have also gone extinct. On the other hand, what would have happened if the law had been passed with incentives for recovery, rather than punitive measures for harming a species? Conceivably, some of the extinct species might still be with us, and the black-footed ferret might have survived without a captive breeding program. There is no way to know for sure. Yet there are three clear areas in which the act has failed.

- First, it has failed to stop the many subsidized federal programs that are harming so many species.

- Second, even where federal agencies are ostensibly cooperating with the Fish & Wildlife Service in protecting species, the agencies put up many inadvertent obstacles to recovery.

- Third, the act not only fails to address the "commons" problem, it actually gives private landowners new incentives to destroy wildlife habitat.

Federal Subsidies

The Endangered Species Act has failed to stop the many subsidized federal programs that are harming species. The Fish & Wildlife Service was able to stop its own animal damage control branch from poisoning a listed species, the Utah prairie dog. But it was not able to stop that program or other federal agencies from poisoning prairie dogs on which another listed species, the black-footed ferret, depended. It was only luck that the federal government had not yet poisoned all the prairie dogs near Meeteetse, Wyoming, before the last population of ferrets was discovered.

Taxpayer's Double Burden, a 1993 report by the Wilderness Society and the Environmental Defense Fund, describes subsidies that promote habitat conversion or degradation as a "double burden," because taxpayers must pay to subsidize a particular industry or activity, and then pay again to recover species and protect them from subsidized activities.[18]

That report was based on a database for all listed species that was developed by staff of the Wilderness Society and the Environmental Defense Fund. Most of its information was derived from the listing packages that Fish & Wildlife Service provides when a species is officially listed. Information that could not be acquired from this source was obtained from the World Wildlife Fund's Guide to Endangered Species.

Taxpayer's Double Burden showed that a majority of listed species on federal lands are threatened by subsidized activities. However, that report considered only species occurring on federal land and those threatened by federal water projects.

In 1996, Jeff Opperman, working for the Thoreau Institute, updated Taxpayer's Double Burden to include species listed since 1993 as well as threats from federally subsidized activities that take place on non-federal land.[19] Environmental Defense Fund ecologist David Wilcove has kept the database up-to-date as new species were listed and generously provided the database to the Thoreau Institute for Opperman's analysis.

Wilcove's database listed all known threats to each species and assessed the threats by magnitude:

- 1 is the only or most significant factor;
- 2 is one of two or more significant factors;
- 3 is a secondary factor;
- 4 is a potential factor; and
- 5 is an historical factor.

Opperman assessed each threat to determine whether it was a federal program or a federally subsidized activity. To do so, he defined subsidy as any government policy where income is directly or indirectly transferred from taxpayers in general to specific recipients, or where the beneficiaries of a specific policy do not pay full costs for a project, access to resources, or for a service. Programs that are largely or completely under government control, such as highway construction and defense, were also counted as federal activities.

Opperman estimated that a species was primarily threatened by federal activities if all magnitude 1 and 2 threats were subsidized. It was mainly threatened by federal activities if a majority of magnitude 2 threats were subsidized. It was partly threatened by federal activities if half or fewer magnitude 2 threats were subsidized.

Out of 956 species listed when Opperman did his analysis, 55 had no threats listed and 375 were not threatened by federal programs. Of the 526 that were threatened by federal activities, 112 were primarily threatened, 104 were mainly threatened, and 310 were partly threatened by federal programs. In other words, for the species for which threats are known, 58 percent are at least partially threatened by federal programs and 24 percent are mainly threatened by federal programs.

Advocates of the Endangered Species Act often call it "the most powerful environmental law ever written. "But if the Endangered Species Act were really so powerful, all of these threats would have ended. Clearly, the act has failed to lead the federal government to apply the most important rule of the Hippocratic Oath: "First, do no harm."

Organizational Obstacles

Under the Endangered Species Act, species recovery is the number one goal of all federal agencies. Yet the literature about endangered species recovery projects is replete with examples of resistance from the federal managers whose primary job is supposed to be endangered species recovery.

Richard Reading, with the Bureau of Land Management, and Brian Miller, with the Smithsonian Institution, say that "professional and organizational weaknesses" have hindered ferret recovery. In fact, they worry that the very success of the ferret captive breeding program tends to mask such organizational problems. This reduces the pressure to fix the organizational problems. "If organizational considerations are not better addressed," note Reading and Miller, "species whose biology and ecology are less amenable to recovery may go extinct."[20]

The ferret is not unique in suffering from conflicts among federal and state agencies. Efforts to protect the spotted owl foundered on conflicts within the Bureau of Land Management between the Congressional mandate to save species and the BLM's own history, orientation and incentives towards timber cutting.

In 1991, a team of experts known as the "gang of four"—Jack Ward Thomas, Jerry Franklin, John Gordon and Norman Johnson—wrote what was then considered to be a state-of-the-art plan for protecting the owl. The plan included old-growth reserves. But it also insisted that the Forest Service and BLM should manage its other forests in compliance with what became known as the "50-40-11 rule." This rule stated that, at all times, at least 50 percent of the managed forests should be at least 40 years old and at least 11 inches in diameter.

The Forest Service, which had always planned to grow trees to at least 80 years of age before final harvest, had no problem with this rule. But the BLM had planned final harvests in many forests when they were as young as 50 or even 40 years. When they made this plan in the 1970s, it allowed them to step up the rate of old-growth cuttings. After cutting at this higher rate for well over a decade, the BLM found that adoption of the 50-40-11 rule would force it to virtually cease timber sales in western Oregon.

The BLM's western Oregon timber program was the pride of the agency. Naturally, and in spite of the Endangered Species Act's mandate to give rare species a priority above all else, the agency rebelled against the 50-40-11 rule. The rebellion took the form of a petition to the god squad to exempt BLM sales from the law. The god squad denied the petition, but the President's forest plan made the political decision to drop the 50-40-11 rule. Resentment against the owl still smolders within Oregon offices of the BLM.

Recovery efforts all over the country are plagued with similar problems. "Land management agencies" says Ken Alvarez, a biologist involved in the effort to recover the Florida panther, "will not readily depart from established practice when presented with a novel challenge." The story of the Florida panther recovery, says Alvarez, is one of "resistance," or at least a "lack of official enthusiasm," on the part of public land agencies ranging from the Florida Department of Natural Resources to the National Park Service.[21]

"Problems are clearly evident in the professional and organizational systems involved in endangered species conservation," says Jerome Jackson, a biologist at Mississippi State University who has worked with the red-cockaded woodpecker for more than 25 years. He describes "professional obstacles" to woodpecker recovery raised by the Forest Service, the Army and even the Fish & Wildlife Service.[22]

Noel Snyder, who led efforts to save the California condor from 1980 to 1986, notes that conflicts between the Fish & Wildlife Service and the California Department of Fish & Game, as well as the National Audubon Society, which helped raise money for and participated in the recovery program, some-times led to a near gridlock in the program's efforts.

"Organizations are not mere mechanisms," concludes Alvarez. It is not enough to simply command them to protect species, as the Endangered Species Act attempts to do; you have to build into their organizational structures incentives for them to do it. As Snyder says, "the system of rewards and benefits in government organizations and many NGOs [non-profit organizations] needs restructuring to favor efficiency and decentralization of authority and to punish proliferation of bureaucracy."[23]

Incentives for Private Landowners

The Endangered Species Act not only failed to fix the problem of wildlife being a commons, it made the problem worse by giving landowners incentives to destroy habitat in order to avoid federal regulation of their land.

Tang Ming-Lin, a California farmer, owned land that was habitat for the Tipton kangaroo rat. After one of his employees plowed a field without obtaining an incidental take permit—possibly killing a few kangaroo rats—the Fish & Wildlife Service, in criminal charges, threatened Ming-Lin with prison and a $300,000 fine, convinced the Immigration Service to threaten his family with deportation, and demanded forfeiture of half his acres for wildlife habitat.

Eventually the agency settled for a $5,000 "donation" without any admission of wrongdoing. But it didn't turn many of Ming-Lin's workers or neighbors into friends of rare species.[24]

Is this type of encounter with the Endangered Species Act unusual? "Yes," say many endangered species advocates. According to John Kostyack, an attorney for the National Wildlife Federation, "the act has never prevented property owners from developing their land."

Kostyack's claim is true only in a limited sense. The Fish & Wildlife Service won't deny private property owners the "use" of their land, it just denies or regulates certain uses. The uses that are denied are often much more valuable than the ones that are allowed, but the agency never offers to compensate property owners whose land loses value when a species is listed.

Margaret Rector owned 15 acres of land near Austin, Texas. She sold it in 1984, but the buyer went bankrupt and she repossessed in April 1990. In May 1990, the Fish & Wildlife Service listed the golden-cheeked warbler as "endangered" and told Rector that her land provided warbler habitat.

Her property had been appraised at more than $830,000 when she repossessed it in 1990. But after the listing, a new appraisal reduced the value to $30,000. The Fish & Wildlife Service blamed the decline on the savings and loan crisis. But before that crisis her property had been worth $1.5 million and Rector says that Austin property values had adjusted to the savings and loan debacle long before 1990.

The Fish & Wildlife Service responds that people in such situations can develop their land if they get an "incidental take" permit. Rector didn't want to develop; she only wanted to sell, and so wasn't eligible for a permit. But others who have tried to get permits found the process time-consuming and expensive.

Jester Development Company, also in Austin, Texas, was building houses in golden-cheeked warbler habitat. When the species was listed, the Fish & Wildlife Service told the company it could get an incidental take permit after two annual surveys for birds. No birds were found. But by the time the Fish & Wildlife Service finally granted the permit, Jester's lack of income for two years led the company's banker to foreclose.

The bank sold the acres to other developers, but Fish & Wildlife Service rules prevented them from building homes on all sites planned by Jester. Undevelopable sites were eventually sold as a preserve—for less than a quarter of their value as developable lots.

The Fish & Wildlife Service has also prevented people from farming their land. The Stephens' kangaroo rat was listed as endangered in 1988. In 1990, the agency told the Domenigoni family that it would not be allowed to plow hundreds of acres of family farmland in southern California.

After three years of remaining idle, the Domenigoni's fields grew thick with brush. In 1993, a fire swept through and destroyed 29 nearby homes. Shortly after, the Fish & Wildlife Service told the Domenigonis that they could farm their acres, saying that the land was no longer suitable kangaroo rat habitat. Ironically, it was not the fire that made the land unsuitable, but the thick brush that had grown prior to the fire.

Sometimes the Fish & Wildlife Service will let people farm or develop some of their property, but only if they give up or buy many acres more to mitigate the effects on habitat. The Morian family owned land in Texas that was habitat for the black-capped vireo. Before the bird was listed, they donated 74 acres of habitat for use as a nature preserve and put conservation easements on 62 more acres before planning a housing development on 69 other acres. Then the bird was listed as a threatened species. The Fish & Wildlife Service told the Morians that they could continue with their development only if they bought at least 100 more acres of habitat somewhere else.

The requirement that people purchase land for mitigation is often accompanied by a requirement that the purchasers also fund the land's management. Marj and Roger Krueger understood that, before they could build their dream home on a 1.7-acre parcel in Texas golden-cheeked warbler habitat, they would have to buy at least three acres elsewhere and provide funds to maintain those acres. After major protests, the Fish & Wildlife Service replaced these requirements with a flat fee of $1,500 per acre. Similar requirements or fees exist for other species.

Ultimately, all of these people have been or might be allowed to use their land—but only after paying substantial costs for surveys, mitigation or reduced property values as a result of limits on the development. The Endangered Species Act has clearly proven costly to numerous private landowners, while the people who have already destroyed most of the habitat for many species often pay little or nothing for species restoration.

Wildlife advocates downplay the costs to landowners and insist that the act doesn't violate private property rights. But they can't have it both ways. If landowners aren't affected by the act, then how can the act—which offers no new incentives—save endangered species? If every landowner who complains gets a special exemption, then what good is the law?

This nation is wealthy enough that it can afford to save habitat for the Tipton kangaroo rat, golden-cheeked warbler, Stephens' kangaroo rat, black-capped vireo and other diminishing species. But we are not so wealthy that we can afford to give up constitutional protections for property owners any more than we can afford to give up freedom of speech or freedom of assembly. The cost of saving rare species habitat should be shared by everyone, not imposed on a few unlucky landowners.

An Alternative Approach

The major reason why the Endangered Species Act has failed is that it is based on command, not incentives. While proponents argue that some incentives were added in the 1982 amendments to the act, these are merely incentives to comply with the original commands. Neither the act nor any amendments to date changed the preexisting incentives to destroy habitat. At best, the act puts people in a dilemma: Follow their incentives or follow the law. At worst, the act creates new incentives to destroy habitat.

An alternative approach would be based on incentives and, wherever possible, markets. Markets are superb at doing two things that government does poorly. First, markets allow individuals and societies to easily assess trade-offs between resources. Handmade furniture requires more labor; mass-produced furniture requires more capital. But consumers don't need to worry about the appropriate ratio of labor to capital; all they need to know is the price and their assessment of quality.

Second, markets make sure that people get what they want, given the limits of their income. Some people will pay the extra cost of handmade furniture; others will be satisfied with Ikea or Bargain Mart. Governments tend to limit choices, while markets tend to produce a broad range of alternatives.

Markets provide more choices because, unlike governments, they don't require majority support for any given choice. Most people don't like anchovies, yet every supermarket in your neighborhood carries at least one and possibly three styles of anchovies.

This is a particularly powerful attribute for protecting rare species. Endangered species advocates can barely muster support for such charismatic animals as the wolf or salmon. How can they maintain majority support for seemingly trivial and not-very-appealing species such as the seven salamanders, 22 snails, three quillworts and two lichens on the list? Private ownership and markets may prove the only way to save such species.

Contrary to popular belief, markets will work even if people don't have perfect knowledge about all the options, competition is less than perfect, or incomes aren't evenly distributed. From an environmental viewpoint, the main obstacle to a successful market is when some resources are left out of the market.

All too often, wildlife is left out of the market not through some market flaw, but because the government has prevented the market from functioning for wildlife. As previously noted, U.S. and state hunting and fishing policies have generally discouraged private ownership or management of wildlife.

In some states, for example, it is illegal for private landowners to deny anyone access to fish or wildlife that happen to cross or be on their property. This gives the landowners little incentive to protect habitat and some incentive to destroy it so as to discourage people whom they regard as trespassers.

Ownership of hunting and fishing rights are not the only way that private property rights can be used to protect wildlife. Domestic animals in general enjoy a huge amount of genetic diversity because their owners prize different qualities of the many varieties. No wild species, for example, is as genetically diverse as *Canis domesticus.*

While captive breeding is not the preferred solution for the long run, it may be the best short-run solution for many species whose numbers are very low. In the U.S., only government entities are allowed to hold endangered species in captivity. But historically, many species have been saved from extinction through captive breeding by private individuals.

Wild populations of the Hawaiian goose, or nene, had fallen to about 20 to 30 birds by 1949. But aviculturists had bred captive populations both in the U.S. and in Europe. In the 1960s, these were reintroduced into the wild and within a decade, as many as 600 thrived in their native habitat. Many of the rarest species of pheasants and members of the parrot family have also survived through captive breeding.[25]

In most cases, the people who own such wildlife do so for their own pleasure, not for any expected profit. Just as people have saved and bred hundreds of varieties of domestic dogs, they can get interested in saving and breeding all sorts of other animals.

Wildlife advocates have attempted to use bald eagles, grizzly bear and other charismatic megafauna as poster children representing all endangered species. That tactic seemed to break down when Republicans took over Congress in 1995. Yet it wasn't even successful enough to get the Endangered Species Act reauthorized when the Democrats were in power in 1993 and 1994.

It may seem foolish to think that markets can protect endangered species. Who will buy a spider or a skink? Yet think of the creativity environmental groups have brought to the political process over the last three decades, resulting in a virtual redefinition of political activism. Applying this creativity to the private sector, which has the advantage of being able to work with only minority support, might save just about any species.

Reinventing the Endangered Species Act

The Endangered Species Act is broken. It never really worked very well, and today it has so polarized the public—including landowners and land managers who are critical to efforts to save species—that in some cases it may be doing more harm than good.

A new or revised endangered species law must accomplish two key goals:

- First, a new law must do much more than the current law to protect rare and diminishing species.
- Second, a new law must greatly reduce, if not eliminate, the conflicts over private property rights and the use of publicly owned resources.

In short, the act must take a firmer stance against subsidies and a gentler, more incentive-based stance towards both public land managers and private landowners. To achieve these goals, changes to the Endangered Species Act must:

- Stop or significantly reduce subsidies to destructive activities;
- Give both private landowners and public land managers incentives to protect species and their habitat;
- Encourage endangered species advocates to work with local communities;
- Provide a mechanism for trade-offs among species and between species and other resources.
- Provide protection for uncharismatic species.
- Provide a source of funds for species and habitat protection.
- Provide a funding mechanism that is both steady and adequate.

These objectives could be accomplished by the following five proposals:

1. Create a biodiversity trust fund;
2. Turn the Endangered Species Act into a subsidies killer;
3. Reform public land management;
4. Allow experiments with private property rights in wildlife;
5. Eliminate regulation of private land.

Create a Biodiversity Trust Fund

Imagine that the authors of interstate highway legislation had decided to use a model similar to the Endangered Species Act. Their bill would have called for highway planners in Washington, DC, to draw lines on maps showing where the roads would go. Then it would decree that everyone whose land was crossed by one of those lines would have to build, at their own expense, a highway to federal standards and open that highway to public use.

If someone's house stood in the way of a highway, they would have to tear it down or move it at their own expense. Where the lines crossed public land, the public managers would be required to build the roads without any significant increases in their budgets for such construction.

Such a law would be perfectly rational from the viewpoint that people should act selflessly for the benefit of society. But it is hard to imagine that it would lead to the construction of very many miles of highway. It is much easier to imagine a revolt of landowners, lawsuits, even violence if the government persisted in forcing owners to build roads at their own expense.

Of course, the Interstate Highway System wasn't based on an endangered-species-act model. Instead, fees assessed on highway users were dedicated to a trust fund that bought land at fair market value and paid for road construction. Landowners were fairly compensated and disputes were minor. The system isn't perfect, but it works better than most government programs. If anything, the result is too many highways.

Is it possible to design a biodiversity trust fund that would work as well as, if not better, than the federal highway trust fund? The first problem is to find a source of funds; I will deal with that in the next two sections. The important point to make here is that designated revenues should be off-budget—that is, they should automatically accrue to the biodiversity trust fund and not go through Congressional appropriations.

Just as important is to find an organizational design that will work fairly and efficiently. One possible model is the Diversity Funding Initiative proposed by the International Association of Fish & Wildlife Agencies. Under this proposal, funds would be spent largely by state wildlife agencies and distributed to those agencies based on population and geographic area. As noted earlier, the proposed distribution formula favors large and populous states, which aren't necessarily the states with the most biodiversity problems.

Another problem is that state agencies may not always be the best ones to recover species, especially species whose ranges are either very limited or cover several states. One good thing about this model is that it places a firm limit on the share of funds that can be spent on administrative overhead.

An alternate proposal is to create a biodiversity board of trustees that would allocate funds to federal, state or local agencies or private entities according to priorities set by the board. The board might be conservation biologists appointed by the Secretary of the Interior or director of the Smithsonian, or—like the god squad—it could consist of a set of predesignated federal officials such as the directors of the Fish & Wildlife Service and National Marine Fisheries Service.

The law should place limits on the share of funds that could be spent on overhead and research. Otherwise, the funds should be available for any activity that would enhance biodiversity or help recover endangered species. These activities might include but are not limited to:

- Buying land;
- Buying conservation easements on private land;
- Buying timber sales or other permits on public land and then not using them;
- Paying private landowners or public land managers to use certain practices, such as "New Forestry," or avoid certain practices, such as clearcutting.
- Contracting with private entities to recover a listed species;
- Paying "bounties" on listed species—that is, pay landowners or managers if their land is supporting breeding pairs of a listed species.

The two major sources of revenues proposed below should provide between $750 million and $1 billion per year to spend on biodiversity. While some may argue that this is not enough, it is far more than is being spent today or that Congress is likely to appropriate to endangered species at any time in the foreseeable future. Moreover, since the fund will be independent of the appropriations process, it will not be subject to the political whims of whatever party happens to be in charge.

Turn the Law into a Subsidy Killer

Under the Endangered Species Act, the federal government is supposed to protect rare species from human threats. But we have seen that the greatest single threat to endangered species is the federal government itself.

Congress itself is facing a dilemma over federal spending. On one hand, most members of Congress know that the government cannot run up $300 billion annual deficits forever. In just a few years, interest on the national debt will be the largest item in the federal budget; soon after that, it will be more than all available discretionary income.

On the other hand, since pork is such an important part of reelection strategies, Congress hasn't been able to figure out a way to stop spending. The Gramm-Rudman Act, the line-item veto and balanced budget amendments are all ways of Congress saying, "Stop me before I spend again!"

One successful technique for reducing spending was conceived by House majority leader Richard Armey. Armey knew that the Pentagon wanted to close hundreds of obsolete military bases, but that they were kept open to please members of Congress. So Armey proposed, and Congress created, a base closures commission.

The commission decided that nearly 100 bases should be closed. Under Armey's law, Congress could overrule this decision only if both houses voted to do so. Since the proposed closures did not affect a majority of the members, attempts to overrule the commission failed. The only problem with the process was that the commission dissolved after one year, so many obsolete bases remain open.

Armey's device can be used as a model for the Endangered Species Act. The act already includes a "god squad" that can exempt a species from protection. Why not also include a "budget squad" that can impound federal funds if it finds that those funds are being used to subsidize an activity that is harmful to any listed species?

The budget squad would be a standing committee consisting of, perhaps, the director of the Smithsonian, the director of the Fish & Wildlife Service (or Secretary of the Interior), the director of the National Marine Fisheries Service (or Secretary of Commerce), the chair of the Council of Economic Advisors, and the director of the U.S. Employment Service (or Secretary of Labor). The committee would meet at the beginning of each fiscal year to review the upcoming year's budget.

Any citizen could petition the squad to review a federal program, and the squad could decide to review programs on its own. If it finds that a program is directly or indirectly harmful to any listed species or its habitat, the squad could decide to impound some or all of the program's funding. Congress might exempt certain defense department and other national security programs from review.

Impounded money might be split three ways. First, a share could go into a biodiversity trust fund that would be used to give managers and landowners incentives to restore and maintain habitat. Another share could go to the U.S.

Employment Service to be used to help people whose jobs might be lost as a result of the funding cuts. The remainder could be dedicated to paying off the national debt.

Unlike the base closures commission, the budget squad would be a standing committee that would meet every year. After it makes its decisions, Congress would have 30 days to overrule any impoundment. Since few impoundments are likely to affect many members of Congress, such vetoes would be rare. As with base closures, this takes advantage of the fact that it is much more difficult for a member of Congress to get other members to act to save a program than it is to keep Congress from acting to kill a program.

How much money could the budget squad provide for the biodiversity trust fund? The federal government spends about $40 billion per year on agricultural subsidies and natural resources, almost all of which could be detrimental to rare species. Other spending on transportation and community development, such as the Tennessee Valley Authority, might also be open for impoundment.

Of course, the budget squad would not try to impound all of these funds in the first year, both for political reasons and because immediate evidence of harm to endangered species might be lacking. But it is likely that it could impound at least $1 billion per year, adding several hundred million per year to the biodiversity trust fund.

Once funds have been impounded, Congress might not try to fund the same activities in future years. But as the budget squad reviews more activities, it is likely to find impoundable funds for many years.

Would Congress agree to such a scheme? As noted, many members of Congress would like to get out of the pork-barrel rat race. A budget squad would allow them to tell their constituents, "I worked as hard as I could for you, but I was overruled." Moreover, the initial law would please both liberal voters who like endangered species and conservative voters who like cutting budgets.

Reform Public Land Agencies

Endangered species and federal land management are generally seen as two distinct issues. In fact, problems with endangered species and controversies over federal lands have the same ultimate source: Congressional micromanagement.

Endangered species advocates are counting on federal lands to provide most of the habitat for many rare species. Yet federal subsidies, Congressional output targets, and manipulations by appropriations committees are the main obstacle to both sound federal land management and habitat protection on those lands.

Even though reforms of the Forest Service, Bureau of Land Management, and other federal resource agencies might require separate legislation from endangered species reforms, it makes sense to contemplate such reforms as a package. For one thing, the proposed biodiversity trust fund could have little influence over the agencies as they exist today. Public land laws do not forbid conservation easements, but the budgetary process—which is focused on commodity output targets—discourages such easements.

Nor is it clear that the agencies would get to keep any of the revenues from easements or from other payments made by a biodiversity trust fund. If managers don't get to add a share of the revenues to their budgets, they will prefer to emphasize timber, grazing or other resources that do add to their budgets.

The one public land reform that is absolutely vital is to fund agencies out of the same fixed share of all of their receipts. If they get the same share of recreation fees as timber fees and the same share of conservation easement fees and grazing fees, managers will not be biased towards any single resource.[26]

A refinement to this reform is to fund agencies out of their net user fees. Agencies funded out of gross fees are certain to make a profit from some of their activities. Since they get to keep a share of the gross, they must make up for their profits by losing money on other activities. Such cross-subsidies are likely to be bad for biodiversity.

A second refinement is to fund agencies exclusively out of their net user fees. If Congressional appropriators are allowed to spend tax dollars on federal lands, they are most likely to spend them on activities hazardous to endangered species, because such activities will provide the greatest political payoff.

Finally, agencies should be allowed to charge fair market value for recreation as well as all other resources in their care. This will level the playing field among marketable resources, and some forms of recreation are likely to make good proxies for the habitat needs of many species.

Taken together, these reforms will produce multiple benefits. First, they will encourage agencies to produce more net receipts, and thereby to produce more revenues for a biodiversity trust fund. Second, funding out of net income will discourage activities destructive to many species. Third, funding agencies out of a share of all their income will allow them to respond to incentives offered by the biodiversity trust fund.

Finally, allowing the agencies to charge market value for recreation and other resources should significantly add to their revenues, which in turn would provide another source of income for the biodiversity trust fund. Since such fees might otherwise go into the U.S. Treasury, they would effectively be "paid" by every U.S. resident. But since the payment of such fees is made by people who are using public lands—and affecting public land biodiversity—such "abuser fees" would seem fair to both users and taxpayers.

In recent years, total revenues to the four major public land agencies—Forest Service, Park Service, Bureau of Land Management and Fish & Wildlife Service—have been around $1.3 to $1.5 billion per year. Most of these revenues have been retained by the agencies or passed on to some other agency, such as counties or (in the case of some BLM revenues) the Bureau of Reclamation.

The Treasury retains about $600 million per year from renewable resources, plus additional public land receipts collected by the Minerals Management Service. Dedicating a fifth of the total receipts to the biodiversity trust fund would add well over $250 million per year to that fund while still leaving some returns for the Treasury.

Funding to both biodiversity and the Treasury could be significantly increased by allowing federal agencies to charge fair market value for recreation. The four public land agencies host well over 450 million visitor days of recreation per year. The Corps of Engineers and Bureau of Reclamation provide 220 million more. If these recreationists paid an average of just $3 per day—half the price of a two-hour movie—total revenues would be about $2 billion per year. A fifth of those revenues would add $400 million per year to the biodiversity trust fund.

To the extent that recreation makes a fairly reasonable proxy for at least some species, federal recreation fees would have another benefit: Such fees would encourage private landowners to charge recreationists, giving those landowners an incentive to protect habitat as well. To the extent that recreation makes a poor proxy for some species, the revenues generated for the biodiversity trust fund should more than offset any problems.

Allow for Experiments with Private Property Rights in Wildlife

Congress should give the Fish & Wildlife Service, biodiversity trust fund or other appropriate agency the authority to assign property rights in a particular species to individuals, non-government organizations or perhaps even for-profit companies. This may improve the chances of recovering some species that the federal government might not have the resources—or political will—to protect.[27]

Several types of species could be prime candidates for such experiments:

- Potential game or commercial species, such as salmon and Columbian white-tailed deer, that could provide their owners an incentive to ensure sustainable management;
- Species that themselves are not game species but which have easily defined proxies, such as other game species;
- Species that require captive breeding and might be successfully bred by private parties; and
- Species whose range is limited to the property of one or a handful of people. Various types of property rights could be conveyed, including:
- The right of landowners to hunt or charge fees for hunting game animals on their property;
- The right to own in captivity individual members of a particular species;
- The right to own all members of a particular species; and
- The right to own a species as well as some rights to its habitat.

At the simplest level, landowners could be given the exclusive right to hunt, or lease hunting rights to others, for animals that happen to be on their land. This would require changes in the wildlife policies of some states. But it would give landowners powerful incentives to protect game habitat—and the habitat of animals whose needs are similar to game.

The next step is to give private parties or organizations the right to own in captivity individual members of a particular species. Distributing captive members of a rare species to more locations could lead to better methods of, say, conditioning juveniles to better survive after they are released into the wild.

The next step up would be to grant private parties or organizations the right to own all members of a particular species, whether they are in the wild or in captivity. The owners would be responsible for maintaining habitat for the species, which might require land purchases or compensation to private landowners.

Private ownership of a species could take advantage of the fact that a few people may love many species that most people would not even notice. Botanically minded people, for example, might enthusiastically purchase the habitat for a species of lichens, whereas convincing Congress—or even a biodiversity trust fund that may have other priorities—to make such a purchase could be difficult.

Private recovery efforts wouldn't always be free: The Fish & Wildlife Service or biodiversity trust fund might offer to pay someone to recover another species and seek the lowest bid for such a recovery. On the other hand, if a species of plant in private ownership were found to be a source of some medicine, the owner of that species would reap the benefits.

In an extreme case, a private organization might be granted, or sold, the rights to own a species as well as certain rights to its habitat that are currently in the public domain. A hypothetical Salmon Trust could own all rights to a particular variety of salmon as well as the streams in which it migrates and spawns (which are now considered public). The trust could sell fishing rights, negotiate water rights with irrigators, and go to court to defend the fish against polluters.

Not all experiments would be successful, but many experiments would result in creative new techniques for species and habitat protection. The law should be amended to specifically allow such experiments.

These experiments could be initiated by the agencies now administering the act—the Fish & Wildlife Service and the National Marine Fisheries Service. But if proposal #1 is passed, it makes more sense to have them administered by the biodiversity trust fund. Whichever federal agency is involved, it would have to negotiate with state agencies to promote changes in state wildlife rules or laws to as to allow these experiments to take place.

Eliminate Private Land Regulation

The fact that qualifiers such as "where practicable" were eliminated from the 1973 version of the Endangered Species Act has often been touted as its strength. In practice, the absolute terms in the law have done little good.

- Activities harmful to many endangered species continue to receive billions of dollars of federal subsidies each year.
- The Fish & Wildlife Service has done little to stop such subsidies even when prompted by citizen lawsuits.
- Other federal agencies that are supposed to give listed species their highest priority instead place numerous obstacles in the way of habitat protection.
- The record of species recovery is dismal: At most, three U.S. species have recovered as a result of the act, while at least eight have gone extinct since the law was passed. Arguably, the act's regulation of private land has done considerable harm.
- Private landowners have an incentive to "shoot, shovel and shut up."
- Any proposal to list a species is followed by a rush to cut trees, bulldoze grasslands or otherwise develop habitat while it is still legal to do so.
- Most significantly, the wise-use and property rights movements have developed a powerful following, in part by playing on people's fears of the Endangered Species Act. Whether or not those fears are valid is less important than the fact that the act has, as Montana economist Richard Stroup says, "made enemies of innocent species."

The other reforms proposed here do not absolutely require the repeal of this regulatory language. But, on balance, endangered species are better off without such language, at least as applied to private lands.

The supposed value of such language is the certainty it gives to protection, especially when dealing with public agencies that are easily monitored and seemingly have to obey the law regardless of the cost. Actual experience suggests that this certainty is more apparent than real, especially since it seems to depend on citizen enforcement through lawsuits: Environmentalists lack the resources to file repeated lawsuits on each of more than a thousand listed and candidate species.

The cost of such language is the hostility to wildlife that it generates among landowners and the political opposition to the law itself that it generates among rural people whose livelihoods depend on either public or private lands.

Repealing the regulatory provisions will force wildlife advocates to find creative new solutions to diminishing species problems. While this will require more work, the creative ideas they develop will ultimately be more successful than simply commanding uncaring public land managers and hostile private landowners to protect habitat.

Eliminating regulatory language will make cooperation with local communities and landowners much more likely than ever before. For one thing, endangered species advocates will have more of an incentive to seek cooperation. But more important, the willing cooperation of landowners can be better assured by offering them carrots than by holding a gun to their heads.

Weighing these benefits and costs, the balance is tipped by the extreme inequities of requiring a relatively few landowners to pay most of the costs of protecting most of the listed species. Ask the American public if they believe in protecting endangered species, and most will say "yes." Ask if they believe in making a few people pay the costs of things that everyone will benefit from, and most will say "no."

In the long run, changing the law to fix these problems will do more to save endangered species than defending a law that has proven more successful at provoking controversy and polarization than at recovering species. A new law must provide more funding for species recovery. It must be given more teeth to end subsidies that are draining our economy as they damage species habitat. But most important, it must rely on carrots rather than sticks, or it will continue to fail.

It may still be appropriate to retain regulatory language in parts of the law applying to federal agencies. But never forget that 23 years of having such language on the books has done little for most listed species. While the spotted owl may be a prominent exception, even in that case other laws and changes within the Forest Service made more of a difference than the Endangered Species Act.

Even on public lands, carrots work better than sticks. Endangered species advocates would do well to ensure that any carrots they put into the law will work on both public and private lands.

The Politics of Endangered Species

Property rights advocates and Endangered Species Act advocates seem to be deadlocked in Congress. One result is the Kempthorne bill, which didn't seem to satisfy either of the two groups.

But the politically realistic view is that most Americans want to save endangered species and are willing to accept major job losses and other costs to do so—even if, or perhaps especially if, those costs are unfairly imposed on a few landowners.

At the turn of this century, when the states banned market hunting and regulated sports hunting, the vast majority of Americans lived in rural areas and had what might be described as a rural land ethic, which can be described as "wise use." The idea of conservation as wise use of the land appealed to these Americans.

Today, the vast majority of Americans live in cities and have an urban land ethic, which can be described as "nature knows best." This ethic views land users as land destroyers and prefers preservation over conservation. It is this stark view that led to the writing of a command-based Endangered Species Act. The nature-knows-best view can also be seen in proposals to end all logging on federal forests, to ban livestock from federal range, and to close federal lands to motorized uses.

But a new paradigm is growing within the environmental movement. This view recognizes that nature does not always know best, and that some management is needed even in wilderness areas if those areas are to play a role in protecting diminishing species and other values.

This "new conservation" can be seen in collaborative groups such as the Quincy Library Group, a group of environmentalists and timber industry leaders that proposes to plan the future of several national forests in northern California. Other collaborative groups work on endangered species issues, such as a group that is planning the reintroduction of grizzly bears into central Idaho.

The new conservationists favor decentralization over command and control. While they are not strong proponents of markets, they have fewer objections to them than the traditional environmentalists.

A bill like the Kempthorne bill, if it ever passes Congress, will be at best a stop-gap measure that fails to solve any of the real problems with the law. Genuine reform of the Endangered Species Act will come when the new conservation paradigm becomes the dominant paradigm within the environmental movement. Advocates of incentive-based reforms should do what they can to nurture and promote this paradigm.

Conclusions

Endangered species advocates must recognize that saving species, like anything else, involves trade-offs: trade-offs among the species we try to save and trade-offs between species recovery and other resources. Refusing to admit those trade-offs won't make them go away.

Endangered species advocates must also admit that, fundamentally, people will save rare species because they want to, not because of a law (which is repealable) or some moral or ethical value (which is debatable). A majority of Americans want to save whales, grizzly bear, bald eagles and other charismatic megafauna. Whether a majority would go out of their way to save the black-spored quillwort, rock gnome lichen or other enigmatic microflora (or fauna) is another question.

In the long run, changing the law to reflect these facts will do more to save endangered species than defending a law that has proven more successful at provoking controversy and polarization than at recovering species. A new law must provide more funding for species recovery. It must be given more teeth to end subsidies that are draining our economy as they damage species habitat. But most important, it must rely on carrots rather than sticks, or it will continue to fail.

Acknowledgment

The author wishes to thank Karl Hess, Jr., and Jeff Opperman for their help in preparing this paper.

Notes

1   U.S. Department of Agriculture. Black-Tailed Prairie Dog Management for the Nebraska National Forest, Samuel R. McKelvie National Forest, Oglala National Grassland, Buffalo Gap National Grassland, and Fort Pierre National Grassland, Forest Service, Rocky Mountain Region, 1989.

2   Merriam, C.H. 1902. "The Prairie Dog of the Great Plains," U.S. Department of Agriculture Yearbook of Agriculture, pp. 257-270, 1902.

3   U.S. Department of the Interior. Black-Footed Ferret Recovery Plan, U.S. Fish and Wildlife Service, August 1988.

4   Roemer, David M. and Steven C. Forrest. Prairie Dog Poisoning in the Northern Great Plains: An Analysis of Programs and Policies, Unpublished Research Paper, 1995.

5   Ibid.
6   Clark, Tim W., Dan Hinckley, and Terrell Rich (eds.). The Prairie Dog Ecosystem: Managing for Biological Diversity, Montana Bureau of Land Management Wildlife Technical Bulletin No. 2, August 1989.
7   U.S. Department of the Interior. Proceedings of the Symposium on the Management of Prairie Dog Complexes for the Reintroduction of the Black-Footed Ferret, U.S. Fish and Wildlife Service, Biological Report 13, July 1993.
8   Thorne, E. Tom and Bob Oakleaf. "Species Rescue for Captive Breeding: Black-Footed Ferret as an Example," Symposium Zoological Society London 62:241-261, 1991.
9   Seal, Ulysses S., E. Tom Thorne, Michael A. Bogan, and Stanley H. Anderson, eds. Conservation Biology and the Black-Footed Ferret, Yale University Press, New Haven, 1989.
10   Clark, Tim W. "Restoration of the Endangered Black-Footed Ferret: a 20-Year Overview," in M.L. Bowles and C.J. Whelan, Restoration of Endangered Species, Cambridge University Press, London, 1994.
11   U.S. Department of the Interior. Black-Footed Ferret Recovery Plan, U.S. Fish and Wildlife Service, August 1988.
12   Clark, Tim W. "Restoration of the Endangered Black-Footed Ferret: a 20-Year Overview," in M.L. Bowles and C.J. Whelan, Restoration of Endangered Species, Cambridge University Press, London, 1994.
13   Karl Hess, Jr., Saving the Black-Footed Ferret (Oak Grove, OR: The Thoreau Institute, 1996), p. 14.
14   Ruth Musgrave and Mary Anne Stein, State Wildlife Laws Handbook (Bethesda, MD: Government Institutes, 1993), pp. 8–9.
15   R. J. Smith, "Resolving the Tragedy of the Commons by Creating Private Property Rights in Wildlife," Cato Journal, 1981. Reprinted by the Competitive Enterprise Institute in 1996.
16   USDI Fish & Wildlife Service, Restoring America's Wildlife (Washington, DC: USDI, 1987), 394 pp.
17   The numbers in the following paragraphs are based on Charles Mann and Mark Plummer, Noah's Choice: The Future of Endangered Species (New York, NY: Alfred Knopf, 1995). A few of the numbers are updated to take into account changes through 1996.
18   Elizabeth Losos, Justin Hayes, Ali Phillips, Carolyn Alkire, and David Wilcove, Taxpayer's Double Burden: Federal Resource Subsidies and Endangered Species (Washington, DC: The Wilderness Society, 1993).
19   Jeff Opperman, The Impacts of Subsidies on Endangered Species (Oak Grove, OR: The Thoreau Institute, 1996).
20   Tim Clark, Richard Reading, and Alice Clarke, Endangered Species Recovery: Finding the Lessons, Improving the Process (Covelo, CA: Island Press, 1994).
21   Ibid.
22   Ibid.
23   Ibid.
24   This and subsequent stories about property owners' encounters with the Endangered Species Act were provided by Ike Sugg of the Competitive Enterprise Institute.
25   R. J. Smith, "Resolving the Tragedy of the Commons by Creating Private Property Rights in Wildlife," Cato Journal, 1981. Reprinted by the Competitive Enterprise Institute in 1996.
26   The reform ideas in this section are taken from Randal O'Toole, Run Them Like Businesses (Oak Grove, OR: The Thoreau Institute, 1995).
27   Many of the ideas in this section are from Terry Anderson and Peter Hill, Wildlife in the Marketplace (Washington, DC: Rowman and Littlefield, 1997) and Brent Schearer, Incentives for Wildlife (Oak Grove, OR: The Thoreau Institute, 1996).

For Product Safety Concerns and Information please contact our EU
representative GPSR@taylorandfrancis.com Taylor & Francis Verlag GmbH,
Kaufingerstraße 24, 80331 München, Germany

Printed and bound by CPI Group (UK) Ltd, Croydon, CR0 4YY
08/05/2025
01864406-0005